Feminist and (

MW01026344

Related titles from Palgrave Macmillan

Sue-Ellen Case: *Feminism and Theatre* (reissued edition)

Feminist and Queer Performance

Critical Strategies

Sue-Ellen Case

First published 2009 by
PALGRAVE MACMILLAN

Palgrave Macmillan in the UK is an imprint of Macmillan Publishers Limited, registered in England, company number 785998, of Houndmills, Basingstoke, Hampshire RG21 6XS.

Palgrave Macmillan in the US is a division of St Martin's Press LLC, 175 Fifth Avenue, New York, NY 10010.

Palgrave Macmillan is the global academic imprint of the above companies and has companies and representatives throughout the world.

Palgrave® and Macmillan® are registered trademarks in the United States, the United Kingdom, Europe and other countries.

ISBN-13: 978–0–230–53754–5 hardback
ISBN-10: 0–230–53754–5 hardback
ISBN-13: 978–0–230–53755–2 paperback
ISBN-10: 0–230–53755–3 paperback

This book is printed on paper suitable for recycling and made from fully managed and sustained forest sources. Logging, pulping and manufacturing processes are expected to conform to the environmental regulations of the country of origin.

A catalogue record for this book is available from the British Library.

A catalog record for this book is available from the Library of Congress.

10   9   8   7   6   5   4   3   2   1
18   17   16   15   14   13   12   11   10   09

Printed and bound in China

Contents

Acknowledgments		vi
Introduction		1

Part I: Queer Theory and Performance

1	Making Butch: an Historical Memoir of the 1970s	17
2	Toward a Butch–Femme Aesthetic	31
3	Toward a Butch-Feminist Retro-Future	49
4	Tracking the Vampire	66
5	The Queer Globe Itself	86

Part II: Feminist Performance

6	Feminism and Performance: a Post-Disciplinary Couple	101
7	The Masked Activist: Greek Strategies for the Streets	111
8	Performing Feminism on the International Stage	125
9	The Screens of Time: Feminist Memories and Hopes	133

Part III: Gendered Performance and New Technologies

10	Performing the Cyberbody on the Transnational Stage	149
11	Dracula's Daughters: In-Corporating Avatars in Cyberspace	170
	Index	188

v

Acknowledgments

1 'Making Butch: an Historical Memoir of the 1970s', *butch/ femme: Inside Lesbian Gender*, ed. Sally Munt (London: Cassell, 1998), pp. 37–45.
2 'Toward a Butch-Femme Aesthetic', *Making a Spectacle: Feminist Essays on Contemporary Women's Theatre*, ed. Lynda Hart (Ann Arbor: University of Michigan Press, 1989), pp. 282–99.
3 'Toward a Butch-Feminist Retro-Future', *Cross Purposes: Lesbians, Feminists, and the Limits of Alliance*, ed. Dana Heller (Bloomington: Indiana University Press, 1997), pp. 205–20.
4 'Tracking the Vampire', *Differences* (Providence, RI: Brown University Press), vol. 3, no. 2 (Summer 1991), pp. 1–20.
5 'The Queer Globe Itself', *Staging International Feminisms*, ed. Elaine Aston and Sue-Ellen Case (Basingstoke: Palgrave Macmillan, 2007), pp. 52–64.
6 'Feminism and Performance: a Post-Disciplinary Couple', *Theatre Research International* (Cambridge: Cambridge University Press), vol. 26, no. 2 (July 2001), pp. 145–52.
7 'The Masked Activist: Greek Strategies for the Street', *Theatre Research International* (New York: Cambridge University Press), vol. 32, no. 2 (July 2007), pp. 119–29.
8 'Performing Feminism on the International Stage', *Theatre Research International* (Cambridge: Cambridge University Press), vol. 24, no. 3 (Autumn 1999), pp. 235–40.
9 'The Screens of Time: Feminist Memories and Hopes', *Feminist Futures? Theatre, Performance, Theory*, ed. Elaine Aston and Geraldine Harris (New York: Palgrave Macmillan, 2006), pp. 105–17.
10 'Performing the Cyberbody on the Transnational Stage', *Gramma: Journal of Theory and Criticism: Theatre in the Age of New Technologies* (Thessaloniki: Aristotle University, English Department), vol. 10 (2002), pp. 41–57.

11 'Dracula's Daughters: In-Corporating Avatars in Cyberspace', *Critical Theory and Performance*, ed. Janelle Reinelt and Joseph Roach (University of Michigan Press, 2007).

The author and publisher wish to thank the following for permission to use copyright material:

Cambridge University Press, for 'Feminism and Performance: a Post-Disciplinary Couple' (*Theatre Research International*, vol. 26, no. 2, July 2001); 'Introduction: Performing Feminism on the International Stage' (*Theatre Research International*, vol. 24, no. 3, Autumn 1999); and 'The Masked Activist: Greek Strategies for the Street' (*Theatre Research International*, vol. 23, no. 2, July 2007);

Continuum International Publishing, for 'Making Butch: an Historical Memoir of the 1970s' (*butch/femme: Inside Lesbian Gender*, ed. Sally Munt, 1998);

Elsi Sakellaridou, for 'Performing the Cyberbody on the Transnational Stage' (*Gramma: Journal of Theory and Criticism*, vol. 10, 2002);

Indiana University Press, for 'Toward a Butch–Femme Retro-Future' (*Cross Purposes*, ed. Heller, 1997);

Palgrave Macmillan, for 'The Screens of Time: Feminist Memories and Hopes' (*Feminist Futures? Theatre, Performance, Theory*, ed. Elaine Aston and Geraldine Harris, 2006); and 'The Queer Globe Itself' (*Staging International Feminisms*, ed. Elaine Aston and Sue-Ellen Case, 2007);

University of Michigan Press, for 'Dracula's Daughters: In-Corporating Avatars in Cyberspace' (*Critical Theory and Performance*, revised and enlarged edition, ed. Janelle Reinelt and Joseph Roach, 2007); and 'Toward a Butch–Femme Aesthetic' (*Making a Spectacle: Feminist Essays on Contemporary Women's Theatre*, ed. Lynda Hart, 1989);

Adriene Jenik and Lisa Brenneis, for the screenshots from waitingforgodot.com on p. 177 and riverofsalsa on p. 184;

Dona McAdams, for the image of Kate Bornstein on p. 173;

Eva Weiss, for the image of Lois Weaver, Peggy Shaw and Deb Margolin in _Upwardly Mobile Home_ on p. 45;

Masami Teraoka, for the images of _Geisha in Bath_/AIDS series on p. 160, and _Eva and Three Blind Mice_ on p. 162, and _Adam and Eve/Mousetrap_ on p. 163.

Note

Where the chapters in this book have previously been published, the original spelling and punctuation and the original notes and references have been retained.

Introduction

The articles collected in this volume were written to intervene in the politics of the moment, consciously inscribing the social agendas and critical strategies of the times. Although I have written books and edited anthologies in the areas of feminist and lesbian performance and new technologies, a large part of my work in the field resides in articles that have been printed and reprinted in numerous journals and anthologies. Journal articles can do what books cannot: they go to press more quickly and they appear in publications that have established a focused readership. For these reasons, some of the articles gathered here are even more polemical and pointed in nature than the work that appears in books. They are responding to lively debates of the moment and appealing directly to a particular audience. Many feminist and lesbian authors from the early years of the political movements were in a rush to publish, sensing the urgency and potential for "breaking the silence." Moreover, the activist movements as well as the performers were working at lightning speed, organizing around contemporary issues that defined the lives of women. My article here "Feminism and Performance: a Post-Disciplinary Couple" (Chapter 6) tries to recapture some of the ways in which academics pursued a relation to these activist challenges. Until now, I have never had the opportunity to bring some of them together to see how they contradict and reinforce the assumptions and interests they represent.

The project of collecting some of these works together has allowed me to review the historical shifts they represent as well as my own inspirations, contradictions, depressions, and hopes. Relax, dear reader, this is not an opportunity for me to indulge in the "talking cure." However, my psychic register does come into play, or rather than "play," perhaps I should suggest that my psychic register "comes" into "critical scenarios" that compose these articles. "Critical scenarios" may be only a postmodern term that repeats the old adage "the personal is the political," but I think it also suggests a way in which engaged writings may be scenarios; let's say performative scenes. I don't mean, necessarily, "performative" in the sense that

1

Judith Butler has suggested, i.e. it is the codes that perform, although codes do set the stage. I mean that critical writings about performance and about politics "voice" calls to action, lay out plans of escape, suggest risky capers, insult the opposition, etc. These critical scenarios borrow from other traditions in order to persuade. They resemble stories told around the home fires, recounting the brave adventures of mythical and historical feminist ancestors, telling horror stories of patriarchal suppression, and delivering homilies about feminist critical practice, just before the lesbian bedtime. They spin off into the netherland of theory only to break traditions of thought.

Whatever may be imagined here as history, or interpretation, or theorizing is realy a wolfy polemic in the sheep's clothing of academic robes. Take the article "The Masked Activist: Greek Strategies for the Streets" (Chapter 7), or any of my several articles on Greek tragedy. These articles have made lots of traditional scholars angry. In this one, the invention of tragedy is made to seem a fundamentalist apparatus for quelling women's demonstrations in the streets. Now, traditional scholars have rested secure for centuries in believing that those scant extant materials on classical Greece are records of glorious democracy and that tragedy is indeed a brilliant, universal form. In continuing to read against this tradition, I hope to make clear that these guys have been doing nothing more than sitting around their own fires, telling stories of mythical ancestors toward their own ends. In other words, their history, their understanding of Greek tragedy is also nothing more than a polemic. Martin Bernal's *Black Athena* reveals how the invention of the Greeks as a source of Western culture was part of a racist project to invent Aryan roots. I work to reveal how the reception of the tragic form went hand in hand with the establishment of an elite all-male culture. The continuing success of this patriarchal invention of the Greeks continues today – even in the realm of popular culture. The enormous box office success and production budget of the new film *300* (2007), for example, illustrate how US investments in Iraq set the stage for recounting the Battle of Thermopylae in which those brave little Spartans, with moral right on their side, battle the evil hordes of Persia. *The Persians*, after all, was the so-called "first" tragedy to organize a moral reception for Spartan hyper-masculinity and the military. So, we might ask, even if tomes of histories work to stop us from asking, what does the form of Greek tragedy actually represent? Once we have managed to break free from the hold of, in this case, years of English public school attitudes towards the classics, at one time the jewel in the crown of academic pursuits, we can hopefully break free from any traditions of learning, when we understand the self-interest invested in their strategies.

If the strategy in deconstructing historical traditions is a particularly feminist one, imagining subcultural delights, "real" or not, is a specifically lesbian one. Writing lesbian theory is, for me, a critical scenario that displaces hanging out in lesbian bars. These scenarios are replete with some good bar fights (with other critics) and some seductions (both being seduced and attempting to seduce). The writing is drunk with metaphorical cadenzas, apoplexies of shame, and attempts to wend my way back home to the feminist hearth. The articles on butch and femme roles are written to foreground a performative voice. I already knew, from the beginning days of the feminist critique, that the so-called objective voice of history writing or interpretation was understood as a patriarchal voice. From feminist theory, I understood that the "objective" voice of discursive writing was actually the vocalizing of the "universal man" who could stand in for all researchers and could speak in a language so transparent that one could clearly observe how things really are. Years later, Donna Haraway described this voice of empiricism as that of the "modest witness," who, in the white clerical robes of the laboratory, could deploy his findings as if through the focal lens of observation. In the feminist critique, discursive strategies to thwart this tradition created a performative voice of location to contradict the universal perspective, and thereby to displace the tradition of absolute knowledge with partial knowing. In order to foreground one's own location, activists and academics began sentences with such identificatory incantations as "I am speaking as a middle-class, white, academic from an urban area," or, "as a Black woman who was raised in the South, but educated in the North," or "as a working-class lesbian, who only came out through the feminist movement." These incantations, vocalized for political effect, were what we now term "performative" language rather than, as they have been termed, "essentialist." They may have deployed the terms of ontology, of being, in the sense of "I am" but they were meant to function as a linguistic tool to break through the centuries-long tradition of patriarchal, unmarked language.

So, I ruminated, what would a lesbian voice sound like? Thinking back on the best times in the dyke bars in San Francisco, I decided to channel the campy, witty, sassy voice I had often heard there. I first used this particular lesbian voice to write "Toward a Butch–Femme Aesthetic" (Chapter 2). I was invited to give a keynote

address to the Women in Theatre Program of the American Theater Association in 1987. I suddenly realized I would be speaking to a
basically heterosexual audience, with maybe two or three other "out"
dykes amongst them. I felt I needed somehow to foreground the
difference between lesbian subcultural practices and heteronormative
feminist ones. I was acutely aware of the way in which heterosexual issues and forms had dominated the activist and artistic scene.
I wanted to mark that there was a different "life" from which some
of us came to the bourgeois, "straight" notion of the feminist "dinner party," as Judy Chicago would install it, or Caryl Churchill would
portray it in *Top Girls*. A bar is not a dinner party. I also sought a form
of self-protection. Jokes have long served both to shield and to give
voice to the "Other," so I thought to employ the campy style as well
as detail how it has been used to protect and to proffer. I decided the
biggest joke, in terms of sexual subcultures and working-class access
to ideas, would be to bring high theoretical concepts down to street
slang. One editor asked me to revise the article, insisting that the style
was spoiling the basically sound theoretical argument of the piece.
I refused. I felt that some of these "high" concepts, ensconced in
academic translations of French ruminations, could be duly expressed
in campy slang: thus, the oft-cited turn of the Lacanian slash into a
lesbian bar.

   The voice of the article has often been attacked by those who
would argue that "camp" was not a lesbian, but a gay male style.
I agree that it did not seem to be the voice of lesbian feminists
who gathered in womens' bookstores, or at womens' music con-
certs. Locally, the campy style was not Berkeley, but San Francisco.
The bars were full of drag queens on Hallowe'en. My cohort did not
listen to, say, Meg Christian, but to a dyke rock group called The
Contractions; did not dance together in a circle, but in a sexualized
style; did not practice serial monogamy, but one-night stands; were
not earnest, but ironic. So were they not feminists? If lesbian feminism was a, shall we say, a particular lifestyle, then they were not. If
feminism was, in part, an all-woman counterculture, then they were.
I was not entranced with ethnography, as some were in this period,
but I did want to tell the stories of Lesbian life. I guess I did set myself
up as a "native informant," though, in articles such as "Making Butch
in the '70s," which is even accompanied by a photo of the author. In
my defense, the article was written to be published in a special edition of butch-femme writings by performers and artists, rather than
academics. My critical scenarios, though, remained in the form of

"quippies," which was probably the written form of "quickies," as they were performed in the bar culture.

This performative voice is, however, particularly an American one. Although some of the later works attempt to dialogue with new globalizing, transnational agendas, the majority of the earlier critical strategies are woefully EuroAmerican-centric, as are many feminist and queer materials from these earlier periods. The substance of the feminist/lesbian articles was derived from autonomous activist movements and minoritized fields of study. At this point in history, however, it is difficult to see anything coming out of the US as other than invasionary. Looking through the haze of destruction mounted by a war-mongering administration, I perceive those volumes of feminist and queer texts that line university bookstores abroad as subversive, on the one hand, and taking part in cultural imperialism, on the other. I have published this critique in several places, careful to celebrate, but also to indict, our subversive, interventionary critical practices as necessarily linked to national politics and economies. The long version of this thought appears in the section titled "Bringing Home the Meat" in my book *The Domain-Matrix: Performing Lesbian at the End of Print Culture*. There, I even argue that several of the leading theories of the 1980s actually structurally embody the dynamics of globalization at that time. While these articles register conditions here in the US, I regret that my attention to long traditions of feminist and lesbian work in Africa, Asia, and the Americas has been only recently informed by the fervent transnational/international work now being done in this field. I will return to this subject later in the Introduction.

I now want to speak in the tongues of decades. Yes, I, too, have fallen victim to the idea that there is some politico-cultural phenomenon called, say, "the '60s." If read carefully, annals and chronicles can preserve partial knowledges. Moreover, these articles answered various "calls" to write. Feminist and lesbian theory does not float in the ether of "truth," so beloved of traditional male philosophers. So reader beware, I am going to march through the decades in which these articles were written as if they really can collect, in groups of ten, what are known as "eras." I want to argue that, in the US, the era of the 1980s witnessed the establishment of the field of feminist critical theory, both broadly configured and focused in the area of performance; the 1990s witnessed the rise of queer theory, and the early years of the twenty-first century signaled the rise of transnational and new media studies. Of course, these are absurdly vague and sweeping claims, but, I think not without some historical merit. What is theory, anyway, but the science of making sweeping claims meritorious? So, like my mother and my grandmother, I will continue to sweep.

Sweeping along, then: feminist theorizing in the 1980s was excited to incorporate new, critical methodologies into studies of performance. I remember teaching one of my first graduate seminars, in which I had assigned the chapter "Suddenly an Age of Theory" from *Beautiful Theories: The Spectacle of Discourse in Contemporary Criticism*, by Elizabeth Bruss (1982). I thought the title of the chapter said it all. Once more, European culture had arrived on the American soil of academe, but this time from France. Columbus's great ships, the *Nina*, the *Pinta* and the *Santa Maria*, were the Kristeva, the Cixous, and the Irigaray of critical theory. No longer would our study of performance be dominated by historical accounts, but it would work to reveal the very base meaning-making. At the break, several of the women students fled crying into the bathroom and the male students retreated to the front lawn of the building. They had never read anything like this theorizing. It was difficult, it shifted the sense of referents, it referred not, dear reader, to Oscar Brockett, but to Jacques Lacan! After this introductory episode, a faculty discussion ensued, questioning my ability to teach graduate students. After all, it was my first seminar after graduate school. I think this incident registers some of the trauma and the intensity in confronting theory in this period. Theory wars broke out everywhere. Later, when I served as an editor of the major journal in the field, *Theatre Journal* (1985–89), the inclusion of articles using critical theories caused many scholars to move to remove it from its role as the official journal of the national organization of theater scholarship. They could understand neither the meaning or the significance of such theorizing. These scholars were mostly male historians who had ruled the scholarly roost for years, so I have no idea what these theories caused them to do in the bathroom, but I certainly encountered their ire at conferences. Janelle Reinelt and I record some of this battle in our introduction to *The Performance of Power: Theatrical Discourse and Politics*.

So what were some of these theories? Semiotics was first introduced to US scholars in 1980 with *The Drama Review* publication of Umberto Eco's "Semiotics of Theatrical Performance" and Keir Elam's *The Semiotics of Theatre and Drama*. Semiotics offered a vocabulary for reading (as we still called it) the production of meaning in performance itself, rather than just text. Lighting effects could be "signs" that had referents, as well as gestures, and performance spaces. Feminist theaters, but more, feminist performance art had been circulating in museums, in clubs, and in site-specific locales since the 1970s. Suddenly, a way to interpret these performances as signs of social coding became available. In feminist criticism, semiotics converged with Lacanian psychoanalytic theory to provide a critical vocabulary for studies of sexuality, so key to the social programming of women. In the late 1970s several seminal texts were translated: Hélène Cixous's *Laugh of the Medusa*; Gayatri Spivak's translation of Derrida's *Of Grammatology*, and Lacan's *Seminar XI*. Feminist film studies brought these semio-psychoanalytic theories in proximity to performance, with books like Kaja Silverman's *The Subject of Semiotics* and Teresa de Lauretis's *Alice Doesn't: Feminism, Semiotics, Cinema*, both published in 1984. Many of us were working across disciplines to knit together (yes, we were sweeping and knitting) some critical approach to performance. In this volume, my article "Toward a Butch-Femme Aesmetic" directly reflects the influences of psycho-semiotics. The burden of both explaining the semio-Lacanian paradigm and applying it to performance is writ large in these articles. We were forging something new called "feminist criticism." Sometimes it was rough-hewn (rough-hewn knitting?) and sometimes underwritten, in the invention of new terminology. As we discovered new critical paradigms in theory, we were also searching for new forms of performance that acted out what we were beginning to understand.

I was flying to another one of those Women in Theater meetings, in the 1980s, when a very sexy blonde in the next seat leaned over and asked me what I was reading. I was reading one of those heady Lacanian books by Jane Gallop at the time (*The Daughter's Seduction: Feminism and Psychoanalysis*), and, stereotyping that blonde, I replied that she would not be interested in my book, but that I'd like to buy her a drink. She replied that she might, indeed, be interested in that book and that drink. It turned out she was (and still is) Lois Weaver. Peggy Shaw was sitting a row away on the aisle. This is how I met the performance group known as Split Britches. Talk about luck! They were going to be performing both at the conference I was flying to attend and in their theatre at WOW (Women's One World) in New York. I became an immediate fan: their sense of humor, their postmodern composition, lesbian politics, and feminist critique completely seduced me. They were the perfect match for the new theory.

Following that serendipitous encounter, the work of this group and its relation to new approaches to feminist/lesbian performance became a critical scenario of seduction in many of my works. I must admit, though, that the divine femme, Lois Weaver, had a great deal to do with that seduction. At a recent LGBT (Lesbian, Gay, Bisexual, and Transgender) conference I asked some panelists if they could distinguish between fan fiction and queer research. I mean, someone once started a fan 'zine called *Judy!* for Judith Butler fans.

Beyond my critical scenario of seduction, though, in writing about the butch-femme performances of Weaver and Shaw, I was arguing for lesbian visibility. Butch-femme relations challenged feminist rejections of lesbian subcultural practices, not only through my own theoretical articles here, but through influential historical accounts, such as Kennedy and Davis's *Boots of Leather, Slippers of Gold: The History of a Lesbian Community* and Joan Nestle's *A Restricted Country*. At first, feminists and lesbian feminists rejected this role-playing as a mere imitation of heteronormative gender roles. Later, these roles became understood as part of a centuries-long tradition of transgender identification: one way to subvert the normative regime. Some critics took issue with the political efficacy of visibility politics and associated them with the so-called essentialism of identity politics. One can read this critique in Peggy Phelan's *Unmarked: The Politics of Performance*, published in 1993. The title word "unmarked" offers an alternative strategy of performance to the marked roles of butch and femme.

While arguing for lesbian visibility, in some circumstances, I also perceived how lesbian INvisibility offered a way in which to critique, from a deconstructive perspective, the short-sighted (ahem) feminist critiques that ignored it. I first met Teresa de Lauretis when she came to give a talk at the University of Washington in the late 1980s. I had already read *Alice Doesn't* and was seduced by the rigor and sophistication of her theorizing. She later organized the first conference in Queer Theory at the University of California at Santa Cruz in 1990 and invited me to speak. At the time, I was interested in alliances with gay men, known then as a "queer alliance," through which a new perspective for theory could be forged. "Tracking the Vampire" (Chapter 4) was the talk I gave there. The vampire offered me a way out of the feeling that I was called upon to represent "lesbian." I had the feeling that straight liberals wanted me to initiate lesbians into their inner circles by marking oppression. I just didn't feel like singing that song from *West Side Story*: "Gee, Officer Krupke, we're very upset; we never had the love that every child oughta get. We ain't no delinquents, we're misunderstood. Deep down inside us there is good!" As someone said at the time, the movement split into "we're just like you only different," in striving for civil rights, and "we're nothing like you and don't want to be," in marking transgression. Along with invisibility, my vampire was an image of perversion, damnation, and other darker delights. The irony of the campy voice could, like the vampire, evade mimesis. Sometimes style is content. At the same time, invisibility could be noted as a site of loss in feminist theory, which seemed to both seduce and abandon the lesbian subject position.

Two years after Teresa de Lauretis's conference, Joseph Roach invited me to join the prominent queer theorists Michael Moon, Eve Sedgwick, Sylvia Molloy, and others for a mini-conference at Tulane University in 1992. It was there that I suffered my academic breakdown. In those two years between the Santa Cruz conference and this one, the meaning of "queer" had radically altered. I can remember lying prone on a bench outside the conference hall, unable to motivate myself back into the conference and thinking I would never be able to write again. OK, so maybe I'm a drama queen, but the anti-essentialist attack brought down a lot of people. I won't name them here, but you could easily discover who stopped publishing around this time. Teresa de Lauretis's 1990 article "Sexual Indifference and Lesbian Representation" creates a history of lesbian work in its footnotes, carefully citing key works in the field. It partakes in the feminist politics of citation that helped to build an academic community of scholars. The new queer theorists quoted primarily male European philosophers, with little or no mention of the feminist and lesbian work that had gone before. This violent break made a community disappear. "Star" scholars rose to take its place. Conferences seemed to circulate around "stars." At the breaks, people rushed out to get Starbuck's coffee, rather than locally-brewed ones, which they drank from a mug with a pink triangle on it that they had bought at one of the many booths selling logos at the enormously popular Pride Parade, where the mayors of major cities were pleased to be photographed. At the same time, there was a renewed interest in masculinity, rather than the category of "women."

In the 1990s, sexuality studies split off from feminism, moving in the direction of gay male and transsexual, transgender critiques. The alliance we had sought with gay male critics turned out to be a one-way street to studies of masculinity. This was partially the result of the AIDS crisis, which put gay men in peril, and the fact that, well, lots of gay male cultural producers were more famous than women. Take Henry James, for example, as Eve Sedgwick did, or Walt Whitman, as Michael Moon did, or Roland Barthes, as D. A. Miller did, or Oscar Wilde, as Alan Sinfield did; well, the list goes on. This was not the same approach as in early feminist critiques that exalted Shakespeare for his treatment of women's roles or damned the Greeks for theirs. It was "queering" otherwise normatively fashioned famous men by revealing how they perversely performed or represented masculinity. These works were brilliant and engaging. They enjoyed a history of critical treatments of these works, in contrast to the meager critical reception of many women writers and performers. Studies of queer masculinity helped to dismantle how the patriarchy had reconstructed the lives and writings of men. It also produced the sense of what I call "the dowdy dyke" in "Towards a Butch-Feminist Retro-Future" (Chapter 3).

In the early years of the 1990s, the transsexual movement provided an important amplification to the understanding of gender. At this time transgender identification still remained in dialogue with feminism. Articles and performances by male-to-female (or M to F) transsexuals marked the first period of the transgender movement. Allucquere Roseanne Stone, an M to F student of the feminist theorist Donna Haraway, published "The Empire Strikes Back: a Posttranssexual Manifesto" in 1991, and the M to F performer Kate Bornstein opened *Hidden: A Gender*, a cabaret-type performance about historical and personal accounts of gender-reassignment surgery, in 1989. Bornstein deconstructed the masculinity she had left behind, while taking on a specifically feminist version of "female." However, later in the decade, the movement emphasized female-to-male transgender identification, with an emphasis on notions of masculinity. The term "butch," specifically associated with lesbian practices, was displaced by a notion of "female masculinity," a term launched by the book of that title by Judith ("Jack") Halberstam in 1998. Now women not only became transgendered men, but some even preferred the gay lifestyle to living with women. Transgendered identifications by women were no longer understood as subversions of women's roles, but amplifications of men's. For example, I heard a paper recently that argued for a version of "tomboy" that would be understood on an axis of masculinity that ran toward heterosexual men, rather than in relation to women. In visual culture, transgender photographers Della Grace, now Del Lagrace

Volcano, and Loren Cameron published brilliant photo shots of F to M bodies that revealed the success of their transformation. A new performance style was launched within this environment: Drag Kings. Within this exciting new movement I was disturbed by performances of hyper-masculinity and violence that, in spite of claiming the trans-gender appearance as subversive, did not seem that critical of the performance of masculinity.

Feeling that the materialist, class critique had disappeared with the lesbian/feminist voice, I could write nothing more in the field. You see, I had begun my studies by writing a dissertation on an East German playwright, Heiner Mueller. As a graduate student, I lived in a collective in Berlin for a year, crossing the border every day to watch rehearsals of Mueller's play *The Construction* (*der Bau*). I had co-translated and directed his play *Cement*, about the begin-nings of communism and feminism in Russia after the Revolution. The socialist/materialist critique was buried deep in the base of my approach. While I disagreed with many of the socialist femi-nist authors, I felt closest to their politics. The shame I had felt in life was not only because of my sexual orientation, but because of my working-class upbringing. These experiences prompted me to question transgender politics in the late 1990s. It seemed to me that cross-dressing, or sex-reassignment surgery, in itself, was not enough of a political platform. How, I wondered, could this stance come into an alliance with poor women in the world? Basically, I left the queer movement.

So, in the 1990s, a refugee from queer discourses, and still searching for a materialist critique, I turned to the study of new technologies. The new "information" culture had radically altered the material base of social communication, the form of writing, the performance of gender, and the dynamics of globalization. My book *The Domain-Matrix* provided a way back to writing. Yet, in spite of my resolve to write about something else, the book begins with a temper tantrum against the anti-essentialist attack. It turned out that I needed a crit-ical laxative in order to continue. After that book, I found my way back to lesbian work. I wrote "Making Butch in the 1970s" as an historical memoir aimed at critiquing the embrace of masculinity. I thought I could make a polemical point by returning to the time of the Vietnam war, when images of military maneuvers tried to look like heroism and thus encourage hyper-masculinist identifications. But in the 1970s, even heterosexual, anti-war men "wore flowers" in their long, hippie hair. I wanted some image of "butch" that could contradict the new fetish for big muscles, "hood-like tattoos", and the adoption of the male. More directly, I launched a verbal attack on what I perceived as the anti-lesbian, exclusively middle-class gay male, commodity fetishism of the queer movement, in a keynote address at the Fifth Annual National LGBT Graduate Student Conference at USC. The auditorium was packed. Maybe 400 students had come to hear my "campy" intonations. By the end of the talk, here repro-duced as "Toward a Butch-Feminist Retro-Future" (Chapter 3), not one of those students approached me at the podium. Only two of the organizers, Joseph Boone and Tania Modleski, were pleased with my performance. As I wandered the conference, looking for panels on "lesbian," or "woman," I found none. This year, at the LGBT conference at UCLA, I moderated the only one.

So I was "out," having once been "in," both by my own choice and by that of others. In contrast, however, I also found that if fem-inism was dead to sexuality studies in the US, it was still very much alive in other parts of the world. I began working with the Interna-tional Feminist Working Group within the International Federation of Theatre Research and that brought me new hope. With a new set of alliances, I could hear about the street theaters that women like Padma Venkataraman were leading in the streets of India, what feminist performances Ashe Panda was producing in Rajasthan, the teaching of feminist criticism Jung Soon Shim was providing in South Korea, or Tiina Rosenberg's gender work in Stockholm. The article "Performing Feminism on the International Stage" (Chapter 8) intro-duced the volume of *Theatre Research International* that was dedicated to the scholarship of that group. In 2007, Elaine Aston and I pub-lished an anthology of manifestos, interventions, and theories created by the Working Group, titled *Staging International Feminisms*. I have now enjoyed over six years of work with that group, and, as in the old days of the Women and Theatre Program, I continue to write queer politics into the feminist venture. The article that appears here as "The Queer Globe Itself" (Chapter 5) was inspired by our meet-ings. It still marks my critique of commodity fetishism, while also finding some good purpose for queer politics in the transnational flow. I think this sensitivity to the struggles for and against transna-tional cultural flows marks the major critical investment of the early years of the twenty-first century.

Meanwhile, the study of new technologies has developed rapidly and widely as a field of theoretical pursuit. Once I turned my inter-est to the topic, I found I could not turn away. I have just published a second book in the field: *Performing Science and the Virtual*, which produces another pseudo-history that accounts for the relationship between the "new" science and theater. The two articles I have included here take two very different approaches to the field. One tries to account for the body in the corporate, transnational space constructed by new technologies. This approach puts together studies in globalization with those of new technology. Globally, women have been assigned specific tasks in this field, both in its production and in its system of representation. The other article takes off from a witty paradigm offered by Friedrich Kittler, more in the tradition of the vampire (Kittler's book entitled *Dracula's Vermächatnis* or *Dracula's Legacy*) in its deconstructive approach. Perhaps they both continue to mark my earlier approach to things as striving to make certain relations visible and marking invisibility in the process. The feminist struggle in the studies of new technology, led by theorists such as Donna Haraway, Katherine Hayles, and Vivian Sobchack, is to retain a materialist base in a study of cyberspaces that would announce themselves as "transcendent." These critics clarify how that desire for transcendence has historically accompanied specifically masculinist pursuits. They critique those works that would figure cyberspace as a place where we can flee the material world into a timeless, globally embracing, playful sphere of gender exchange.

Now at the end of this sweeping account of decades, I can turn to my article printed here as "The Screens of Time: Feminist Memories and Hopes" (Chapter 9), which appeared in a volume titled *Feminist Futures?* I think the question mark following the suggestion of a future is uncannily appropriate. Thinking on time and feminism, I suggested a slipstream of time, a wormhole of time, a palimpsest of times in which the past, present, and future intermingle. This notion contradicts the march through decades I have just offered here, for it has a different purpose. If my decade march was dedicated to locating critical interventions within their specific historical space in the past, in the article on time I was seeking to find a way to install the feminist as a subject of time that could continue into the future. My meditation on time was inspired, in part, by the works of Sarah Kane, who installs a psychotic subject of time through time's wasting. I tried to imagine a kind of negative dialectic, in which a subject might glimmer, once in a while, more positive than the vampire, but not necessarily more instantiated. I tried to imagine how it would be if the past, if history, as Ernst Bloch suggests, is actually here in the present, as is the future. Then we could no longer doubt the efficacy of past deeds because they would be helping to form the very shapes we see, and we could no longer doubt activism, as it brings the future into the present. In this way, I could imagine something like "hope."

But the question now begins to emerge as simply *Futures?* Will there be a future at all? Will there be sustainable life on this planet? If not, how important are these other concerns? Perhaps this question is prompted by my current condition. There are sixteen wildfires raging in Southern California as I write this Introduction. The air is heavy with smoke and pollutants. We have finally begun to publicly admit what we have known for several decades: there will not be enough water. As long ago as the 1980s, I read in a German newspaper that water would be the oil of the twenty-first century. "They" have known it for some time. Today's paper (finally) reports that states as far away as New Mexico are beginning to seek water from the Great Lakes near Chicago. The water wars are beginning. Large parts of Africa have become arid and the glaciers are massively receding in most parts of the world. They feed the rivers. In a documentary film on religious practices in India, I saw a naked, ashen-covered holy man, living in a hut near the river, say he was worried that the Ganges would dry up because the glaciers are receding. I was shocked to see that even this guru-type, who had dedicated his life to a strict set of religious practices, was aware of the ecological future or non-future of his holy river. In my recent book *Performing Science and the Virtual*, I try to develop some sense of how humans began to imagine themselves as THE subject, to the detriment of other species.

Ecofeminism has not offered much in the way of an activist agenda. Generally, it installs an essentialist notion of "woman" alongside neoRomantic notions of "nature." I must admit, I don't know how to write about ecological activism from a feminist or lesbian perspective. But I think I must try. Sustaining life on this planet will be my next subject. In the 1980s, the feminist critique alerted me to the condition of my sisters and my responsibility for their welfare. Now, I look around me at the devastation of the natural resources in my region and the effect it is having on other species of plants and animals. Humans have already caused the extinction of around 1,000 bird species. Scientists predict 400 more species will disappear by 2050. Have you looked at the sky lately? Listened for the birds in the morning? This is only one signpost. These facts are all around us, but they don't even make the front page of the paper. What can we do?

Part I

Queer Theory and Performance

1

Making Butch: an Historical Memoir of the 1970s

While watching the film *Last Call at Maud's*, I remembered my first night at Maud's: more, my many nights at Maud's.[1] For Maud's was my first bar, my coming-into-the-life bar, the bar I frequented several nights a week, the bar that centered my obsessive fantasies of a lesbian (under)world – the bar that loomed behind my article "Toward a Butch-Femme Aesthetic".[2] The film was about Maud's. In part, it depicted a Maud's that did not exist, since the film was peopled by well-known feminist authors whom I had never seen there, but whose inclusion in the film seemingly added legitimacy to the bar's claim to centrality in the lesbian scene in San Francisco. In part, the film focused on the later Maud's, in which baseball provide some innocent centre around which the drinking, drugs, and cruising could be relegated to more marginal roles. Perhaps all that cheery team-playing was partially a result of the feminist clean-up of the lesbian scene. At any rate, Maud's, the oldest women's bar in San Francisco, was my training ground, was the social centre of the lesbian scene in the city, and now is no more.

My first night at Maud's was in the late 1960s. I pushed open its plain black door to discover two rather dimly lit rooms. The long bar occupied the first room. It was illuminated by various neon ads for beers, the warm, orange light from the juke box, and the garish surround of the pinball machine. The other room afforded a central view of the pool table, with its low-hanging lamp and a few tables along the walls. The old butch–femme scene hunkered down at the end of the bar itself, while a few hippie dykes straggled in to sit at the tables. The classical butches still played the pinball machine and occupied the central pool table. The hippie dykes played the juke box (demanding

new tunes) and talked endlessly among themselves. Their conversation was not like anecdotal monologues delivered by the classical
butches, after a few beers, but were sometimes drug-inspired, enthusiastic descriptions of altered perception. The two groups regarded
one another with suspicion.

It is this sharped, but contested gaze that defines the intersection,
the historical moment of this memoir. The time when hippie neo-
butches encountered the classical ones. At Maud's: where lifestyle
politics met ghettoized, closeted behavior; where middle-class drop-
outs, students, and sometime professionals met working-class people
who had slim, but tenacious hopes of doing better; where the "sexual
revolution" broke the code of serial monogamy; where costume and
hallucination affronted sober dress codes and drink. Outside that dark
retreat, feminism was constructing other social spaces and the student movement at San Francisco State was wiping the sidewalk with
the canon and the exclusionary curriculum that produced "whiteness" with its every assignment. Inside, a new historical moment was
being forged whose legacy of confrontations proceeds down into the
contemporary scene.

At the time, I was a grad student in an experimental program at
San Francisco State College. The program offered a version of the history of ideas, with young junior professors just out of the places like
Brandeis University, where Herbert Marcuse was teaching and Angela
Davis was studying. Even without the later wisdom of cultural studies programs, studying notions of history by day and standing around
in the bar by night did not seem to contradict one another. Student
activism encouraged a necessary relationship between the streets and
the classroom. Later, in my PhD studies in drama at Berkeley, I completed a course which combined dramatic theory with the practice
of directing. I knew, even then, that I was just sublimating my earlier
pleasure in books by day and bars by night – text and performance. I
continue to do so, perhaps most literally in this piece. This particular
combo currently defines the field, where gender dresses up in the glad
rags of the performative and lesbian bars go as "queer" watering holes.

Like many others, I wore long, straight, hippie hair and bell-
bottom hip-huggers, but felt I was "butch" (though I had never
heard the term). They were men's pants, after all, with broad leather
belts, and hippie men when sporting long hair as well. Nevertheless, I had to depend on the kindness of classical butches in order
to learn the ropes of bar culture. They seemed quite obliging –
I think it was my long hair. They drove me around in their big

American cars, showing me the route of four bars which composed the itinerary of a weekend night. Maud's was both the starting
place and the end-point along a route that included two bars in
the Mission district and one over on the the North Beach side of
town. After the bars closed, the hearty might add an after-hours
joint (for members only) in the Tenderloin district. Brunches at the
boys' bars on Sunday provided an opportunity to see who had gone
home with whom, and all that together composed a weekend in
the life.

The butch–femme people included "Whitey" whom some may
remember from the film *The Word is Out* – her parents had her confined to a mental institution for her sexual proclivity. I dated one of
her girlfriends, a young innocent from Kansas City, who had met
Whitey in the bars in her first two-week discovery of San Francisco
and whom Whitey had rescued from the Midwest by arriving at her
parents' door in Kansas City to whisk her off on the back of her
motorcycle. That young girl later committed suicide. Other femmes
I knew also went down: one who had worked in the publishing film
Little, Brown, until she ran off to join a lesbian commune and become
addicted to pills; a sex worker (called prostitutes at the time) who had
her own "shop" in her apartment and sold stained glass windows on
the side; the beautiful Eileen, the bar server, and Janice Joplin, who
(it was said) sometimes frequented the place. Of course, lots of people
were dying from drug use in the hippie culture and its environment.
So there were mourning rituals in the hippie culture and in the bar
culture.

Strangely, among those, I knew, it was the femmes who died. These
were actually the neo-femmes, who somehow crossed the two cultures. The classic ones did better – they survied. One was called "the
fox" because of her dyed red wig – she waited tables at a hamburger
place called Zim's. She might still be there. She had already been
there for several years. Some classic butches included "Red", who
once won the pool championship with one hand, having broken her
other in a bar fight, and "Ace" who drove a cab and had lived for
years with a beautician, whose teased, dyed hair was truly monumen-
tal. I can remember one femme–femme couple, actually. They were
both beauticians. No butch–butch couples, though – well, not until
the androgynous look came into fashion. Then everyone looked like
butches – "Girl Scout counselors", some of us called them, who wore
plaid shirts and REI pants. They could be camping in a minute. They
had their back packs close at hand.

The crowed was almost exclusively "white", a fact I did not notice at the time, even though, by day, I was involved in the student strike at San Francisco State which broke out over bringing ethnic studies onto campus. I could yell at a cop in riot gear about needing to break the "white" composition of the campus and then fail to notice its hold in the bars. My semi-closeted student status must have helped to isolate my political critique from my social one. In fact, as I remember, there was little discussion of the student strike in the bar. Of course, I didn't discuss the writings of Marcuse in there either. Somehow, my own working-class upbringing had taught me to confine school words and concerns to the schoolyard. Still, I knew that the "black" women, as they were then called, hung out over in Oakland at their own bars and the Filipinas hung out in a place out by the Avenues. I don't remember any Latinas. Hippies were also a pretty white bunch, seemingly ignorant of the racist element in their "new world" of love and understanding. It doesn't seem to be much better today. Oh, *Diva*, for instance, includes that one article on, say, Andrea Stuart, but look at the ads. The "white" image of the "queer" or the sex radical pervades the videos and the hair-styles. Or, as one of my students has written, the butches are women depicted as women of colour, but the femmes are white.[3] Maybe it's a consequence of the heritage of lifestyle politics. I mean, who has a lifestyle, anyway?

We were beginning to develop a sense of ourselves in representation – we were discovering with the camera. My friend Lili Lakich, the neon artist, was on the cover of *The Ladder*, for instance, looking all brooding and hot. Judy Grahn, over in Oakland, was writing the poetry and helping to found a women's press and bookstore. Barbara Hammer was making underground films. In 1979, I wrote a play about Maud's called *Jo: A Lesbian History Play*. It was produced at a straight theater in San Francisco. It wasn't very good play, but it was a big event, since no such play had ever appeared on a regular stage there. The show was sold out night after night to roaring, screaming, clapping lesbian audiences who loved seeing Maud's depicted on the stage. Fortunately, their catcalls drowned out much of the dialogue. Meanwhile, the reviewer for the *San Francisco Chronicle* reported that it "told us nothing new about about being a lesbian". He presumably had a good "deep throat".[4] Anyway, Meg Christian went to see the play and looked me up later to ask why, in my humorous and alluring depiction of the bars, I had not detailed the alcoholism and drug abuse, which had so challenged her life and which she attributed to the fact that lesbians could only gather in bars. I guess that's why I want to bring it up here.

I, too, when writing out into the straight culture, want to idealize the bars for political purposes. Make them jealous. But writing within the new fashionable context of pro-sex and butch–femme lifestyle politics, I do want to make a point the community, as it was then called, discovered was valuable. Many elements and substances in the bars and bar life are addictive. I, myself, started going out four and five nights a week. I watched lots of people drop out, go on welfare, or gain some kind of disability pay, in order to live their whole lives there. Why not? It was painful to live under the dominating culture. And wearing a damned skirt in an office was confining. There was a dress code at San Francisco State, for example, stating that skirts and hose were required for all female instructors. I had a couple of knit suits that made riding a motor scooter to work rather treacherous. Inside, in the remove of the bar, it seemed like being a waitress, all decked out, and the centre of dyke attention, was a really glamorous job. In my earlier article, "Toward a Butch–Femme Aesthetic", I try to undo the class assumptions behind the upward mobility required by groups such as the Daughters of Bilitis. I realize I might be promoting that same attitude now. More to the point, however, is the feeling that the ghetto nature of our social life at that time encouraged us to collapse many of our aspirations and dreams into the mythic landscape of the bar, sometimes to the detriment of our futures.

Drinking accompanied the socializing and for some, that was life-threatening. I have two friends from those days who are still struggling with alcoholism. Eroticizing commodity fetishism, as lifestyle politics will do, is also addictive. It's like Edie Sedgwick said in her book *Edie*, about life in the Warhol factory: after a while, with the drugs, they just spent all their time getting dressed up and ready to go out – eventually they never even made it out the door. The most fun was the dressing up, the make-up, the hair-styles. Saturdays were about getting ready, Saturday night partying and picking up, and Sundays about seeing who had done what with whom. The weekend was gone. So When the feminist movement came up with the idea called "substance abuse" it didn't seem as prudish and antique as it does now. In fact, it was an eye-opener. The organization called "sober dykes" was founded with great pride. Most drugs were put away, except for cocaine, which was touted then to be non-addictive. We later found out about that one, too. I'm not promoting an anti-alcohol, anti-drug attitude, nor even a 12-step approach to life. However, for some, the fact that the social life occurred only around alcohol was dangerous – even life-threatening. As corny and middle-class as those early feminist coffee houses appeared to many of us, they at least provided a safer place for some.

During the later 1970s, feminist coffee houses began opening in the city, along with a women's centre, which included a lesbian space. So suddenly there were options for places to gather. If you couldn't afford to be around drinking, but still wanted to meet dykes, you had another possibility. People began exploring social relationships outside of the context of drinking and sexual practice. Anyway, all these discoveries would later suffer their own correction back to the pro-sex perspective. Contradictions create healthy politics, as Mao once said. But it is important to keep in mind that early on in those changing years, bars were still the only places to hang out and sex was the centre of social relations. Addictions abounded and were explored with great gusto and we all kept returning to the magic circle that bounded those rites. In one way, it was a grand time. The imagination that would celebrate myth and ritual could find wonderful dreams in those bars. Yet constructing a ghetto out of choice, as some bars currently do, has a different valence from having no option but the ghetto.

Now, I just want to take this opportunity to excuse myself if I seem to be name-dropping while recounting these times. I do not mean to imply that I was running around with the in-crowd. I enjoyed only a nodding acquaintance with most of the people I want to mention. On the contrary, I was rather shy, leaning/hiding by my favorite pillar near the bar. Hopefully, the name-dropping can serve as another kind of footnote – a different way to cite the community. Esther Newton had said about my "Toward a Butch–Femme Aesthetic" that it is not historical, so in this piece I want to display the nature of my evidence. As we now know, however, as constitutive a role as they may play, experience and memory cannot claim much real empirical power. I'd like to think I could take my cue from Audre Lorde's notion of "a biomythography". Lorde's invention in *Zami* helps to inform my uncertianty about how much memory is constructed out of my desire, how much is observation, and how much is reconstructed to make a timely politicial point.[5] Of those possibilities, the mythic nature of the construction is its most authentic component. Memory's maids of honour, nostalgia, mourning, vindicating and celebrating colour most of what is written here. Anyway, about the name-dropping, the riskiest part of the venture, we spent a lot of time at the bar gossiping about certain well-known names and claiming sightings of them in the scene. That's what I want to report here. Perhaps namings places and people can lend a candour to this report if not the kind of proof the -ologies so admire. Anyway, name-dropping can also recreate the sense that just everyone was seen at Maud's. Herb Caen even included it in his trend-setting column in the *Chronicle* as the "place where beautiful women meet women".

Maud's location, about three blocks from Haight Street, influenced the mix of people in the bar. The woman who wrote the book *Going Down on Janice* had opened a kind of sexy, hippie clothing store on Haight and could be seen in the bar on a Friday night. I felt comfortable going into her store to buy the men's clothes. She had the exciting reputation of peeking around the dressing-room curtain when you were undressing. Her butch lover, in full leathers, could be seen riding her Triumph chopper down Haight Street in the early evening. She was one of the few butch images to intrude into the het, hippie flower look. You see, hippies were into strong gender roles, with women baking bread and having bavies, while men chopped wood and rolled joints. They didn't mix with the homosexual crowd, but many of the lesbians around that scene emulated some of its practices, such as living in communes. Theirs were as separatist communes, though. People at the bar often moved "out into the country" for a while, but many returned in a hurry. Some lesbian communes still persist in the south of Oregon. Others were founded in Grass Valley in California and in northern New Mexico. They were the subject of many conversations in the bars. We would pack up our cars and go out there for a week, just to look. The ones up in Sonoma County were close enough for the girls to come into town on the weekend and report on their successes with goat grazing and wood chopping. It was exotic. We were interested in flirting with these "milk maids", as we called them. I was having fantasies out of Restoration comedies. Fop that I would be.

So, anyway, I learned butch in the heart of this cauldron, which was brewing alternative subcultures in San Francisco. A new butch was born then, combining certain characteristics of the classical style with other influences. Because of feminism, cloning was already happening, toning down the masculine stance. Likewise, middle-class and student conventions altered the gestures, in terms of how you held your cigarette, for example, no longer between the thumb and first finger, which was definitely working-class, but more like Virginia Woolf, in that famous smoking photo of hers. Your seated posture was different as well. You might cross your legs and lean forward at the table, rather than hook your big shoes on the rungs of the bar stool and lean back. The volume of speech diminished, no more yelling "Hey, Red" when your friend entered the bar, while the volume of music rose, with the new electro sounds of the Jefferson Airplane, for instance. Dancing freed up, releasing one from the bondage of partnering – like sexual freedom, the flirtation was opened out into a wider, more flexible space on the dance floor. Finally, walking the walk definitely altered. Although we might have ridden motorcycles (I certainly did) we did not stomp about in our boots. Everyone was wearing boots, after all. If you had shoulders, you didn't need to mark the fact. Feminism made us interested in women and allowed us to be uninterested in men.

While we were butch, an identification with men would have seemed sordid. Many hippie men, with their long hair and soft ways, who were anti-Vietnam activists, running from the draft, were also trying to put aside the masculine. The idea of a politics around gays in the military would have been strange, indeed, to those against national military forces. Replicating what were perceived as the gestures of power and dominance had no attraction to those concerned with "equals rights", so to speak. We were "flower children" who were against all aggression. The vietnam war made weaponry and hints of violence seem obscene. Hulking about, or strutting one's stuff would have been aggrandizing space and aping dominance. Thus, butch was about giving sexual pleasure, taking pride in a lesbian identification, and being attracted to femmes. We were seeking to be "gentlemen", in the best sense of the word, if we understood butch to have any referent among men. A sense of gallantry could mark gestures as butch. You know, there was that Brit fashion of puffy sleeves – the courtier style. Listening to the Stones' "my sweet lady Jane" encouraged fantasies as pages – exquisite ceremonies for butch bottoms.

However, the butch I learned was not acceptable to the classical butches. Sherman, who appears in a chapter in the novel *Sita*, laughed derisively at my long hair, my silly hippie pants, my flowered shirts, and my "execrable" taste in music. She had been elected the "king" of North Beach, in her men's long-sleeved shirts, her tough ways, and her abstract-expressionist painting style. She wore boxer shorts and men's pajamas and was probably "stone". We were not. We had been a part of the "sexual revolution", after all and wanted to experience it all. Sherman told me to just forget it and, by the way, to forget her beautiful girlfriend. I didn't. Some of those femmes liked the new-style butches. For one thing, we could "pass" when necessary, both in terms of sexual orientation and class manners. For another, we were struggling with some kind of feminist notion of equality and shared practices. But then, Kate Millett agreed with Sherman, telling me, as a butch, I was just missing a certain something – maybe I just wasn't tall enough.

At the other end of the spectrum, the clone thing was around, compromising a too-rigid stance on role-playing. Barbara Hammer's ground-breaking films represented, as sexual and chic, women in bib overalls, in the country. She associated the nude body with "nature", cutting from scenes of clitoral manipulation to caves, or whatever. Even though some of us called out 'What is that?' in the dark, alternative cinema showings, protesting the vanilla portrayal of sex, we were still somewhat disciplined by these initial lesbian films. Caught somewhere between being too soft for the Shermans and too tough for the Hammers, we forged a style that referred to hippie anti-masculine male fashions, while still distancing ourselves from new feminist representations which would have us dancing in the meadow in our bib overalls.

Some called us "nelly butches" as a way to accommodate the new style. We took to wearing 1930s men's clothes from the thrift stores, with flowing, Dietrich-type pants and silk bow-ties. Why, we wondered, did butch necessarily mean dressing down, playing baseball, or poker? To be honest, sometimes, when we watched those traditional butch–femme couples waltz around the floor, they resembled our parents, saying the same things, like "cut your hair" and don't listen to that loud, horrible music'. We were alternatively amused and frustrated by the classic rhetoric of serial monogamy: repetitively "falling in love", "getting married", and then living with a "roommate" who, as they loved to insist, "used to be my lover but we don't sleep together anymore". This was the signal that they were moving on. It occasioned those bar fights and couple-identified postures. Hippie free love shred a devotion to sexual pleasure with the classic butches and femmes around the bars, but without the thrill of sneaking around. Bar fights just didn't fit with the idea of "make love not war". And then, those classic couples seemed so apolitical, at the time of street demonstrations. They didn't join them.

Perhaps it was because they couldn't yet feel comfortable in the streets.

Rather than enjoying tradition, hippie dykes felt themselves part of a modernist movement, I gueses you could say, dedicated to creating the new. Whether it was actually new or not, that was the rhetoric of the subculture. Let me remind the reader again that I am here correcting my stance in my first butch–femme article. At that point in the history of writing about lesbian subculture (the mid-1980s), I felt it was important to emphasize the connection with classical butches in the face of feminism's intrusion into the discourse. Now, I sense a certain mythologizing of butch–femme, which is made to serve an anti-feminist stance, which I believe misinterplets certain historical moments in the history of the feminist movement. I have revised my earlier stance at length in a new article, "Toward a Butch-Feminist Retro-Furture", in hopes of retaining the debates within feminism and its dedication to coalitions among women.[6] Part of the polemic behind this essay is to understand a different reception around issues of "female masculinity" (now enjoying a privileged status in some critical circles) by historicizing the markers of masculinity at the time of the Vietnam war.

While we're on contested critical terrian, let me return to the much-debated issue of the lesbian relationship to "camp", which I celebrated in the first article. When I asserted that such a practice was common, I neglected to locate that practice within San Francisco. It probably did not play in, say, Buffalo. In San Francisco, lesbians and gay men did suffer some social intercourse with one another. Perhaps that is how camp came into the lesbian bar discourse. Crowning the king and Queen of North Beach was an annual joint event. The boys' bars hosted some wonderful women entertainers whom the lesbians poured in to ogle. Tapes by the fabulous Ann Weldon circulated in both bars. The drag ball brought the leading queens around in their limos to visit the annual drag party at Maud's. And, as I mentioned before, the boys' bars hosted those Sunday brunches we all attended. Moreover, several of them served cheap dinners on certain nights of the week. We often met our gay friends there early in the evenings before making our way out into our gender-specific clubs. So, the pratice of drag and the enjoyment of multiple sexual partners circulated between gay and lesbian bar cultures. Show people were on the fringes of the scene. Some girls who worked as "exotic dancers", as they preferred to be called, cynically performed flirtations with men on the stages of topless/bottomless clubs. Costumes were playing

on the sidewalks of the Haight. Hallucination dis-jointed the "real".
Some of us had seen not only Barbara Hammer's films, but Andy
Warhol's as well. Kenneth Anger was around in the city. His movie,
which begins with a big biker putting on his leathers and chains to
"Blue Velvet", was the talk of the town. I talked with him once about
trying to do some homosexual version of *Oedipus*. Shortly after that,
he jumped, nude onto the altar of Glide Memorial Church. Meanwhile, back at Maud's, the brutal, clipped discourse of bar butches
still circulated among the hippie descriptions of visions and hallu-
ciantions. Opening in there, between the clip and the float, in an
environment of self-ironic flirtation within an urban homosexual
scene, was a space for masquerading thoughts and inverting social
codes. Clipped, ironic, playful travesties cast the mantle of camp across
the scene. Not the whole scene, of course, but this particular graft of
hippie and traditional.

At the same time as this permissive environment held great sway,
violent homophobic pratices still penetrated the removed spaces of
the bars. Paying off the cops at the bar could be seen by anyone
who wanted to look over there on party nights. It was still illegal
to dance together in close contact and the local beat cops had to be
encouraged not to come around. The raids around election time as
"moral clean-ups" enforced a sense of the frailty of official liberality.
One of the bars in Oakland allowed dancing in a back room, where
a large red light blinked when the vice cops entered the front door.
Everyone flew to their seats. A certain butch badge of daring could
be sported by getting "86ed", or thrown out of the bar for a certain
period of time. The owners had to be careful about the vice cops, so
they would police untoward physical proximity, when we enjoyed in
various dark corners. Frighteningly, there were still repeated episodes
of male gangs hiding around the corner at the time of the bar's closing
ready to gang rape the women who dared to walk down the pavement
alone. This happened to two of my friends. We might swagger in the
bars, sporting our butch outfits, but we put on a coat and hurriedly
got on our bikes out in front, when we left the safety of the bar's
confines.

In many ways, a certain sense of "butch" did not survive
this moment. The lesbian feminist movement turned away from
role-playing into a privileging of androgyny, or non-gendered, or
non-patriarchal, or "natural" styles, as they insisted. When butch
re-emerged out the other side of that betrayal, it did so with a
vengeance – so vengeful, in fact, that it associated its demeanour with

gay men and the masculine, rather than with styles among women. Daddy boy dykes and F2M associated with men in new, more fleshly ways. The swagger was back. Images of dominance were eroticized. Working-class styles were sported, even though, often, by middle-class butches. Leather harnesses, dildos, and piercings don't exactly suggest the gestures of gallantry, the way page haircuts and puffy sleeves once had done. In those days, I think the gyno-centric (as it was called then in feminist circles) was the magnetic pole of the imaginary, rather than the masculine. The masculine had been contaminated by its proximity to war.

Well, I am not calling for a vote on which is better. Instead, I want to make a different point, to conjecture that it was in the constrast between these two styles that the notion of style itself became visible in the subculture. Before hippies, butch and femme were not perceived as a style, but as "the way we are". At this point in history, one might argue, when hippies and butches actually regarded one another across the room, both became aware of a contest of styles. They were on their way to constructing a sense of lesbian "lifestyle". Their comparative practices redefined lesbian sexual practice as style and began to construct a sense of a serlf-conscious lesbian sociality, grounded first in the bars and later, in various kinds of locations. At the same time, because of the poets, the filmmakers, and the dress-shop owners, there arose a sense that there was a style of lesbian self-representation. Lesbians could begin to see themselves in the mirror in a way that only a few novels had provided them before. Now, they were represented in a certain way – partially influenced by the underground cinema pratices in women's and gay films at the time, partially by the styles of the subculture itself. Now, by the time "lesbian style wars", as Arlene Stein called them in her article by the same title, were taking place in the late 1980s, the 1970s had become cast as a pre-style moment.[7] Although Stein makes some acute observations about the politics of "lifestyle", she grounds its emergence in the 1980s by reducing the 1970s to what she calls the "anti-fashion" movement within lesbian feminism. I think this has become a kind of commonplace assumption that I want to adjust here by introducing the hippie butch. At least in the urban centre known as San Francisco, with its Haight–Ashbury hippie culture, its "Love-Ins", its Fillmore Auditorium, its local groups such as The Jefferson Airplane, its singers such as Joan Baez and Janis Joplin, its anti-war demonstrations, its student uprisings such as the one at San Francisco State and other events of the late 1960s and the 1970s, more than a strict hairy-legged, overall-wearing lesbian feminist was walking through the bar door. Sure, she was around and she was influential. But the encounter between the classic butch and the hippie butch was perhaps even more prescient in its focus on style, on issues or representing masculinity and sexual desire.

Hippies also presented the subculture with an interest in perception (via hallucination) and in the structuring of internal processes. If you look around now, these elements, although reconfigured, are still recognizably present. The student movement brought these kinds of studies onto the campus. Some people think we got them from importing French psychoanalytic studies. But I think they developed out of a subculture which smoked marijuana and indulged in long monologues about inner processes, or dropped acid and then dealt with the nature of perception, and out of a militant student movement that insisted that the streets, with all their priorities and social exigencies become part of the "student body".

Of course, organizing observations around something designated as a historical moment is really only a familiar disguise for a polemic. I think I already copped to that. Every time I see those crowds at Pride pushing for gays in the military, with those uniformed colour guards marching by, and those lesbians cheering on Margarethe Cammermeyer in her drive to get her much-deserved promotion in the US Army, I think of those flowered banners that read "Make love not war!" Cammermeyer served in Vietnam, I believe. Allen Ginsburg recently died, a gay brother who led that ferocious "ooohm" out in front of the Pentagon, never running from those cops who were restoring order, but standing quietly his anti-way ground, his long, hippie hair just blowing in the winds of war. Those are the issues in their most aggressive form. Watching some styles of butching it up today, though, I find they still carry for me, a one-time hippie butch, the same associations with masculinity I learned then. I can't shake those countercultural images of talking on the feminie as the devalued, unAmerican, anti-militaristic style. An interest in the masculine still smells of Agent Orange.

So, in spite of what the *X Files* advertises, I am ulitmately unconvinced, when discussing the lesbian subculture, that "the truth is out there". I don't claim any truth in this matter, only my own strong opinions, memories, vindictive parries, and iconoclastic mythologies. I'm trying to replicate my opinions at the time. But intertextuality, as we call it, among all the articles on butch–femme, queer dykes, lesbian history and attendant topics has penetrated my associations.

"Hippie" is thus a position to hold a certain ground in the terrain of lesbian studies. Still, it does serve to correct the misapprehension that "lesbian feminists" as they are now constructed against stylish queer dykes define the representation of lesbian in the 1970s.

Notes

1. *Last Call at Maud's/The Maud's Project* (New York: Water Bearer Films, 1993). The bar was Maud's on Cole Street in San Francisco, also known as The Study.
2. This article has been published in many places, to my embarrassment. I did not retain the copright and it was released by the press. One accessible collection is Henry Abelove, Michèle Barale and David Halperin (eds), *The Lesbian and Gay Studies Reader* (New York and London: Routledge, 1993), pp. 294–306. [Reproduced here as Chapter 2.]
3. This idea occurred thanks to a class paper written by Tricia Slusser.
4. The critic was named Bernard Weiner, who was pretty good on other political theatre.
5. Audre Lorde, *Zami A New Spelling of My Name: A Biomythography* (Freedom, CA: The Crossing Press, 1982).
6. In Dana Heller (ed.), *Cross-Purposes: Lesbians, Feminists, and the Limits of Alliance* (Bloomington: Indiana University Press, 1997), pp. 205–20.
7. Arlene Stein, "All dressed up but no place to go? Style wars and the new lesbianism", *Outlook* (Winter 1989), 1 (4), pp. 34–42.

2

Toward a Butch–Femme Aesthetic

In the 1980s, feminist criticism has focused increasingly on the subject position: both in the explorations for the creation of a female subject position and the deconstruction of the inherited subject position that is marked with masculinist functions and history. Within this focus, the problematics of women inhabiting the traditional subject position have been sketched out, the possibilities of a new heterogeneous, heteronomous position have been explored, and a desire for a collective subject has been articulated. While this project is primarily a critical one, concerned with language and symbolic structures, philosophic assumptions, and psychoanalytic narratives, it also implicates the social issues of class, race, and sexuality. Teresa de Lauretis's article "The Technology of Gender" (in *Technologies of Gender*, 1987) reviews the recent excavations of the subject position in terms of ideology, noting that much of the work on the subject, derived from Foucault and Althusser, denies both agency and gender to the subject. In fact, many critics leveled a similar criticism against Foucault in a recent conference on postmodernism, noting that while his studies seem to unravel the web of ideology, they suggest no subject position outside the ideology, nor do they construct a subject who has the agency to change ideology ("Postmodernism," 1987). In other words, note de Lauretis and others, most of the work on the subject position has only revealed the way in which the subject is trapped within ideology and thus provides no programs for change.

For feminists, changing this condition must be a priority. The common appellation of this bound subject has been the "female subject," signifying a biological, sexual difference, inscribed by dominant cultural practices. De Lauretis names her subject (one capable of change and of changing conditions) the feminist subject, one who is "at the same time inside and outside the ideology of gender, and conscious of being so, conscious of that pull, that division, that doubled vision" (1987, 10). De Lauretis ascribes a sense of self-determination at the micropolitical level to the feminist subject. This feminist subject, unlike the female one, can be outside of ideology, can find self-determination, can change. This is an urgent goal for the feminist activist/theorist. Near the conclusion of her article (true to the newer rules of composition), de Lauretis begins to develop her thesis: that the previous work on the female subject, assumes, but leaves unwritten, a heterosexual context for the subject and this is the cause for her continuing entrapment. Because she is still perceived in terms of men and not within the context of other women, the subject in heterosexuality cannot become capable of ideological change (1987, 17–18).

De Lauretis's conclusion is my starting place. Focusing on the feminist subject, endowed with the agency for political change, located among women, outside the ideology of sexual difference, and thus the social institution of heterosexuality, it would appear that the lesbian roles of butch and femme, as a dynamic duo, offer precisely the strong subject position the movement requires. Now, in order for the butch-femme roles to clearly emerge within this sociotheoretical project, several tasks must be accomplished: the lesbian subject of feminist theory would have to come out of the closet, the basic discourse or style of camp for the lesbian butch-femme positions would have to be clarified, and an understanding of the function of roles in the homosexual lifestyle would need to be developed, particularly in relation to the historical class and racial relations embedded in such a project. Finally, once these tasks have been completed, the performance practice, both on and off the stage, may be studied as that of a feminist subject, both inside and outside ideology, with the power to self-determine her role and her conditions on the micropolitical level. Within this schema, the butch-femme couple inhabit the subject position together – "you can't have one without the other," as the song says. The two roles never appear as . . . discrete. The combo butch-femme as subject is reminiscent of Monique Wittig's "j/e" or coupled self in her novel *The Lesbian Body*. These are not split subjects, suffering the torments of dominant ideology. They are coupled ones that do not impale themselves on the poles of sexual difference or metaphysical values, but constantly seduce the sign system, through flirtation and inconstancy into the light fondle of artifice, replacing the Lacanian slash with a lesbian bar.

However, before all of this *jouissance* can be enjoyed, it is first necessary to bring the lesbian subject out of the closet of feminist history. The initial step in that process is to trace historically how the lesbian has been assigned to the role of the skeleton in the closet of feminism; in this case, specifically the lesbian who relates to her cultural roots by identifying with traditional butch-femme role-playing. First, regard the feminist genuflection of the 1980s – the catechism of "working-class-women-of-color" feminist theorists feel impelled to invoke at the outset of their research. What's wrong with this picture? It does not include the lesbian position. In fact, the isolation of the social dynamics of race and class successfully relegates sexual preference to an attendant position, so that even if the lesbian were to appear, she would be as a bridesmaid and never the bride. Several factors are responsible for this ghosting of the lesbian subject: the first is the growth of moralistic projects restricting the production of sexual fiction or fantasy through the antipornography crusade. This crusade has produced an alliance between those working on social feminist issues and right-wing homophobic, born-again men and women who also support censorship. This alliance in the electorate, which aids in producing enough votes for an ordinance, requires the closeting of lesbians for the so-called greater cause. Both Jill Dolan and Alice Echols develop this position in their respective articles.

Although the antipornography issue is an earmark of the moralistic 1980s, the homophobia it signals is merely an outgrowth of the typical interaction between feminism and lesbianism since the rise of the feminist movement in the early 1970s. Del Martin and Phyllis Lyon describe the rise of the initial so-called lesbian liberatory organization, the Daughters of Bilitis (DOB), in their influential early book, *Lesbian/Woman* (1972). They record the way in which the aims of such organizations were intertwined with those of the early feminist, or more precisely, women's movement. They proudly exhibit the way in which the DOB moved away from the earlier bar culture and its symbolic systems to a more dominant identification and one that would appease the feminist movement. DOB's goal was to erase butch-femme behavior, its dress codes, and lifestyle from the lesbian community and to change lesbians into lesbian feminists.

Here is the story of one poor victim who came to the DOB for help. Note how similar this narrative style is to the redemptive, corrective language of missionary projects: "Toni joined Daughters of Bilitis . . . at our insistence, and as a result of the group's example, its unspoken pressure, she toned down her dress. She was still very butch, but she wore women's slacks and blouses... one of DOB's goals was to teach the lesbian a mode of behavior and dress acceptable to society.... We knew too many lesbians whose activities were restricted because they wouldn't wear skirts. But Toni did not agree. 'You'll never get me in a dress,' she growled, banging her fist on the table." The description of Toni's behavior, her animal growling noise, portrays her as uncivilized, recalling earlier, colonial missionary projects. Toni is portrayed as similar to the inappropriately dressed savage whom the missionary clothes and saves. The authors continue: "But she became fast friends with a gay man, and over the months he helped her to feel comfortable with herself as a woman" (*Lesbian/Woman* 1972, 77). Here, in a lesbian narrative, the missionary position is finally given over to a man (even if gay) who helps the butch to feel like a woman. The contemporary lesbian-identified reader can only marvel at the conflation of gender identification in the terms of dominant, heterosexual culture with the adopted gender role-playing within the lesbian subculture.

If the butches are savages in this book, the femmes are lost heterosexuals who damage birthright lesbians by forcing them to play the butch roles. The authors assert that most femmes are divorced heterosexual women who know how to relate only to men and thus force their butches to play the man's role, which is conflated with that of a butch (*Lesbian/Woman* 1972, 79). Finally, the authors unveil the salvationary role of feminism in this process and its power to sever the newly constructed identity of the lesbian feminist from its traditional lesbian roots: "The minority of lesbians who still cling to the traditional male-female or husband-wife pattern in their partnerships are more than likely old-timers, gay bar habituées or working class women." This sentence successfully compounds ageism with a (homo)phobia of lesbian bar culture and a rejection of a working-class identification. The middle-class upward mobility of the lesbian feminist identification shifts the sense of community from one of working-class, often women-of-color lesbians in bars, to that of white upper-middle-class heterosexual women who predominated in the early women's movement. The book continues: "the old order changeth however" (here they even begin to adopt verb endings from the King James Bible) "as the women's liberation movement gains strength against this pattern of heterosexual marriages, the number of lesbians involved in butch-femme roles diminishes" (*Lesbian/Woman* 1972, 80).[1]

However, this compulsory adaptation of lesbian feminist identification must be understood as a defensive posture, created by the
homophobia that operated in the internal dynamics of the early
movement, particularly within the so-called consciousness-raising
groups. In her article with Cherríe Moraga on butch-femme relations, Amber Hollibaugh, a femme, described the feminist reception
of lesbians this way: "the first discussion I ever heard of lesbianism
among feminists was: 'We've been sex objects to men and where
did it get us? And here when we're just learning how to be friends
with other women, you got to go and sexualize it'... they made
men out of every sexual dyke" (1983, 402). These kinds of experiences led Hollibaugh and Moraga to conclude: "In our involvement
in a movement largely controlled by white middle-class women, we
feel that the values of their culture... have been pushed down our
throats...," and even more specifically, in the 1980s, to pose these
questions: "why is it that it is largely white middle-class women
who form the visible leadership in the anti-porn movement? Why
are women of color not particularly visible in this sex-related single
issue movement?" (1983, 405).

When one surveys these beginnings of the alliance between the
heterosexual feminist movement and lesbians, one is not surprised at
the consequences for lesbians who adopted the missionary position
under a movement that would lead to an antipornography crusade
and its alliance with the Right. Perhaps too late, certain members
of the lesbian community who survived the early years of feminism
and continued to work in the grass-roots lesbian movement, such as
Joan Nestle, began to perceive this problem. As Nestle, founder of the
Lesbian Herstory Archives in New York, wrote: "We lesbians of the
1950s made a mistake in the 1970s: we allowed ourselves to be trivi-
alized and reinterpreted by feminists who did not share our culture"
(1981, 23). Nestle also notes the class prejudice in the rejection of
butch-femme roles: "I wonder why there is such a consuming interest in the butch-fem lives of upper-class women, usually more literary
figures, while real-life, working butch-fem women are seen as imita-
tive and culturally backward... the reality of passing women, usually
a working-class lesbian's method of survival, has provoked very little
academic lesbian-feminist interest. Grassroots lesbian history research
is changing this" (1981, 23).

So the lesbian butch-femme tradition went into the feminist closet.
Yet the closet, or the bars, with their hothouse atmosphere have
produced what, in combination with the butch-femme couple, may

provide the liberation of the feminist subject – the discourse of camp. Proust described this accomplishment in his novel *The Captive*:

> The lie, the perfect lie, about people we know, about the relations we have had with them, about our motive for some action, formulated in totally different terms, the lie as to what we are, whom we love, what we feel in regard to those people who love us . . . – that lie is one of the few things in the world that can open windows for us on to what is new and unknown, that can awaken in us sleeping senses for the contemplation of the universes that otherwise we should never have known.   (Proust, 213; in Sedgwick 1987)

The closet has given us camp – the style, the discourse, the *mise en scène* of butch-femme roles. In this history of the development of gay camp, Michael Bronski describes the liberative work of late-nineteenth-century authors such as Oscar Wilde in creating the homosexual camp liberation from the rule of naturalism, or realism. Within his argument, Bronski describes naturalism and realism as strategies that tried to save fiction from the accusation of daydream, imagination, or masturbation and to affix a utilitarian goal to literary production – that of teaching morals. In contrast, Bronski quotes the newspaper *Fag Rag* on the functioning of camp: "We've broken down the rules that are used for validating the difference between real/true and unreal/false. The controlling agents of the status quo may know the power of lies; dissident subcultures, however, are closer to knowing their value" (1984, 41). Camp both articulates the lives of homosexuals through the obtuse tone of irony and inscribes their oppression with the same device. Likewise, it eradicates the ruling powers of heterosexist realist modes.

Susan Sontag, in an avant-garde assimilation of camp, described it as a "certain mode of aestheticism . . . one way of seeing the world as an aesthetic phenomenon . . . not in terms of beauty, but in terms of the degree of artifice" (1966, 275). This artifice, as artifice, works to defeat the reign of realism as well as to situate the camp discourse within the category of what can be said (or seen). However, the fixed quality of Sontag's characteristic use of camp within the straight context of aestheticization has produced a homosexual strategy for avoiding such assimilation: what Esther Newton has described as its constantly changing, mobile quality, designed to alter the gay camp sensibility before it becomes a fad (1972, 105). Moreover, camp also protects homosexuals through a "first-strike wit" as *Fag Rag* asserts: "Wit and irony provide the only reasonable modus operandi in the American Literalist Terror of Straight Reality" (1984, 46).

Oscar Wilde brought this artifice, wit, irony, and the distancing of straight reality and its conventions to the stage. Later, Genet staged the malleable, multiple artifice of camp in *The Screens*, which elevates such displacement to an ontology. In his play, *The Black*, he used such wit, irony and artifice to deconstruct the notion of "black" and to stage the dynamics of racism. *The Blacks* displaced the camp critique from homophobia to racism, in which "black" stands in for "queer" and the campy queen of the bars is transformed into an "african queen." This displacement is part of the larger use of the closet and gay camp discourse to articulate other social realities. Eve Sedgwick attests to this displacement when she writes: "I want to argue that a lot of energy of attention and demarcation that has swirled around issues of homosexuality since the end of the nineteenth century . . . has been impelled by the distinctly indicative relation of homosexuality to wider mappings of secrecy and disclosure, and of the private and the public, that were and are critically problematical for the gender, sexual, and economic structures of the heterosexist culture at large. . . . 'the closet' and 'coming out' are now verging on all-purpose phrases for the potent crossing and recrossing of almost any politically-charged lines of representation. . . . The apparent floating-free from its gay origins of that phrase 'coming out of the closet' in recent usage might suggest that the trope of the closet is so close to the heart of some modern preoccupations that it could be . . . evacuated of its historical gay specificity. But I hypothesize that exactly the opposite is true." Thus, the camp success in ironizing and distancing the regime of realist terror mounted by heterosexist forces has become useful as a discourse and style for other marginal factions.

Camp style, gay-identified dressing and the articulation of the social realities of homosexuality have also become part of the straight, postmodern canon, as Herbert Blau articulated it in a special issue of *Salmagundi*: "becoming homosexual is part of the paraphilia of the postmodern, not only a new sexual politics but the reification of all politics, supersubtilized beyond the unnegotiable demands of the sixties, from which it is derived, into a more persuasive rhetoric of unsublimated desire" (1983, 233). Within this critical community, the perception of recognizable homosexuals can also inspire broader visions of the operation of social codes. Blau states: "there soon came pullulating toward me at high prancing amphetamined pitch something like the end of Empire or like the screaming remains of the return of the repressed – pearl-white, vinyl, in polo pants and scarf – an englistered and giggling outburst of resplendent queer . . . what was there to consent to and who could possibly legitimate that galloping specter I had seen, pure ideolect, whose plunging and lungless soundings were a full-throttled forecast of much weirder things to come?" (1983, 221–2). Initially, these borrowings seem benign and even inviting to the homosexual theorist. Contemporary theory seems to open the closet door to invite the queer to come out, transformed as a new, postmodern subject, or even to invite straights to come into the closet, out of the roar of dominant discourse. The danger incurred in moving gay politics into such heterosexual contexts is in only slowly discovering that the strategies and perspectives of homosexual realities and discourse may be locked inside a homophobic "concentration camp." Certain of these authors, such as Blau, even introduce homosexual characters and their subversions into arguments that conclude with explicit homophobia. Note Blau's remembrance of things past: "thinking I would enjoy it, I walked up Christopher Street last summer at the fag end of the depleted carnival of Gay Pride Day, with a disgust unexpected and almost uncontained by principle. . . . I'll usually fight for the right of each of us to have his own perversions, I may not, under the pressure of theory and despite the itchiness of my art, to try on yours and, what's worse, rather wish you wouldn't. Nor am I convinced that what you are doing isn't perverse in the most perjorative sense" (1983, 249). At least Blau, as in all of his writing, honestly and openly records his personal prejudice. The indirect or subtextual homophobia in this new assimilative discourse is more alluring and ultimately more powerful in erasing the social reality and the discursive inscriptions of gay, and more specifically, lesbian discourse.

Here, the sirens of sublation may be found in the critical maneuvers of heterosexual feminist critics who metaphorize butch-femme roles, transvestites and campy dressers into a "subject who masquerades," as they put it, or is "carnivalesque" or even, as some are so bold to say, who "cross-dresses." Even when these borrowings are nested in more benign contexts than Blau's, they evacuate the historical, butch-femme couples' sense of masquerade and cross-dressing the way a cigar-store Indian evacuates the historical dress and behavior of the Native American. As is often the case, illustrated by the cigar-store Indian, these symbols may only proliferate when the social reality has been successfully obliterated and the identity has become the private property of the dominant class. Such metaphors operate simply to display the breadth of the art collection, or style collection, of the straight author. Just as the French term *film noir* became the name for B-rate American films of the forties, these notions of masquerade and cross-dressing, standing in for the roles of working-class lesbians, have come back to us through French theory on the one hand and studies of the lives of upper-class lesbians who lived in Paris between the wars on the other. In this case, the referent of the term Left Bank is not a river, but a storehouse of critical capital.

Nevertheless, this confluence of an unresolved social, historical problem in the feminist movement and these recent theoretical strategies, re-assimilated by the lesbian critic, provide a ground that could resolve the project of constructing the feminist subject position. The butch-femme subject could inhabit that discursive position, empowering it for the production of future compositions. Having already grounded this argument within the historical situation of butch-femme couples, perhaps now it would be tolerable to describe the theoretical maneuver that could become the butch-femme subject position. Unfortunately, these strategies must emerge in the bodiless world of "spectatorial positions" or "subject positions," where transvestites wear no clothes and subjects tread only "itineraries of desire." In this terrain of discourse, or among theorized spectators in darkened movie houses with their gazes fixed on the dominant cinema screen, "the thrill is gone" as Nestle described it. In the Greenwich Village bars, she could "spot a butch 50 feet away and still feel the thrill of her power" as she saw "the erotic signal of her hair at the nape of her neck, touching the shirt collar; how she held a cigarette; the symbolic pinky ring flashing as she waved her hand" (1981, 21–2). Within this theory, the erotics are gone, but certain maneuvers maintain what is generally referred to as "presence."

The origins of this theory may be found in a Freudian therapist's office, where an intellectual heterosexual woman, who had become frigid, had given way to rages, and, puzzled by her own coquettish behavior, told her story to Joan Riviere sometime around 1929. This case caused Riviere to publish her thoughts in her ground-breaking article entitled "Womanliness as a Masquerade" that later influenced several feminist critics such as Mary Russo and Mary Ann Doane and the French philosopher Jean Baudrillard. Riviere began to "read" this woman's behavior as the "wish for masculinity" which causes the woman to don "the mask of womanliness to avert anxiety and the retribution feared from men" (1929, 303). As Riviere saw it, for a woman to read an academic paper before a professional association was to exhibit in public her "possession of her father's penis, having castrated him" (1929, 305–6). In order to do recompense for this castration, which resided in her intellectual proficiency, she donned the mask of womanliness. Riviere notes: "The reader may now ask how I define womanliness or where I draw the line between genuine womanliness and the 'masquerade'... they are the same thing" (1929, 306). Thus began the theory that all womanliness is a masquerade worn by women to disguise the fact that they have taken their father's penis in their intellectual stride, so to speak. Rather than remaining the well-adjusted castrated woman, these intellectuals have taken the penis for their own and protect it with the mask of the castrated, or womanhood. However, Riviere notes a difference here between heterosexual women and lesbian ones – the heterosexual women don't claim possession openly, but through reaction-formations; whereas the homosexual women openly display their possession of the penis and count on the males' recognition of defeat (1929, 312). This is not to suggest that the lesbian's situation is not also fraught with anxiety and reaction-formations, but this difference in degree is an important one.

I suggest that this kind of masquerade is consciously played out in butch-femme roles, particularly as they were constituted in the 1940s and 1950s. If one reads them from within Riviere's theory, the butch is the lesbian woman who proudly displays the possession of the penis, while the femme takes on the compensatory masquerade of womanliness. The femme, however, foregrounds her masquerade by playing to a butch, another woman in a role; likewise, the butch exhibits her penis to a woman who is playing the role of compensatory castration. This raises the question of "penis, penis, who's got the penis," because there is no referent in sight; rather, the fictions of penis and castration become ironized and "camped up." Unlike Riviere's patient, these women play on the phallic economy rather than to it. Both women alter this masquerading subject's function by positioning it between women and thus foregrounding the myths of penis and castration in the Freudian economy. In the bar culture, these roles were always acknowledged as such. The bars were often abuzz with the discussion of who was or was not a butch or femme, and how good they were at the role (see Davis and Kennedy 1986). In other words, these penis-related posturings were always acknowledged as roles, not biological birthrights, nor any other essentialist poses. The lesbian roles are underscored as two optional functions for women in the phallocracy, while the heterosexual woman's role collapses them into one compensatory charade. From a theatrical point of view, the butch-femme roles take on the quality of something more like a character construction and have a more active quality than what Riviere calls a reaction-formation. Thus, these roles qua roles lend agency and self-determination to the historically passive subject, providing her with at least two options for gender identification and with the aid of camp, an irony that allows her perception to be constructed from outside ideology, with a gender role that makes her appear as if she is inside of it.

Meanwhile, other feminist critics have received this masquerade theory into a heterosexual context, retaining its passive imprint. In Mary Ann Doane's influential article entitled "Film and the Masquerade: Theorising the Female Spectator," Doane, unfortunately, resorts to a rather biologistic position in constructing the female spectator and theorizing out from the female body. From the standpoint of something more active in terms of representation such as de Lauretis's feminist subject or the notion of butch-femme, this location of critical strategies in biological realities seems revisionist. That point aside, Doane does devise a way for women to "appropriate the gaze for their own pleasure" (1982, 77) through the notion of the transvestite and the masquerade. As the former, the female subject would position herself as if she were a male viewer, assimilating all of the power and payoffs that spectatorial position offers. As the latter, she would, as Riviere earlier suggested, masquerade as a woman. She would "flaunt her femininity, produce herself as an excess of femininity – foreground the masquerade," and reveal "femininity itself . . . as a mask" (1982, 81). Thus, the masquerade would hold femininity at a distance, manufacturing "a lack in the form of a certain distance between oneself and one's image" (1982, 82). This strategy offers the female viewer a way to be the spectator of female roles while not remaining close to them, nor identifying with them, attaining the distance from them required to enter the psychoanalytic viewing space. The masquerade that Doane describes is exactly that practiced by the femme – she foregrounds cultural femininity. The difference is that Doane places this role in the spectator position, probably as an outgrowth of the passive object position required of women in the heterosexist social structures. Doane's vision of the active woman is as the active spectator. Within the butch-femme economy, the femme actively performs her masquerade as the subject of representation. She delivers a performance of the feminine masquerade rather than, as Doane suggests, continues in

Rivere's reactive formation of masquerading compensatorily before the male gaze-inscribed-dominant-cinema-screen. *Flaunting* has long been a camp verb and here Doane borrows it, along with the notion of "excess of femininity," so familiar to classical femmes and drag queens. Yet, by reinscribing it within a passive, spectatorial role, she gags and binds the traditional homosexual role players, whose gender play has nothing essential beneath it, replacing them with the passive spectatorial position that is, essentially, female.

Another feminist theorist, Mary Russo, has worked out a kind of female masquerade through the sense of the carnivalesque body derived from the work of Mikhail Bakhtin. In contrast to Doane, Russo moves on to a more active role for the masquerader, one of "making a spectacle of oneself." Russo is aware of the dangers of the essentialist body in discourse, while still maintaining some relationship between theory and real women. This seems a more hopeful critical terrain to the lesbian critic. In fact, Russo even includes a reference to historical instances of political resistance by men in drag (1985, 3). Yet in spite of her cautions, like Doane, Russo's category is once again the female subject, along with its biologically determined social resonances. Perhaps it is her reliance on the male author Bakhtin and the socialist resonances in his text (never too revealing about gender) that cause Russo to omit lesbian or gay strategies or experiences with the grotesque body. Instead, she is drawn to depictions of the pregnant body and finally Kristeva's sense of the maternal, even though she does note its limitations and problematic status within feminist thought (1985, 6). Finally, this swollen monument to reproduction, with all of its heterosexual privilege, once more stands alone in this performance area of the grotesque and carnivalesque. Though she does note the exclusion, in this practice, of "the already marginalized" (6), once again, they do not appear. Moreover, Russo even cites Showalter's notion that feminist theory itself is a kind of "critical cross-dressing," while still suppressing the lesbian presence in the feminist community that made such a concept available to the straight theorists (1985, 8). Still true to the male, heterosexual models from which her argument derives, she identifies the master of *mise en scène* as Derrida. Even when damning his characterization of the feminist as raging bull and asking "what kind of drag is this," her referent is the feminist and not the bull . . . dyke (1985, 9). This argument marks an ironic point in history: once the feminist movement had obscured the original cross-dressed butch through the interdiction of "politically incorrect," it donned for itself the strategies and characteristics of the role-playing, safely theorized out of material reality and used to suppress the referent that produced it.

In spite of their heterosexist shortcomings, what, in these theories, can be employed to understand the construction of the butch-femme subject on the stage? First, how might they be constructed as characters? Perhaps the best example of some workings of this potential is in Split Britches' production of *Beauty and the Beast*.[2] The title itself connotes the butch-femme couple: Shaw as the butch becomes the Beast who actively pursues the femme, while Weaver as the excessive femme becomes Beauty. Within the dominant system of representation, Shaw, as butch Beast, portrays as bestial women who actively love other women. The portrayal is faithful to the historical situation of the butch role, as Nestle describes it: "None of the butch women I was with, and this included a passing woman, ever presented themselves to me as men; they did announce themselves as tabooed women who were willing to identify their passion for other women by wearing clothes that symbolized the taking of responsibility. Part of this responsibility was sexual expertise . . . this courage to feel comfortable with arousing another woman became a political act" (1981, 21). In other words, the butch, who represents by her clothing the desire for other women, becomes the beast – the marked taboo against lesbianism dressed up in the clothes of that desire. Beauty is the desired one and the one who aims her desirability at the butch.

This symbolism becomes explicit when Shaw and Weaver interrupt the Beauty/Beast narrative to deliver a duologue about the history of their own personal butch-femme roles. Weaver uses the trope of having wished she was Katharine Hepburn and casting another woman as Spencer Tracy, while Shaw relates that she thought she was James Dean. The identification with movie idols is part of the camp assimilation of dominant culture. It serves multiple purposes: (1) they do not identify these butch-femme roles with "real" people, or literal images of gender, but with fictionalized ones, thus underscoring the masquerade; (2) the history of their desire, or their search for a sexual partner becomes a series of masks, or identities that stand for sexual attraction in the culture, thus distancing them from the "play" of seduction as it is outlined by social mores; (3) the association with movies makes narrative fiction part of the strategy as well as characters. This final fiction as fiction allows Weaver and Shaw to slip easily from one narrative to another, to yet another, unbound by through-lines, plot structure, or a stable sense of character because they are fictional at their core in the camp style and through the butch-femme roles. The instability and alienation of character and plot is compounded with their own personal butch-femme play on the street, as a recognizable couple in the lower East Side scene, as well as within fugitive narratives onstage, erasing the difference between theatre and real life, or actor and character, obliterating any kind of essentialist ontology behind the play. This allows them to create a play with scenes that move easily from the narrative of beauty and the beast, to the duologue on their butch-femme history, to a recitation from *Macbeth*, to a solo lip-synced to Perry Como. The butch-femme roles at the center of their ongoing personalities move masquerade to the base of performance and no narrative net can catch them or hold them, as they wriggle into a variety of characters and plots.

This exciting multiplicity of roles and narratives signals the potency of their agency. Somehow the actor overcomes any text, yet the actor herself is a fiction and her social self is one as well. Shaw makes a joke out of suturing to any particular role or narrative form when she dies, as the beast. Immediately after dying, she gets up to tell the audience not to believe in such cheap tricks. Dies. Tells the audience that Ronald Reagan pulled the same trick when he was shot – tells them that was not worth the suturing either. Dies. Asks for a Republican doctor. Dies. Then rises to seemingly close the production by kissing Weaver. Yet even this final butch-femme tableau is followed by a song to the audience that undercuts the performance itself.

Weaver's and Shaw's production of butch-femme role-playing in and out of a fairy tale positions the representation of the lesbian couple in a childhood narrative: the preadolescent proscription of perversity. Though they used *Beauty and the Beast* to stage butch-femme as outsiders, the quintessential childhood narrative that proscribes cross-dressing is *Little Red Riding Hood*, in which the real terror of the wolf is produced by his image in grandmother's clothing. The bed, the eating metaphor, and the cross-dressing by the wolf, provide a gridlock closure of any early thoughts of transgressing gender roles. Djuna Barnes wrote a version of this perspective in *Nightwood*. When Nora sees the transvestite doctor in his bed, wearing women's nightclothes, she remarks: "God, children know something they can't tell; they like Red Riding Hood and the wolf in bed!" Barnes goes on to explicate that sight of the cross-dressed one: "Is not the gown the natural raiment of extremity? ... He dresses to lie beside himself, who is so constructed that love, for him, can only be something special...." (1961, 78–80).[3] *Beauty and the Beast* also returns to a childhood tale of taboo and liberates the sexual preference and role-playing it is designed to repress, in this case, specifically the butch-femme promise. As some lesbians prescribed in the early movement: identify with the monsters!

What, then, is the action played between these two roles? It is what Jean Baudrillard terms *séduction* and it yields many of its social fruits. Baudrillard begins his argument in *De la séduction*, by asserting that seduction is never of the natural order, but always operates as a sign, or artifice (1979, 10). By extension, this suggests that butch-femme seduction is always located in semiosis. The kiss, as Shaw and Weaver demonstrate in their swooping image of it, positioned at its most clichéd niche at the end of the narrative, is always the high camp kiss. Again, Baudrillard: seduction doesn't "recuperate the autonomy of the body . . . truth . . . the sovereignty of this seduction is transsexual, not bisexual, destroying all sexual organization. . . . " (1979, 18). The point is not to conflict reality with another reality, but to abandon

Figure 1 Lois Weaver, Peggy Shaw and Deb Margolin appear in *Upwardly Mobile Home*, a Split Britches production (photograph by Eva Weiss)

the notion of reality through roles and their seductive atmosphere and lightly manipulate appearances. Surely, this is the atmosphere of camp, permeating the *mise en scène* with "pure" artifice. In other words, a strategy of appearances replaces a claim to truth. Thus, butch-femme roles evade the notion of "the female body" as it predominates in feminist theory, dragging along its Freudian baggage and scopophilic transubstantiation. These roles are played in signs themselves and not in ontologies. Seduction, as a dramatic action, transforms all of these seeming realities into semiotic play. To use Baudrillard with Riviere, butch-femme roles offer a hypersimulation of woman as she is defined by the Freudian system and the phallocracy that institutes its social rule.[4]

Therefore, the female body, the male gaze, and the structures of realism are only sex toys for the butch-femme couple. From the perspective of camp, the claim these have to realism destroys seduction by repressing the resonances of vision and sound into its medium. This is an idea worked out by Baudrillard in his chapter on pornography, but I find it apt here. That is, that realism, with its visual organization of three dimensions, actually degrades the scene; it impoverishes the suggestiveness of the scene by its excess of means (1979, 49). This implies that as realism makes the spectator see things its way, it represses her own ability to free-associate within a situation and reduces the resonances of events to its own limited, technical dimensions. Thus, the seduction of the scene is repressed by the authoritarian claim to realistic representation. This difference is marked in the work of Weaver and Shaw in the ironized, imaginative theatrical space of their butch-femme role-playing. Contrast their freely moving, resonant narrative space to the realism of Marsha Norman, Beth Henley, Irene Fornes's *Mud*, or Sam Shepard's *A Lie of the Mind*. The violence released in the continual zooming-in on the family unit, and the heterosexist ideology linked with its stage partner, realism, is directed against women and their hint of seduction. In *A Lie of the Mind*, this becomes literally woman-battering. Beth's only associative space and access to transformative discourse is the result of nearly fatal blows to her head. One can see similar violent results in Norman's concerted moving of the heroine toward suicide in *'night, Mother* or Henley's obsession with suicide in *Crimes of the Heart* or the conclusive murder in Fornes's *Mud*. The closure of these realistic narratives chokes the women to death and strangles the play of symbols, or the possibility of seduction. In fact, for each of them, sexual play only assists their entrapment. One can see the butch Peggy Shaw rising to her feet after these realistic narrative deaths and telling us not to believe it. Cast the realism aside – its consequences for women are deadly.

In recuperating the space of seduction, the butch-femme couple can, through their own agency, move through a field of symbols, like tiptoeing through the two lips (as Irigaray would have us believe), playfully inhabiting the camp space of irony and wit, free from biological determinism, elitist essentialism, and the heterosexist cleavage of sexual difference. Surely, here is a couple the feminist subject might perceive as useful to join.

Notes

A version of this article appears in the journal *Discourse* 11, no. 1, from the Center for Twentieth Century Studies, University of Wisconsin-Milwaukee.

1. It is interesting to note here, that when same-sex marriage was legalised in California (June 2008), the first ceremony performed in San Francisco was of Del Martin and Phyllis Lyon now in their eighties.
2. There is no published version of this play. In fact, there is no satisfactory way to separate the spoken text from the action. The play is composed by three actors, Deborah Margolin along with Shaw and Weaver. Margolin, however, does not play within the lesbian dynamics, but represents a Jewish perspective. For further discussions of this group's work see Kate Davy, "Constructing the Spectator: Reception, Context, and Address in Lesbian Performance," *Performing Arts Journal* 10, no. 2 (1986): 43–52; Jill Dolan, "The Dynamics of Desire: Sexuality and Gender in Pornography and Performance," *Theatre Journal* 39, no. 2 (1987): 156–74; and Sue-Ellen Case, "From Split Subject to Split Britches," *Feminine Focus: The Women? Playwrights*, ed. Enoch Brater (Oxford: Oxford University Press, 1989), pp. 126–46.
3. My thanks to Carolyn Allen, who pointed out this passage in Barnes to me in discussing resonances of the fairy tale. In another context, it would be interesting to read the lesbian perspective on the male transvestite in these passages and the way he works in Barnes's narrative. "The Company of Wolves," a short story and later a screenplay by Angela Carter, begins to open out the sexual resonances, but retains the role of the monster within heterosexuality.
4. The term *hypersimulation* is borrowed from Baudrillard's notion of the simulacrum rather than his one of seduction. It is useful here to raise the ante on terms like artifice and to suggest, as Baudrillard does, its relation to the order of reproduction and late capitalism.

References

Barnes, Djuna (1961) *Nightwood* (New York: New Directions).
Baudrillard, Jean (1979) *De la séduction* (Paris: Editions Galilee).
Blau, Herbert (1983) "Disseminating Sodom." *Salmagundi* 58–9: 221–51.

Bronski, Michael (1984) *Culture Clash: The Making of Gay Sensibility* (Boston, MA: South End Press).

Davis, Madeline, and Kennedy, Elizabeth Lapovsky (1986) "Oral History and the Study of Sexuality in the Lesbian Community: Buffalo, New York, 1940–1960." *Feminist Studies* 12, no. 1:7–26.

de Lauretis, Teresa (1987) *Technologies of Gender* (Bloomington, Ind.: Indiana University Press).

Doane, Mary Ann (1982) "Film and the Masquerade: Theorising the Female Spectator." *Screen* 23:74–87.

Dolan, Jill (1987) "The Dynamics of Desire: Sexuality and Gender in Pornography and Performance." *Theatre Journal* 39, no. 2:156–74.

Echols, Alice (1983) "The New Feminism of Yin and Yang." In *Powers of Desire: The Politics of Sexuality*, ed. Ann Snitow, Christine Stansell, and Sharon Thompson, pp. 440–59 (New York: Monthly Review Press).

Hollibaugh, Amber, and Moraga, Cherríe (1983) "What We're Rollin' Around in Bed With: Sexual Silences in Feminism." In *Powers of Desire: The Politics of Sexuality*, ed. Ann Snitow, Christine Stansell, and Sharon Thompson, pp. 395–405 (New York: Monthly Review Press).

Martin, Del, and Lyon, Phyllis (1972) *Lesbian/Woman* (New York: Bantam).

Nestle, Joan (1981) "Butch-Fem Relationships: Sexual Courage in the 1950s." *Heresies* 12:21–4. All pagination here is from that publication. Reprinted in Joan Nestle (1987), *A Restricted Country*, pp. 100–9 (Ithaca: Firebrand Books).

Newton, Esther (1972) *Mother Camp: Female Impersonators in America* (Englewood Cliffs, N.J.: Prentice-Hall).

"Postmodernism: Text, Politics, Instruction" (1987) International Association for Philosophy and Literature, Lawrence, Kansas, April 30–May 2.

Riviere, Joan (1929) "Womanliness as a Masquerade." *International Journal of Psycho-Analysis* 10:303–13.

Russo, Mary (1985) "Female Grotesques: Carnival and Theory." Working Paper no. 1. Center for Twentieth Century Studies, Milwaukee. Page citations for this text. Reprinted in *Feminist Studies Critical Studies*, ed. Teresa de Lauretis (Bloomington: Indiana University Press, 1986).

Sedgwick, Eve (1987) "The Epistemology of the Closet." Manuscript.

Sontag, Susan (1966) *Against Interpretation* (New York: Farrar, Strauss & Giroux).

Wittig, Monique (1975) *The Lesbian Body*, trans. David LeVay (New York: William Morrow).

3

Toward a Butch-Feminist Retro-Future

After throwing a major temper tantrum about the feminist tradition in my article "Toward a Butch-Femme Aesthetic," I now want to emphasize the fact that the tantrum was intended as a dramatic event that would, hopefully, by the force of its critique, initiate a dialogue to correct what seemed to me to be persistent omissions and oppressions in the history of feminist discourse around lesbian issues.[1] The scenario I sought to write was a butch seduction/bar fight with feminism, with no exit from the feminist arena on my mind. For, dysfunctional as the feminist family of critical notions proved to be, it was still "home" to my lesbian identity. And I mean specifically a "lesbian" identity. If the bar culture had given me "butch," feminism had given me "lesbian." Now maybe the reason I was entangled with feminism had to do with my pre-movement, oppressed habit of bringing out straight women – particularly straight middle-class women, who seemed to best grace my working-class arm. I kept trying to seduce feminism, then, as it toyed with representations of me. Classic behavior for a butch bottom.

Yet, while "butch" provided a way back into the bars, subcultural history, and signs, "feminism" had provided a way out of the bars, onto the streets, in coalitions with other women, and into theories of representation. Theoretical prowess – is that another name for academic upward mobility? Possibly. Barbara Christian and others have revealed the operations of class in such theory building. But, as those very authors have illustrated, it isn't in the theory that the class markers are embedded. After all, they theorize against theory, or theorize through autobiography and poetry. The class-specific signs, then, reside in the language of the theory. Part of an early feminist concern – that. The general proscription was not to

49

duplicate the impersonal, unmarked language of the patriarchal tradition. Refined by some women of color and white-trash lesbians, the creative impulse within the movement was to abandon elitist, class-privileged language for experiments in the personal voice of the author. As in what was once called the arts, an embodiment of the abstracted position of the author was the practice. Author, as floating signifier, presumed access to the realm of timeless, genderless, subjective-less knowledge. In the case of the early feminist critique, the abstract, situated author, apart from "personal" or explicit historical and material attributes, practiced gender, class, and ethnic privilege. Slippage, then, signaled upward mobility. Dorothy Allison, author of *Trash*, quotes, in *Skin*, from a speech delivered by Bertha Harris that contrasts what she calls "lower class" writing with such signs of privilege:

> direct, unequivocating, grabby, impolite, always ready for a fight, and with a nose that can smell bullshit a mile away. The ecumenical, appeasing, side-stepping, middle-class mind never ever produces a great work of art, nor a great work of politics.   (206)

Now, Allison reports that Harris delivered this homily in a manner that "scared" her. Harris "put her hands on her hips, glared out at us." Scared, seduced, and supported in one, Bertha's attitude and her admonition produced a therapeutic effect for Allison. She took them as a challenge to believe in herself – to overcome her class-based insecurities and lack of self-esteem. She then quotes how Harris threw down the gauntlet to stop shuddering and get busy:

> *Remember, the central female organ that makes us different and strong and artists is not the womb but the brain.*   (207; italics hers)

Allison is citing a speech Harris delivered at the Sagaris feminist institute in 1975. Here is an essentialism of 1970s lesbian feminism – an appeal to the biological, delivered through that "unequivocating, grabby" style, aimed at the material practice of writing, and received within the class practices of she who would write. Harris's call to the body (the brain) is a rhetorical strategy, insisting upon a hands-on relation to the meat of mentality. To write, for Allison and Harris, is to work – appeals to the body reference manual labor – a far cry from the elitist notions of "ontology" or "presence" later ascribed to lesbian feminists. But those later charges presume the referents of writing to be philosophical systems. Their distance from the assumption of manual labor and class shame mark more the authors who deploy such charges than those they were set against.

In order to reframe the debates over critiques of lesbian and queer, I want to erect Harris, standing, feet apart, like a feminist butch colossus, overseeing the divide between the tradition of feminism and its *All About Eve* successor – the queer dyke. Allison's Harris, big, bad, gender-and class-specific, seductive and butch in her positioning of writing and the body, challenges the later charge of essentialism that has been channelled through the term *queer* in order to undo that pose of the feminist butch. The charge of essentialism, from those queer quarters, would bury that butch feminist and her likes beneath an image of lesbian feminists that look like button-wearing naive politicas. Queer dykes, flipping through fashion magazines while boarding at North-Eastern private universities, proffer, instead, the semiotic copy of such material practices as a correction to the "essentialist" fallacy. If Allison sees in Harris a kind of *Night of the Living Dead*, starring brain-eating butch writers teaching at a 1970s feminist institute, the queer dyke sees herself seeing k.d.lang on the cover of *Vanity Fair*. How is it that Condé Nast(y) has become more poststructurally correct than Allison's *Skin?* The answer resides in the deployment of the term *queer*.

Queer, not!

Early on, before its assimilation by postsomething or other's positioning of the discourses constructing sexuality, "queer" theorizing still emulated the sense of taking back the insult – inhabiting the "bad girl" – playing the monster – as 1970s lesbian feminism had taught some of us to do. Antiassimilationist in its intent, "queer" moved away from good-girl civil-rights petitioning. Some people thought "queer" originated that pose, but Allison reports, from that 1975 feminist writing institute, that big Bertha admonished them: "*Dare to be monstrous*, she told us in that tone of irony that warned of puns and witticisms to follow" (207). The tradition of antiassimilation, then, could be perceived as emanating from a 1970s working-class butch feminism, rather than a late 1980s New York queer coalition. Embedded in camp irony and wit (a discourse some writers of lesbian history deny to lesbians), these shared moments of Dorothy Allison and Bertha Harris at the feminist writer's institute could promote the kind of move that would embrace the insult of queer, in order to retrieve a contestatory site for political intervention.

Moreover, "queer" might reposition lesbian – moving the term out of its subcategorical position within feminism to one of (hopefully) equal status within discourses and practices of homosexuality. In order to safeguard the status of lesbian within feminist practices, and in association with gay men, Teresa de Lauretis organized a conference in Santa Cruz in 1990, proposing "queer" as a tactic that would so move the lesbian into a queer coalition that would, however, continue to trouble the conjunction between "lesbian AND gay." As de Lauretis explained it, in her introduction to the special issue of *differences* that was culled from the conference, "queer" was set at the site of difference, to call for an articulation of historical/material specificity in regard to sexual and gender practices where "and" had simply conjoined them (iv–vii). In other words, (some of them penned by Mary McIntosh), there is a separate development of lesbian and gay male history inscribed in their shared strategies.[2] Terms such as constructionism and queer, rather than inhabiting a gender-free or beyond-gender theoretical position, would be examined to reveal the uneven development of lesbian/gay politics along the social, historical axis of gender difference, while also forging a common front.

Persuaded by de Lauretis's call through queer to critically explore the homosexual divide, I wrote "Tracking the Vampire" for her conference and to be published in the ensuing collection of articles. For me, queer mobilized a vampiric (in)visibility within systems of representation that would feed along an axis of both gay and lesbian texts which had nourished me prior to feminism. Again, ever in dialogue with feminist constructions, I tried to retrieve "lesbian" from an ill-got *jouissance* that cast her in *Whatever Happened to Baby Jane*. Smarting (hopefully) at the feminist "recreational use of the lesbian" that assigned her to the wings in order to stage mother/daughter conjunctions, I hoped to provide an entrance for lesbian from upstage center by aligning her with homosexuality – the queer. Within that critical context, situating lesbian representational strategies in proximity to those of the gay, or homosexual, man, was intended as a correction to the way in which feminist discourses had subsumed or "topped" the lesbian. The social movement ever in mind, it also seemed high time to end the historical labor relations between the lesbian and the feminist activist movement which had domesticated lesbian labor. After all, the lesbian feminist had provided activist labor in many causes, not necessarily her own, such as abortion rights, and for which the straight feminist

did not return the favor by, say, marching in PFLAG units in
Pride marches. Where were those legions of feminists marching in
support?

When I delivered the paper, "Tracking the Vampire," I was
critiqued by the local community in Santa Cruz for performing
"whiteness" and privileging complex, abstract theorizing, unavailable
to working-class people. I revised may paper by founding the theorizing in my historically-geographically specific experiential situation
that had produced the theory and by working anti-Semitic codes
of blood along with vampiric images. This process of self-criticism
and answerability to the local community seemed a familiar practice within lesbian feminist cultural production. However, the editors
at the Pembroke Center for Teaching and Research on Women,
who would publish the article in *differences*, had (to me) a surprising reaction to what I considered to be a standard materialist feminist
correction. They sought to edit out the initial experiential foundation
of the piece as an example of 1970s feminist essentialism. First they
suggested that I italicize the personal base of the argument, so that
it would read like a biographical sketch of the author, separated out
from the theorizing. Then they sought to cut it entirely. I'm relat-
ing this publishing gossip, not to elevate the stature of my work, nor
to seek some balm for wounds to my ego, nor to *j'accuse* those editors, but to compose a parable, bound in the business of publishing,
that illustrates the shift in the reception of the construction of "lesbian" in representation, and situates that shift specifically within the
rise of the term *queer*. The deconstructive break with the personal as
political sought to reaffirm the author as floating signifier. Slippage,
once perceived as privileged mobility, became the preferred mode
of intellectual travel. The queer call was to return to that unmarked
patriarchal, Eurocentric language of, well, the French and German
philosophical traditions. "Philosophy to the fore!" cheered *queer*.
Queer thus functioned as the sign of sexual politics cut loose from
earlier, grassroots lesbian feminism.

Burial rites of the feminist butch

From the developing perspective of queer, lesbian became conflated
with what was once more specifically identified as radical feminist
politics. The preponderance of socialist/materialist feminist practices in the 1970s was buried in such revisionism, along with the
critique devised by working-class, manual-laboring butch feminists.

Soon, in queer quarters, it seemed that all lesbian feminists had been wearing Birkenstocks and ripping off their shirts at the Michigan Womyn's Music Festival. Some of us chortled at the revisionist image of bar/butch/feminist dykes listening to acoustic guitars. We remembered, for example, the girl group called the Contractions, who whacked their electric instruments at top volume and flirted impossibly with the audience of dykes (sigh). The culture, always variegated by its wildly divergent feminisms was, through the charge of essentialism and the newly organized perspective of queer, being represented by one small subset. Slapping each other on the back, we joked, "was lesbian s/m invented by Gayle Rubin and Pat Califia in an argument with antiporn advocates?" Leafing through our old phone books and photos of friends flamed out in one affair after another, we snorted at the queer dykes' belief that they were originating the practice of multiple sexual partners, s/m scenarios, the use of sex toys, and the habit of hanging around bars. Beebo Brinker, Ann Bannon's 1950s seducer and abandoner, who found someone else's flannel pajamas in the faithful Laura's apartment, took it as a familiar sign of lesbian social practices, and her progeny peopled at least two succeeding decades. What a surprise, then, to learn that queer dykes associated such sexual promiscuity as more narrowly particular to a gay male culture that they would then need to assimilate and imitate. Butch feminists, it seemed, had been having monogamous, vanilla, Saturday-morning slight sex since the 1970s. We snickered. Then it wasn't funny anymore.

Such revisionist history thus promoted a queer ascension, through a valorization of gay male practices, arising from lesbian feminist ashes. The new queer dyke is out to glue on that gay male mustache and leave those dowdy, gynocentric habits behind. The *lesbian* body, perforated by discursive intrusions as early as Monique Wittig's, disciplined by materialist production as early as the manifestos of Ti-Grace Atkinson and the Combahee River Collective, and radiated out through the hard work of coalition-building, was spanked by the queers for its so-called ontological status and antisexual proclivities. Although, by now, we are surely bored with the spectacle of the debate over the essentialist charge, the charge continues to brand "queer" onto the disciplined, upended bottoms of what were once fleshly figures of lesbian desire. Further, queer's consort, "performativity," links "lesbian" to the tarnished sweating, laboring, performing body that must be semiotically scrubbed until the "live" lesbian gives way to the slippery, polished surface of the market manipulation of its sign. Better to circulate the queer dyke body through zines and fashion rags than to travel its orifices and tissues in Wittig's speculum-script. Body-less transcendence is produced through the process of semiosis. Isn't that the same desire for transcendence that was identified earlier by lesbian feminists as a masculine, Eurocentric trope? That gay male mustache, garnishing the lip of the queer dyke, then, also garnishes her critical strategies. Even if, as Peggy Shaw contends, testosterone is better in the hands of women, appropriating the masculine is not, obviously, beyond gender.

Right after those queer dykes slammed the door on the way out of lesbian feminism, the dowdy old women-centered places began to close down: most feminist and lesbian theaters, bookstores, and bars have disappeared. One of the underground movies making the circuit last year is called *Last Call at Maud's* – about the last night at the oldest lesbian bar in San Francisco and the end of many such lesbian bars. I walk the streets of West Hollywood and the Village in New York to jealously observe packed bar after bar of gay men. I stand in the book chain A Different Light on a Saturday night in West Hollywood – one of four or five lesbians among, say, fifty gay men. I'm flipping through the zines. I'm checking out the special photo shots of daddy-boy-dykes in *Quim*. Back on the streets. Everyone is looking good. I stand outside the gym on Santa Monica, in front of the huge picture windows, reminiscent of shop windows, where I can watch everybody working out. The women are looking strong. Slim. Young. I look down at my aging, overweight, academic body. They've cleared us out, I think. It's true – the Birkenstocks are gone, but so are what we used to call "women of size" and well, uh, older women. Two of my gay male friends call me up – they're freaking out because they're now in their 30s – how will they retain their sexual currency – do they have to become tops – do they have to go over to the leather scene, where older men still find them desirable? So now we all have *their* problems, I think.

Never mind, I'll go to the theater. I like *Angels in America* – it has a big cast and a big theme – a critique of nationalism and, well, I'm pretty sure the angel is a lesbian. That's what we used to say about the Holy Ghost – you know, the Father, the Son and. . . . Anyway, there are some great one-person dyke shows making the circuit and lots of new lesbian stand-up comics. Forget Broadway – we have "intimate" sites such as P.S. 122, or I can always go to the movies with my other professor friends and "read," as we say, something like *Single White Female* as signifying, as we also say, lesbian. The privileging of gay male culture by queer dykes, along with the disdain and mis-remembering of lesbian feminism, has produced the dwindling away of lesbian cultural resources – socially and economically and theo-retically. Oh well, I comfort myself with the option of those lesbian luxury cruises sponsored by Olivia – if only I could afford one. Then I'm caught up short with this thought – those old dowdy lesbian feminist hangouts – almost all of them were organized as collectives: theater collectives, bookstore collectives, food collectives, collective living quarters. Lesbian dowdy politics' had been intrinsically tied to collective ownership and collective labor. They locked the mode of material production to cultural production and to the produc-tion of sexual, personal relationships . . . and then there was interactive commodity dildoism. Does it matter that A Different Light is not a collective and is, in fact, a chain? Is someone getting rich? Is Someone not? Does it matter?

Up (your) market

What was once a lesbian or gay community is now becoming a market sector. The *Journal of Consumer Marketing* ran an arti-cle that summarized the finding of several studies to discover just how lesbians and gays consume market goods. Several studies (some produced by gay public relations agencies) concur that gays and lesbians make more money per household than the US average, buy more airline tickets, own more cars, are better educated, and spend more money on consumer goods. Clearly this market sec-tor has disposable income. They are becoming a target market, but how are they accessible to the market? This study suggests that it is primarily through their publications. The article lists the *Advo-cate*, *Deneuve*, *Genre*, *On Our Backs*, *Out* and *10 Percent* as likely venues for effective ads. The new, glossy formats with upscale-looking models and ads encourage corporations to consider buying their pages.

Sarah Schulman has taken such studies to evidence a rising "man-agement class," warning that there is a "class war emerging within the gay and lesbian world" ("Now for a Word from Our Sponsor" 6). She details how some gay organizations are even organizing to profit from HIV-positive buyers. Particularly poignant, notes Schul-man, is the growth of viatical companies that purchase the life insurance policies of persons with terminal illnesses. After all, people with AIDS, who have no children or other heirs, may be eager to spend and thus sell their insurance money, at any percentage, to a viatical company. Schulman details how this new management class creates the image of a gay/lesbian market sector that conceals the class differences within it. She quotes from the literature published by the gay-owned Mulryan/Nash advertising firm – the one that marketed *Angels in America* to gay tourists and worked for the government of Holland to develop advertising that would attract gay tourists. Mulryan/Nash contends that 61 percent of gay people have college degrees, household incomes of $62,000, and CD players, work out in gyms, and drink sparkling water. Schulman contrasts these figures with some published in the *New York Times* asserting that homosexual men earn 12 percent less than heterosexual ones and lesbians 5 percent less than heterosexual women, who earn 45 percent less than heterosexual men. Schulman's conclusion, then, is that a privileged gay class is entering the market economy and creating a fiction that erases the "others" in what was once called a community. The aim is to produce sexual identities as powerful consumers with discretionary incomes and good taste.

The once-activist Queer Nation has formed the Queer Shopping Network of New York. "Queer" may be found on coffee mugs, T-shirts, and postcards sold at Gay Pride parades and in new marketing chains across the country. One can buy queer and wear it. In some circles, "queer" seems to be primarily constituted by body piercings, leather, and spike haircuts. One might applaud such signs of commodification as signs of success. Good. We are not necessarily poor, nor downwardly mobile. Lipstick lesbians are cute. Sex can be fun. We are visible, strong, making more money, dressing better, eating out, and enjoying sex.

Many "queer" academics write this affluent, commodity fetishism. Some are concerned with Rock Hudson's body, some with k. d. lang's and Cindy Crawford's photo display in *Vanity Fair*, others with the radical purchasing of dildoes – "subversive shopping," as Danae Clark refers to it in her article "Commodity Lesbianism." They invent queer discourse out of an addiction to the allure of the mass market. Fandom queered. *Melrose Place* reruns as Castro Street. Class privilege and the celebration of capitalism are compounded with the queer sex industry. Likewise, certain theoretical strategies have been embodied in new, surprising ways. The much-touted practice and theory of masquerade, once written as subversive cross-dressing, has literally turned into a uniform. Recent Gay Pride parades sport a uniformed color guard of Marines and the like, accompanying the flag. The people on the sidewalk cheer as the presumably "queer" or "gay" US flag and military march by. If only we could make the military-industrial complex gay-friendly. From queer planet to queer Pentagon. Antiassimilationist in its move away from pleading civil rights, the queer movement insinuates sexual citizenship through affluence in the market and the willing participation in national agendas. Wouldn't it be victory for the movement if Colonel Margarethe Cammermeyer, mother of four sons, Vietnam vet, could be reinstated into the army?

Mommie dearest

The Reagan 1980s, ushered in by Joan Crawford's attack on any of those hideous wire hangers still found in the closet, produced a routing out of any associations with the iron curtain that continued to inform the political movements concerning alternative sexualities. Contesting capitalism, along with providing alternative economic practices such as collective ownership and labor, in discourses of so-called sexual dissidence was out. Following its successful purge, the privileged compound "queer performativity" ushered in the 1990s, having detonated the ground of lesbian feminism – shattering its socialist roots through the charge of essentialism. The trick was, as post-Berlin Wall discourse also performed, to invert the traditional meanings of political terminology, thereby confusing the actual development of power relationships. After the wall's fall, Euromediaspeak repositioned communism as signifying the Right and the reactionary and global capitalism as the leftist, outsider position. Such sleights of terminology masked material conditions: former property owners in the West appropriated the properties of the former East, while portraying themselves as the oppressed, shaking off the shackles of collective ownership. Similarly, the lesbian feminist position, imbricated with socialist/communist strategies, such as collective practices of ownership and labor, were represented as essentialist, reversing the nature of the critique in order to overcome its materialist practices with formal discursive ones. The rise of "queer performativity," then, accompanied the victory of global capitalism in the new Europe as well as the complete commodification of the sexual movement. The charge of essentialism rousted the iron curtain out of the closet.

The notion of the Bad Binary also functioned to resituate the queer movement within market strategies. Second terms were out. Hetero/homo made homo suspect. Likewise for capitalism/communism. After all, Baudrillard had already depicted the two as the twin trade towers in New York in his *Simulations*. Global capitalism could contain everything, all differences within its shifting economic zones, just as the new Individual could contain multiple subject positions. Down with the binary went oppositional economic and cultural alternatives. Queer emulated global capitalism in order to gain status within it. Certain revisions of history would have to be performed, of course, in order to cleanse any sense of oppositional affiliations from the sexual rights movement. Enter the case of Colonel Cammermeyer. Antiwar demonstrators? Not! Instead, the bid to reinstate the lesbian Vietnam hero into high ranks in the army revised the image and the agenda of the movement. Soldiers and marketeers of global expansion, avid and capable consumers, loyal fans, even (hopefully) good wives and husbands could gather under the banner of queer. Oppositional struggles fade before simple iterations that queer includes everyone who is antinormal and hypernormal all at once. Who could but envy us? At last we're competitive, as they say.

Nevertheless, those of us who were in a relationship, so to speak, with the old dowdy "I" of i-dentity politics, the "I" of dialogue or the dialectic, continue to interpret "presence" as politically showing up. As a base of operations, that "I" signals the old theatrical, the old dare I say communist, the old feminist collective dialogues of contradiction − "I know, let's do a show − I'll play," as Lois Weaver once said onstage to Peggy Shaw, "Katharine Hepburn to your Spencer Tracy." Or, in the old communist sense, "I know, let's redistribute the land − let's collectivize the labor − what? It's not fair, given your college education, your student loan, your expertise? How can we work this out?" Or, in the old feminist sense, I can still hear the voice of the African American activist Bernice Johnson Reagon, speaking to a group of feminists struggling over issues of ethnicity and sexual practice. She described the experience of building coalitions:

The first thing that happens is that the room don't feel like the room anymore. (The audience laughed) And it ain't home no more. It is not a womb no more. And you can't feel comfortable no more. . . . [Yet] the "our" must include everybody you have to include in order for you to survive. . . . That's why we have to live in coalitions. Cause I ain't gonna let you live unless you let me live. Now there's danger in that, but there's also the possibility that we both can live − if you can stand it. ("Coalition Politics," 359, 363)

The sound of dialogue, the collective, resounds in these threats and hurts of the clash of conflicting positions, or the joy of temporary agreement which, like Rome, is not made in a day, or by the fiat of a term like *queer* that sweeps down from the discourse to gather up oppositional positions by force of its own definition AS embracing AS multimulti, acting like the movies, or the old well-made plays that conclude all problems with a kiss, a marriage, or, in this case, a dildo.

And "presence" – showing up – at activist disruptions, at live performances, in collective venues, reclaims the "live" – the body – the visible – looking for lesbians in the political sense. It is "live" performance as politics, as theater, the play of positional masks, sweating flesh and clapping hands that finally animates what cyberpunks call the "meat." For presence as body, as visibility, in the collective, once abandoned, i-dentity once gone, promotes the new sense of performativity in which the body is a trope and performance part of the allure of reading and writing.

Work not, want not

The year 1982 might be regarded as the Great Divide. Along with *Mommie Dearest*, the Barnard conference staged the outbreak of open conflict between the lesbian s/m community and the feminist antiporn adherents – a conflict that was never resolved. The debates were hot and the rifts were deep. What later became the "sex radicals" tired of feminism's het "missionary position," while the feminist critique stalled out in its persistent blindness to heterosexism. Moreover, the socialist critique remained obsessed with labor, ignoring issues around sexual practice and pleasure.

Meanwhile, the beginning of what would become the AIDS crisis was forging new alliances between lesbians and gay men. Patriarchal privilege aside, gay men were in life-or-death struggles around sexual practices. Sex was a given, open focus in their community, while the feminist community, where heterosexism forced a silencing of the debate they were afraid to continue, seemed to be formulating neo-puritanical prescriptions against erotic materials and the exploration of sexual pleasure. So lesbian feminists became queer dykes among gay men. The rise of the fundamentalist Right demanded a new, more aggressive political activism. The failure of government institutions to respond to the need for AIDS treatment became more and more reactionary. ACT UP, formed in the late 1980s in New York, produced "live" agitprop street performances within a coalition. For a while. While some ACT UP organizations survived, others, such as the ones in San Francisco and Seattle, split into ACTS UPS, or whatever. Lesbians split from gay men over the focus of concern: is AIDS a gay male disease, or how do we also address the problems of the category "women," straight or lesbian, of color who bear a high incidence of AIDS? Latent feminist coalitions with other women, particularly women of color, still haunted the new dyke. It seems girls don't just wanta have fun, but they also don't wanta have none. In queer coalitions, proceeding out from New York's urban center, how could those queer dykes still remain in old feminist coalitions with women of color and third-world women?

If queer, as sex-positive and antiassimilationist, claims to cut across differences: bisexuals, transgendered people, s/m practitioners – and all the "antinormal" could be included in its embrace, and if it also claims multicultural representation at its base, then why do we read things like the following? Cherríe Moraga, the lesbian Chicana poet and dramatist writes:

> We discussed the limitations of "Queer Nation," whose leather-jacketed, shaved-headed white radicals and accompanying anglo-centricity were an alien-nation to most lesbians and gay men of color. (*The Last Generation* 147)

Even the queer enthusiast Michael Warner offers a chilling description of the "queer community" in his introduction to *Fear of a Queer Planet*:

> In the lesbian and gay movement, to a much greater degree than in any comparable movement, the institutions of culture-building have been market-mediated. . . . Nonmarket forms of association . . . churches, kinship, traditional residence – have been less available for queers. This structural environment has meant that the institutions of queer culture have been dominated by those with capital: typically, middle-class white men. (xvii)

Terry Castle, in *The Apparitional Lesbian*, adds this dimension:

> As soon as the lesbian is lumped in – for better or for worse – with her male homosexual counterpart, the singularity of her experience (sexual and otherwise) tends to become obscured . . . to the extent that "queer theory" still seems . . . to denote primarily the study of male homosexuality, I find myself at odds with both its language and its universalizing aspirations. (12–13)

Charles Fernández, in "Undocumented Aliens in the Queer Nation," identifies *queer* as a "melting pot" term of "bankrupt universalism."

I think an important clue to the element in the notion and practice of queer that led to its embrace of commodification and its emulation of dominant class and gender practices may be found in Alexander Chee's historical account of the origins of Queer Nation:

> The name stuck simply for the sake of marketing. The original idea was this: choose a name around each action, keep responsibility with each individual and not with an institution. . . . People are tired of groups with egos, processes, personality cults, and politicking. So far Queer Nation is individuals confronting individuals.   ("A Queer Nationalism" 15)

Chee underscores that any practice of continuity was a marketing choice. The queer retention of individualism, changing tactics, venue, and organizations, was designed to invigorate those who are "tired" of group processes. The interest, then, is not in collective agency – in fact, collectives are perceived as infected with "politicking" – but in the individual's action of intervention into the marketing process. In fact, if Chee is correct, Queer Nation arose as a direct contradiction to collective, group-process-oriented politics. At the same time, it does seem to unfurl that same old banner of the individual that liberal democracy keeps hanging out to dry. Sarah Schulman, writing from a slightly different perspective in *My American History*, indicates that the AIDS crisis catalyzed the correction of traditional forms of coalition-building. She offers "processing" as the problem, through which coalition-building became therapizing, continually postponing activism – a delay the new, fatal progress of AIDS could ill afford (6). Yet, when the process is aborted and the coalition simply iterated, the skills that had been learned in antiracist, antisexist training groups become lost and those dominant structures remain intact within the coalition.

Queer coalitions, then, in a hurry to get onto the streets, began to interrogate the "normal," as if outside of the normalizing operations of patriarchy, capital, and nation. For, without arduous attention to dominant contexts, single-issue politics operate within them. The term *queer*, then, circulating out from Queer Nation, asserts itself as an umbrella term without the hard rain of coalition-building. Thus it reinstates the dominant social structures, lending its power to those who are already vested in the system, with the exception of their sexual identification. Not surprisingly, then, white middle-class men will form the constituency. Their culture, sub or not, will continue to be representative.

You have nothing to wear but your chains

Now thoroughly depressed, I wonder if this writing is only nostalgic. The good old days of butch feminism. Not only. I mean, the child whines because she wants something she can't have – in the present. It isn't all fort/da, as the Freudians would have us believe – I mean, it isn't all because mommie left the room. If this writing did begin by wriggling through those spread thighs of the colossal Bertha Harris I erected to guard the portals between butch feminist and queer, it isn't satisfied to remain there, curled up in the fetal position, stammering fort/da to some Freudian who likes to watch. Toward a butch-feminist retro-future seeks an agenda that might animate both a modernist project of doing something historical about the future and the ironic, postmodern sense of retro that, by the conjunction, still performs a critique of the categories of historical past and future.

Employing *retro* in this way is in contradiction to the way the term and the practice are typically theorized. Critics such as Celeste Olalquiaga in *Megalopolis* contend that any retro future is always already

> attracted by an image of progress only possible to an apocalyptical fin de siecle as a melancholic appropriation – one that refuses to accept death, fetishistically clinging to memories, corpses, and ruins.   (23)

Farting the old fetishistic gas, as usual. Crucial to my argument, however, is the way in which Olalquiaga discovers retro as a specifically gay male practice. She contends that the "two most conspicuous subcultures involved in retro fashion are children of the baby-boomer era: yuppies and young gay men" (32). Never to be left out, I want to imply queer dyke subculture in such practices. Here's how Olalquiaga sees it:

> While yuppies use money as a means of neutralizing difference, many young gay men use their bodies as a celebratory means of camouflage and the absorption of difference. Rather than the explicit transvestism of drag...these men are prone to...the body as the territory on which infinite characters and personas can be explored on a daily basis. ... Money and body alike, then, serve as conduits for the circulation of

signs, enabling a swift exchange void of the weight of referentiality. It
is not history or a peculiar culture that is being referred to in this way
of quoting, it is rather an iconographic richness that is being happily
cannibalized.   (32)

Something in the style of retro quoting, then, makes it unspecific –
the general play of signs that, finally, celebrates a significatory empti-
ness. The past is dead. This sense of retro depends upon a rather wide
bandwidth of signs – that is, unlike drag, not signs of a specific historical or collective past. Retro butch feminism is more specific in
its referent, butch feminism, than queer has been in its operations
that would dismantle the generalized, revisionist lesbian feminism.
So first the retro I have in mind requires a knowledge of the specific historical and discursive strategies of butch feminism to cite.
Retro, in this sense, is a kind of discipline. On the one hand, retro
confounds the melancholic nostalgia of a dead retro with an agenda
for the future; on the other, it corrects the tendentious quality of
utopian agendas with a camp citation of history. What does this mean?
Partially, it mandates a reconsideration, back through queer, of a class-
specific, self-consciously gendered political program that situates the
practitioner within coalitional politics while playing out traditionally
lesbian seduction scenarios within the political practice. Economic
structures once again codetermine sexual politics and the inscription of the different histories of gay men and lesbians reconfigure
what now seem to be common, agendered forms, which encourage the belief that there is another, nongendered discursive space
within which such politics may emerge. The composition seeks a
certain playful sobriety, oxymoronic compounds that actually do suggest, once again, agency and responsibility in a time which puts on
a good show in order to distract the audience from the irreparable
damage it inflicts on those who continue to play by its rules.

Notes

I am indebted to the organizers of the conference entitled "Queering the Pitch" in
Manchester and to Karen Quimby and the other organizers of the "Queer Frontiers"
conference at the University of Southern California for inviting me to deliver the
keynote addresses that led to this chapter.

1. Both this chapter and its title overwrite the femme with feminist. Partially, this
    new conjunction means to place the butch and feminism in a similar desiring cou-
    pling, as the earlier butch/femme had suggested. Polemically, the conjunction also
    means to reforge a lost, troubled connection. However, "dropping" the femme is

definitely part of the theoretical process here – an unhappy one. I can only hope
that she will make me regret every minute of it – will force herself back into the
theorizing. Thanks to Laura Harris for pointing out this problem in my article. I
eagerly await her forthcoming femme flirtation with the discourse.
2. See McIntosh's notion of the triad of "queer," "feminist," and "lesbian" strategies
   at the conclusion of her article "Queer Theory and the War of the Sexes."

Works cited

Allison, Dorothy. *Skin* (Ithaca, NY: Firebrand, 1994).

Baudrillard, Jean. *Simulations*. Trans. Paul Foss et al. (New York: Semiotext(e) 1983),
135–36.

Castle, Terry. *The Apparitional Lesbian* (New York: Columbia University Press, 1993).

Chee, Alexander. "A Queer Nationalism." *Out/Look* 12 (1991): 15–20.

Clark, Danae. "Commodity Lesbianism." *The Lesbian and Gay Studies Reader*,
ed. Henny Abelove, Michéle Aina Barale and David M. Halpenin (New York:
Routledge 1993), pp. 186–207.

"Daddy Boy Dykes." *Quim*. Winter 1991: 32–35.

de Lauretis, Teresa. "Queer Theory: Lesbian and Gay Sexualities: an Introduction."
differences 3.2 (1991): iii–xviii.

Fernández, Charles. "Undocumented Aliens in the Queer Nation." *Out/Look* 12
(1991): 20–23.

Fugate, Douglas. "Evaluating the US Male Homosexual and Lesbian Population as a
Viable Target Market Segment." *Journal of Consumer Marketing* 10.4 (1993): 46–57.

McIntosh, Mary. "Queer Theory and the War of the Sexes." In *Activating Theory:
Lesbian, Gay, Bisexual Politics*, ed. Joseph Bristow and Angelia R. Wilson (London:
Lawrence and Wishart, 1993), 30–52.

Moraga, Cherríe. *The Last Generation* (Boston, MA: South End Press, 1993).

Olalquiaga, Celeste. *Megalopolis: Contemporary Cultural Sensibilities*: (Minneapolis:
University of Minnesota Press, 1992).

Reagon, Bernice Johnson. "Coalition Politics: Turning the Century." In *Home Girls:
A Black Feminist Anthology*, ed. Barbara Smith (Brooklyn: Kitchen Table, Women
of Color Press, 1983).

Schulman, Sarah. *My American History: Lesbian and Gay Life during the Reagan/Bush
Years* (New York: Routledge, 1994).

——"Now for a Word from Our Sponsor." Paper delivered at the University of
California at San Diego, January 1995.

Warner, Michael. Introduction. *Fear of a Queer Planet* (Minneapolis: University of
Minnesota Press, 1993), vii–xxxi.

4

Tracking the Vampire

In my teens, when I experienced the beginnings of fierce desire and embracing love for other women, the only word I knew to describe my desire and my feelings was "queer" – a painful term hurled as an insult against developing adolescents who were, somehow, found to be unable to ante up in the heterosexist economy of sexual and emotional trade. "Queer" was the site in the discourse at which I felt both immediate identification and shame – a contradiction that both established my social identity and required me to render it somehow invisible. At the same time, I discovered a book on the life of Arthur Rimbaud. I was astounded to find someone who, at approximately my same age, embraced such an identity and even made it the root of his poetic language. Thus, while brimming with a desire and long-ing that forced me to remain socially silent, I found in Rimbaud an exquisite language – a new way for language to mean, based on reveling in an illegitimate, homosexual state of desire.

This adolescent phase in the construction of my social identity is still marked in the word "queer" for me, with its plenitude and pain, its silence and poetry, and its cross-gender identification. For I became queer through my readerly identification with a male homo-sexual author. The collusion of the patriarchy and the canon made Rimbaud more available to me than the few lesbian authors who had managed to make it into print. Later, a multitude of other experi-ences and discourses continued to enhance my queer thinking. Most prominent among them was the subcultural discourse of camp which I learned primarily from old dykes and gay male friends I knew in San Francisco, when I lived in the ghetto of bars – before the rise of feminism. Then there was feminism, both the social movement and the critique, which became my social and theoretical milieu – after the bars. And finally, my young lesbian students and friends who have taught me how, in many ways, my life and my writing reflect a lesbian "of a certain age." My construction of the following queer theory, then, is historically and materially specific to my personal, social, and educational experience, and hopefully to others who have likewise suffered the scourge of dominant discourse and enjoyed these same strategies of resistance. It is in no way offered as a general truth or a generative model.

My adolescent experience still resonates through the following discursive strategies: the pain I felt upon encountering heterosexist discourse here becomes a critique of heterosexism within feminist theory – a way of deconstructing my own milieu to ease the pain of exclusion as well as to confront what we have long, on the street, called "the recreational use of the lesbian"; the identification with the insult, the taking on of the transgressive, and the consequent flight into invisibility are inscribed in the figure of the vampire; the discovery of Rimbaud and camp enables a theory that reaches across lines of gender oppression to gay men and, along with feminist theory, prompts the writing itself – ironically distanced and flaunting through metaphor. By imploding this particular confluence of strategies, this queer theory strikes the blissful wound into ontology itself, to bleed the fast line between living and dead.

But I am rushing headlong into the pleasure of this wound, an acceleration instigated by the figure that haunts this introduction, the figure that appears and disappears – the vampire. Like the actor peeking out at the audience from the wings before the curtain rises, she rustles plodding, descriptive prose into metaphors whose veiled nature prompts her entrance. Her discursive retinue whets my desire to flaunt, to camp it up a bit, to trans-invest the tropes. But first, the necessary warm-up act of exposition.

The relationship between queer theory and lesbian theory: or, "Breaking Up's So Very Hard to Do"

Queer theory, unlike lesbian theory or gay male theory, is not gender specific. In fact, like the term "homosexual," queer foregrounds same-sex desire without designating which sex is desiring. As a feminist, I am aware of the problems that congregate at this site. These problems are both historical and theoretical. Gay male theory is inscribed with patriarchal privilege, which it sometimes deconstructs and sometimes does not. Lesbian theory is often more narrowly lesbian feminist theory, or lesbian theory arising, historically, from various alignments with feminist theory. Through its alliance with feminism, lesbian theory often proceeds from theories inscribed with heterosexism. I will deal at length with this problem later. But for now, I would contend that both gay male and lesbian theory reinscribe sexual difference, to some extent, in their gender-specific construction. In her article "Sexual Indifference and Lesbian Representation," Teresa de Lauretis has already elucidated some of the problematic ways that sexual difference is marked within lesbian representation. For, while gender is an important site of struggle for women, the very notion reinscribes sexual difference in a way that makes it problematic for the lesbian, as de Lauretis configures it, "to be seen." This gender base also leads to problems for lesbians when a certain feminist theory defines the gaze itself, as will be illustrated later.

In contrast to the gender-based construction of the lesbian in representation, queer theory, as I will construct it here, works not at the site of gender, but at the site of ontology, to shift the ground of being itself, thus challenging the Platonic parameters of Being – the borders of life and death. Queer desire is constituted as a transgression of these boundaries and of the organicism which defines the living as the good. The Platonic construction of a life/death binary opposition at the base, with its attendant gender opposition above, is subverted by a queer desire which seeks the living dead, producing a slippage at the ontological base and seducing through a gender inversion above. Rephrasing that well-known exchange between Alice B. Toklas and Gertrude Stein at Gertrude's death bed, Alice might here ask: "Now that you're dying, tell me Gertrude, what's the answer?" And Gertrude might reply: "What's the queery?" Gertrude, the lesbian on the border of life/death, locked in language with her lover, exits through a campy inversion.

The lethal offshoot of Plato's organicism has been its association with the natural. Life/death becomes the binary of the "natural" limits of Being: the organic is the natural. In contrast, the queer has been historically constituted as unnatural. Queer desire, as unnatural, breaks with this life/death binary of Being through same-sex desire. The articulation of queer desire also breaks with the discourse that claims mimetically to represent that "natural" world, by subverting its tropes. In queer discourse, as Oscar Wilde illustrated, "the importance of being earnest" is a comedy. Employing the subversive power of the unnatural to unseat the Platonic world view, the queer, unlike the rather polite categories of gay and lesbian, revels in the discourse of the loathsome, the outcast, the idiomatically proscribed position of same-sex desire. Unlike petitions for civil rights, queer revels constitute a kind of activism that attacks the dominant notion of the natural. The queer is the taboo-breaker, the monstrous, the uncanny. Like the Phantom of the Opera, the queer dwells underground, below the operatic overtones of the dominant; frightening to look at, desiring, as it plays its own organ, producing its own music.

This un-natural sense of the queer was, of course, first constituted as a negative category by dominant social practices, which homosexuals later embraced as a form of activism. Historically, the category of the unnatural was one of an aggregate of notions aimed at securing the right to life for a small minority of the world's population. This right to life was formulated through a legal, literary, and scientistic discourse on blood, which stabilized privilege by affirming the right to life for those who could claim blood and further, pure blood, and the consequent death sentence, either metaphorically or literally, for those who could not. Against the homosexual, this right was formulated as the seeming contradiction between sterile homosexual sex and fertile heterosexual practice; that is, before recent technological "advances," heterosexuals may have babies because of their sexual practice and queers may not. From the heterosexist perspective, the sexual practice that produced babies was associated with giving life, or practicing a life-giving sexuality, and the living was established as the category of the natural. Thus, the right to life was a slogan not only for the unborn, but for those whose sexual practices could produce them. In contrast, homosexual sex was mandated as sterile – an unlive practice that was consequently unnatural, or queer, and, as that which was unlive, without the right to life.

Queer sexual practice, then, impels one out of the generational production of what has been called "life" and history, and ultimately out of the category of the living. The equation of hetero $=$ sex $=$ life and homo $=$ sex $=$ unlife generated a queer discourse that reveled in proscribed desiring by imagining sexual objects and sexual practices within the realm of the other-than-natural, and the consequent other-than-living. In this discourse, new forms of being, or beings, are imagined through desire. And desire is that which wounds – a desire that breaks through the sheath of being as it has been imagined within a heterosexist society. Striking at its very core, queer desire punctures the life/death and generative/destructive bipolarities that enclose the heterosexist notion of being.

"Was it the Taste of Blood? Nay ... the Taste of Love"

Although, as a queer theorist, I eschew generational models of history, I would like to perform the reading of certain texts, not as precursors, fathers, or mothers of a youthful time, but as traces of she-who-would-not-be-seen, whose movement is discernible within certain discursive equations. The compound of wounding desire, gender inversion, and ontological shift is early configured in mystic writings. The mystic women authors, such as Hrotsvita von Gandersheim, Teresa of Avila, or Hildegard von Bingen write of reveling in the wounding, ontological desire. Yet their precision in marking the social oppression in the feminine position of such desire makes the gendering of that desire mimetic – stable in its historical resonances. Gender slippage, performed through the ontological break, may be found in the writings of an early male mystic – marking both oppression in the feminine and liberation in the adoption of it.

The works of John of the Cross, although not literally queer, begin a tradition that will be taken up later as literal by Rimbaud, Wilde, and more recently Alexis DeVeaux. John's wounding desire is articulated in several ways, but often as a fire, as in his treatise, the *Living Flame of Love*: "had not God granted a favor to [the] flesh, and covered it with his right hand ... it would have died at each touch of this flame, and its natural being would have been corrupted" (49); or, "the healing of love is to hurt and wound once more that which has been hurt and wounded already, until the soul comes to be wholly dissolved in the wound of love" (61). The flame of this desire not only corrupts natural beings, but sears into a world where being is reconfigured. John, the mystic lover, desires a being of a different order – one who does not live or die as we know it. In order to "know" this being, the senses and thus epistemology must be reconfigured. In his poem "The Dark Night of the Soul," John lyricizes this reconfiguring of the senses necessary for his tryst (*Poems*). Then, in "The Spiritual Canticle," where his love finds full expression in the trope of marriage, John inverts his gender, writing his desire as if he were the bride with the other being as the bridegroom. John, the bride, languishes for her lover, seeks him everywhere, finally reaching him: "Our bed: in roses laid/patrols of lions ranging all around. ... There I gave all of me; put chariness aside: there I promised to become his bride" (*Poems* 7–9). And the bridegroom says to John: "I took you tenderly hurt virgin, made you well" (13). The wound of love liberates the lover from the boundaries of being – the living, dying envelope of the organic. Ontology shifts through gender inversion and is expressed as same-sex desire. This is queer, indeed.

Historically, John's queer break-through from "life" also signaled a break with a dominant discourse that legislated the right to life through pure blood. His works were written in Spain during the so-called Golden Age, with its literature and social practice of honor and pure blood: the dominant discourse was spattered with the blood of women and their illicit lovers, but ultimately aimed, in the sub-text, against the impure blood of Jews and Moors (the figure for illicit lovers a cover for *conversos*). The Golden Age tragedies set the scene of desire in the context of the generational model, the family and the potential family, in a verse that conflates racial purity with sexual honor, and spilt blood with the protection of pure blood.[1] Writing his poems in a cramped prison cell designed to torture, John defied the generational, heterosexual mandate by a counterdiscourse that set desire in gender inversion: he countered the conflation of race/love/life in a discourse that imagined and orgiastically embraced the un-dead.[2] Blood, in the dominant discourse which was writing racial laws along with such tragedies, is genealogy, the blood right to money; and blood/money is the realm of racial purity and pure heterosexuality. Looking forward several centuries, one can see the actual tragic performance of this dominant equation in Hitler's death camps, where, among others, both Jews and homosexuals were put to death. More recently, one can see such tropes operating in the anti-AIDS discourse that conflates male homosexual desire with the contamination of blood.

I would like to read from this dominant discourse of blood, death, purity, and heterosexual generation in its most obscene form: Hitler's *Mein Kampf*. I apologize for quoting such a text, for, on the one hand, I can understand the necessity of censoring it as they do in Germany; but, on the other hand, this text sets out the compound I am here addressing in its most succinct form – the horror story of the obscene notion of the right to life for racially pure heterosexuals and death for the others.

> The Jew . . . like the pernicious bacillus, spreads over wider and wider areas. . . . Wherever he establishes himself the people who grant him hospitality are bound to be bled to death sooner or later. . . . He poisons the blood of others but preserves his own blood unadulterated. . . . The black-haired Jewish youth lies in wait for hours on end, satanically glaring and spying on the inconspicuous girl whom he plans to seduce, adulterating her blood and removing her from the bosom of her own people. . . . The

Jews were responsible for bringing Negroes into the Rhineland, with the
ultimate idea of bastardizing the white race.   (quoted in Poliakov 1)

Such discourse invented the vampiric position – the one who waits,
strikes, and soils the living, pure blood; and it is against this bloody
discourse that the queer vampire strikes, with her evacuating kiss that
drains the blood out, transforming it into a food for the un-dead.

The dominant image of the vampire began to appear in Western
Europe in the eighteenth century through tales and reports from small
villages in the East. In literature, Mario Praz observes in *The Romantic
Agony*, the vampire appears in the nineteenth century as the Byronic
hero who destroys not only himself but his lovers. Praz finds "the
love crime" to be essential to the figure, who early in the century
was a man, but in the second half – what Praz calls "the time of
Decadence" (75–7) – was a woman. For the purposes of queer theory,
the most important work in the dominant tradition is "Carmilla" by
Sheridan Le Fanu, the first lesbian vampire story, in which the lesbian,
desiring and desired by her victim, slowly brings her closer through
the killing kiss of blood. In the dominant discourse, this kiss of blood
is a weakening device that played into male myths of menstruation,
where women's monthly loss of blood was associated with their pale,
weak image.[3]

In the counterdiscourse, Rimbaud builds on the elements in John,
writing those revels into a more literally queer poetry. To the gender
inversion Rimbaud adds a moral and metaphysical one. The ontological break remains, but heaven becomes hell, and the saint becomes
the criminal. In his *Season in Hell* such desire once again makes the
male lover into the bride, but Rimbaud's lover is now the "infernal
bridegroom." His wounding love is more literally painful, and this
pain, this love, this ontological shift, as in John, creates a new epistemology – a reorganization of the senses. Along with these inversions,
Rimbaud also revels in the mythical impurities of blood and race.
One example from *A Season in Hell*: "It's very obvious to me I've
always belonged to an inferior race. I can't figure out revolt. My race
never rose up except to loot: like wolves after beasts they haven't
killed" (3–4). His sepulchral, racially inferior, dangerous queer rises
up to walk in *Illuminations*:

Your cheeks are hollow. Your fangs gleam. Your breast is like a lyre, tin-
klings circulate through your pale arms. Your heart beats in that belly
where sleeps the double sex. Walk through the night, gently moving that
thigh, that second thigh, and that left leg.   ("Antique" 25)

This is a fanged creature, who promises the wound of love that pierces the ontological/societal sac.

But it is Oscar Wilde who wrote the queer kiss in *Salome*. At the end of the play, Salome stands with the severed head of Iokanaan in her hand. Herod, who looks on in horror, commands that the moon and the stars, God's natural creation, go dark. They shall not illuminate the transgressive, unnatural kiss. Wilde has the moon and stars actually disappear, and in the vacuum, outside of natural creation, Salome says:

> Ah, I have kissed thy mouth, Iokanaan, I have kissed thy mouth. There was a bitter taste on thy lips. Was it the taste of blood?... Nay, but perchance it was the taste of love.... They say that love hath a bitter taste.... But what matter? What matter? I have kissed thy mouth, Iokanaan, I have kissed thy mouth.   (66–7)

Wilde wrote these lines in 1892 – when they were first uttered on stage, after issues of censorship, Wilde was in prison. The immorality, or the taboo status of this desire, socially expressed in Wilde's incarceration, becomes a life/death break in his writing – the wound that decapitates the natural and delivers it into the hands of the queer who desires it.

Now, in the nineteenth century, this queer compound led by inverted brides and Oscar Wilde in drag as a dancing girl, the feminized gender that shifts ontologies, was also represented as lesbian desire. Baudelaire's lesbians in "Femmes Damnées Delphine et Hippolyte" lay in their chamber: "Reclining at her feet, elated yet calm, / Delphine stared up at her with shining eyes / the way a lioness watches her prey / once her fangs marked it for her own" (304). After their love-making, Baudelaire sends them down to hell, out of this life, desiccated by their dry desire, as he called it, the "stérilité de votre jouissance" (307). At least, in Baudelaire, *jouissance* belongs to the lesbian couple. Nevertheless, once again the fangs, the death, the other world of the living dead. But what was the metaphorical bride of inverted gender is represented here as lesbian desire – the gender trope of the double-feminized.

I read lesbian here, the two "she's" together, as a trope. The term does not mimetically refer to a gender in the world. In queer discourse, "she" is the wounding, desiring, transgressive position that weds, through sex, an unnatural being. "She" is that bride. "She" is the fanged lover who breaks the ontological sac – the pronominal Gomorrah of the queer. When two "she's" are constructed, it is a

double trope – a double masquerade. To read that desire as lesbian is
not to reinscribe it with dominant, heterosexist categories of gender,
for lesbian, in queer theory, is a particular dynamic in the system of
representation: the doubled trope of "she's," constructed in the dominant discourse as the doubly inferior, the doubly impure, and recast
in the queer as Wrigley chewing gum celebrates it: "double your
pleasure, double your fun."

  I realize that this seems to be a move away from the material, historical condition of lesbians. Yet the entry point of this theory rests
upon my entrance, as an adolescent, into the speaking and hearing,
reading and writing about my sexuality. Insofar as I am queer, or lesbian, this identity is in consonance with the discursive strategies that
those words represent historically: my desire and my sexual practice
are inscribed in these words and, conversely, these words – the historical practice of a discourse – are inscribed in my sexual practice. Take,
for instance, my years of furtive pleasure between the sheets, or my
years of promiscuous tweeking and twaddling. Both eras were performances of the double trope of the "she," either as the doubly inferior,
marked by oppression, or as double pleasure, reveling in transgression.
To ask "will the real lesbian please stand up," when she is embedded
in the dominant discursive mandate to disappear, or in the subcultural subversion to flaunt her distance from the "real," is like asking
the vampire to appear in the mirror. (She made me write that. For
now is the time of her entrance.) The double "she," in combination
with the queer fanged creature, produces the vampire. The vampire
is the queer in its lesbian mode.

The en-tranced take: the lesbian and the vampire

So finally, now, the vampire can make her appearance. But how
does she appear? How can she appear, when the visible is not in
the domain of the queer, when the apparatus of representation still
belongs to the un-queer? Thus far, we've had the fun, fun, fun of
imagining the liberating, creative powers of the queer in representation. Unfortunately, daddy always takes the T-Bird away and the
vampire, those two "she's" in the driver's seat, is left standing at the
cross-roads of queer theory and dominant discourse. Although the
"she" is not mimetic of gender, "she" is shaped, in part, by her
pronominal history – that is, how "she" is constructed elsewhere and
previously in language. Along the metaphorical axis, "she" is somehow the queer relative of the other girls. What this "she" vampire

flaunts is the cross – the crossing out of her seductive pleasure, the plenitude of proximity and the break. Thus, the dominant gaze constructs a vampire that serves only as a proscription – is perceived only as a transgression: interpolated between the viewer and the vampire is the cross – the crossing out of her image. Dominant representation has made of the vampire a horror story.

But this site/sight of proscription lingers in the theoretical construction of the gaze in feminist theory as well – specifically in theories of the gaze proceeding from psychoanalytic presumptions. There, the vampire is subjected to the familiar mode of "seduced and abandoned," or "the recreational use of the lesbian," for while such heterosexist feminist discourse flirts with her, it ultimately double-crosses her with the hegemonic notion of "woman," reinscribing "her" in the generational model and making horrible what must not be seductive. The vampire as the site or sight of the undead leads such feminist discourse back to the mother's right to life, where fruition becomes the counterdiscourse of exclusion. For example, taking Kristeva's cue that the birthing mother is transgressive, flowing with the milk of semiosis, the cover photo on Jane Gallop's *Thinking Through the Body* fixes the gaze at the birthing vaginal canal of the author, suggesting that her head may be found inside the book.[4] In other words, Mother Gallop's site of fruition counters discursive exclusion. But does not the feminist political privileging of this sight, designed to empower "women," re-enliven, as the shadowy "other" of this fertile, feminist mother, the earlier categories of the "unnatural" and "sterile" queer, transposed here from dominant discourse to feminist troping on the body?[5] Further, the melding of mother and desire into the hegemonic category of "woman's" plenitude also masks the transgression at the very site of fruition by both the "racially inferior" and the "sexually sterile." Because my desire is for the vampire to appear/disappear, guided by the pain of exclusion, I must now critically read the feminist theory of the gaze and of "woman" in order to reclaim her (the vampire's) role in representation.

Popular lore tells us that if we look at the vampire without the proscriptions that expel her, our gaze will be hypnotically locked into hers and we will become her victims. The feminist theorists, aware of the seductive quality of the vampire's look, excavate the proscription to discover the desire below. For example, Linda Williams's ground-breaking article "When the Woman Looks" constructs a certain dynamic of women looking at monsters. Williams notes that when the woman sees the monster, she falls into a trance-like fascination that "fails to maintain the distance between observer and observed so essential to the 'pleasure' of the voyeur." As the woman looks at the monster, her "look of horror paralyzes her in such a way that distance is overcome" (86). Hers is an en-tranced look, and the fascination in it could be read as a response to lesbian desire.

However, Williams's notion of proximity in the look proceeds from the hegemonic notion of "woman." As Mary Ann Doane phrases it, woman is "[t]oo close to herself, entangled in her own enigma, she could not step back, could not achieve the necessary distance of a second look (75–6). Thus, Williams's reading of woman's trance-like lock into the gaze with the monster is an extension of "woman's" condition in the gaze. How this "woman" is locked in the gaze, or what constitutes her pleasurable proximity, figures Williams, is her identification with the monster – a shared identification between monster and woman in representation: since they both share the status of object, they have a special empathy between them. In other words, this entranced seeing and proximity in the vision, consonant with psychoanalytic theory, rests upon the special status of "woman" as object of the viewer's scopophilia – and hence the shared identification of woman and monster. I want to come back to this premise later, but let us continue for a moment to see how Williams situates sexuality within this monstrous looking.

Within the horror genre, she observes, it is in the monster's body that the sexual interest resides, and not in the bland hero's. The monster's power is one of sexual difference from the normal male; thus, the monster functions like woman in representing the threat of castration. So, as Williams would have it, when the woman looks at the monster and when the cross is removed from before her gaze, they are totally proximate and contiguous, alike in sexual difference from the male and transfixed, outside of scopophilia, in the pleasures of shared sexual transgression. Desire is aroused in this gaze, but Williams quickly defers it to identification. In relegating the proximity and desire in the trance between woman and monster to (female) identification, Williams has securely locked any promise of lesbian sexuality into an Oedipal, heterosexual context.

This "woman," then, in Doane, Williams, and others, is really heterosexual woman. Though her desire is aroused vis-à-vis another woman (a monstrous occasion), and they are totally proximate, they identify with rather than desire one another. Their desire is still locked in the phallocratic order, and the same-sex taboo is still safely in place. What melds monster to woman is not lesbian desire – trance is not entranced – but finally daughter emulating mother in the Oedipal triangle with the absent male still at the apex. By inscribing in this configuration of looking a sexuality that is shared and not male, Williams both raises the possibility of the site of lesbian looking and simultaneously cancels it out. Like the image of the vampire in the currency of dominant discourse, this heterosexist configuration of the gaze seems to derive some power for its formulation by careening dangerously close to the abyss of same-sex desire, both invoking and revoking it. The critical pleasure resides in configuring the look by what it refuses to see. Thus, the revels of transgression enjoyed by the queer remain outside the boundaries of heterosexist proscription. You can hear the music, but you can't go to the party. Nevertheless, the site/sight of the monstrous is invoked and, though horrible, is sometimes negatively accurate and often quite seductive.

The hegemonic spread of the psychoanalytic does not allow for an imaginary of the queer. It simply reconfigures queer desire back into the heterosexual by deploying sexual difference through metaphors. For example, Kaja Silverman's "Fassbinder and Lacan: a Reconsideration of Gaze, Look, and Image" reconstructs the Lacanian "gaze/look" formation through the homosexual films of Fassbinder. For some of us queers, Fassbinder has pioneered a same-sex desiring cinematic apparatus – not only in his narratives, but in his camera. The queer spectator's pleasure in the films is constructed partially through the subcultural signs upon which the camera lovingly lingers (and/or ironizes), partially through the sense of camp and its distance from the real, which he employs for his political critique, and partially through the way he situates homosexual desire within national narratives. In fact, it is the dense overlay of these techniques that makes the films so homosexual in their signification.

For example, in *Querelle* (1982), the remake of Genet's novel, Fassbinder uses painted backdrops for the outdoor scenery. The two-dimensional, highly-saturated-color, painterly drops of the seaport mark the distance of this sexual site from "real" water and "real" boats. Fassbinder visually refers to the camp discourse of sailors, rather than to the reality of the sea. In the foreground, the camera lovingly follows the ass of the muscular seaman, who will later be seen, pants down, bent over the table. The relation of the camera to the ass certainly refigures forms of desire untouched by the Lacanian preoccupation with the penis. The anus is not itself a signifier of lack, and only comes to represent lack when tropes of sexual difference are reinserted into the discourse, feminizing it, while the penis is retained as signifier of the "masculine."[6] This is the move Silverman makes in deploying the heterosexist psychoanalytic model to read a homosexual text:

> Whereas classic cinema equates the exemplary male subject with the gaze, and locates the male eye on the side of authority and the law even when it is also a carrier of desire, *Beware a HolyWhore* [1970] not only extends desire and the look which expresses it to the female subject, but makes the male desiring look synonymous with loss of control. . . . It might be said doubly to "feminize" erotic spectatorship.   (62)

Even though Silverman has placed "feminize" within quotation marks, she must retain the category and the bipolar stability of the phallic male to configure the gaze. At worst, this is the kind of thinking that, in street discourse, produces the male homosexual as effeminate.

This model, if one can read the subcultural signs, is also disrupted by Fassbinder's Petra von Kant, a truly queer creature who flickers somewhere between haute couture butch lesbian and male drag queen, making sexual difference a double drag. In amazonian strength (camped up through her gown with metal Walkyrie-like breastplates) and bondage before the young femme (camped up by the roped fall of the same gown, which forces her to walk, on the make, with bounded steps), Petra performs melodramatic tirades before yet another painted backdrop. The drag show, so emphatically marked, and the lesbian designs of Petra, in sex and fashion, delight the homosexual with codes that seem incongruous with the Lacanian conclusions Silverman draws: "Fassbinder's films refuse simply to resituate the terms of phallic reference. Instead, [they] seek to induce in the viewer a recognition of him or herself as 'annihilated in the form . . . of castration" (79). It seems to me, instead, that Petra's embellished, elegant discourse, flowing before volumetrically rendered, corpulent, half-clothed bodies on the backdrop, suggests a surfeit of subcultural signs of queer desire, glimmering with the ghetto and distanced from both the real and the law of the traditional phallic world.

My point here is not to disallow the heterosexual feminist perspective in theories of representation, but to point out that, when it creates the unmarked category of "woman" as a general one that includes queers, or when it displaces queer desire by retaining, in the gaze/look compound, sexual difference and its phallus/lack polarity, that perspective remains caught in a heterosexist reading of queer discourse. Moreover, I suggest, the pleasure in theorizing the look that such a perspective affords appears dependent on disavowing or displacing what should not be seen.[7]

But now I must once again register the vampire's perturbations in this discourse. She is perturbed by this lengthy encounter with heterosexism and is agitating for her return to the discourse. As far as she is concerned, the heterosexual overlay of the queer is just another version of *Guess Who's Coming to Dinner*. So allow me to return to the site where the vampire appears/disappears, that is, in the configuration of proximity. In vampire lore, proximity is a central organizing principle – not only in the look, but also in the mise en scène.

In his work on the supernatural, Tzvetan Todorov maintains that the central diegetic force in these tales is their atmosphere – an atmosphere of proximity. Settings in fog and gloom connect the disparate elements of the structure through a palpable, atmospheric "touching." Judith Mayne, writing on *Nosferatu* (1922), agrees, describing the twilight as a "dangerous territory where opposing terms are not so easily distinguishable" (27). From the entranced look, through the mise en scène, to the narrative structure, proximity pervades the vampire lore. But why is this proximate potential represented as horror by the dominant culture? There is a supernatural tale that unlocks the code of the prohibition against this proximity – Freud's paper on the Uncanny. Freud's entry, so to speak, into the uncanny is through the notion of the double and of doubling processes, such as the feeling that we have been somewhere before. Thus, the uncanny for Freud is a kind of haunting proximity. In fact, Freud's endpoint is in a haunted house.

> To many people the idea of being buried alive while appearing to be dead is the most uncanny thing of all. And yet psycho-analysis has taught us that this terrifying fantasy originally had nothing terrifying about it at all, but was filled with a certain lustful pleasure – the fantasy, I mean, of intrauterine existence.   (397)

For in German *unheimlich* (uncanny) implies, on one level, un-homely. So, Freud continues, "this *unheimlich* place, however, is the entrance to the former *Heim* [home] of all human beings [and] the prefix '*un*' is the token of repression" (399).

So this proscribed proximity, the very world of vampires and of the "entranced" women who view them, is the desire for what Freud calls intrauterine existence. More than the fog, the gloom, the cobwebs, and the twilight, Freud's article serves as an exact description of the vampire's sleep in her coffin: toward the end of every night, she races back there, to her native soil, and enjoys the lustful pleasure of being buried alive and dead – her intrauterine recreation. However, while Freud unlocks one repressive code to liberate a certain pleasure, his notion of intrauterine pleasure further defers the actual pleasure proscribed here. And the feminist psychoanalytic theorists carry on his tradition: his intrauterine pleasure, this *jouissance*, can only be enjoyed as a pre-Oedipal *jouissance* with the mother.

If, for Lacan, sexuality is dominated by the phallus in a trench coat, for Kristeva and her ilk, it is the masked mother. The feminist allocation of this lascivious pleasure of proximity with the mother is simply a bad hangover from too much Freud – it shares his anxieties and proclivities. When Freud imagined this lustful recreation, he imagined the mise en scène as dirty and musty, with the sense of an old vampire who's about to exhibit her true wrinkled self. That's Freud's sexist anxiety about the wrinkled, musty vagina displaced onto an ageist fantasy of the old mother. Moreover, the idea of this pre-Oedipal *jouissance* with the mother reinscribes Freud's patriarchal obsession with genealogy and sexuality as generative – part of the nineteenth-century proscription against homosexuality. Locating *jouissance* in a mother keeps heterosexuality at the center of the picture – the son can insert him self into the site of *jouissance*. As Hamlet gleefully puts it in Müller's "Hamletmaschine," "the mother's womb is not a one-way street."[8]

Yet the history of anti-Semitism is also marked in Freud's preoccupation with "home" here; the founder of what the Nazis termed the "Jewish science" locates a so-called primal desire in returning to the home – a desire that became painfully identificatory for the Jews in the following years, forced into exile, as even Freud himself.[9] Similarly, the vampires, often from Eastern Europe as well, who sought their lustful sleep in dirt from their *Heimat* are marked as the wandering tribe and the despised. Thus, Freud's is both a dominant discourse and a counterdiscourse: while interpolating the heterosexual into the lesbian vampiric, it is also haunted by the outsider position of a myth of "race" that violently denied the pleasure of "home." This intersection of racism and notions of *Heim* or more dangerously *Heimat* seems crucial once again, as the term and the danger reappear in this time of Germany's reunification.

On the brighter (or the darker) side of things, in tracking the vampire, we can here re-imagine her various strengths: celebrating the fact that she cannot see herself in the mirror and remains outside that door into the symbolic, her proximate vanishing appears as a political strategy; her bite pierces platonic metaphysics and subject/object positions; and her fanged kiss brings her the chosen one, trembling with ontological, orgasmic shifts, into the state of the undead. What the dominant discourse represents as an emptying out, a draining away, in contrast to the impregnating kiss of the heterosexual, becomes an activism in representation.

Now, if you watch some recent vampire films, it may seem that things are getting better. Surely, you offer, the confining nineteenth-century codes are liberalized in the late twentieth century. For example, if you watch some recent vampire films, you may note that the vampire is actually portrayed as a lesbian. But this move only reflects a kind of post-Watergate strategy of representation; that is, don't keep any secrets because they can be revealed, just reveal the repression and that will serve to confirm it. So the vampire is portrayed as lesbian, but costumed in all the same conventions, simply making the proscription literal. The strategic shift here is in revelation, not representation. Whether she is the upper-class, decadent, cruel Baroness in *Daughters of Darkness* (1971; played by the late Delphine Seyrig, who was marked in the subculture as a lesbian actor), whose coercive lesbian sex act is practiced behind closed doors and whose languorous body proscribes the lesbian as an oozing, French dessert cheese; or whether she is the rough-trade, breast-biting Austrian lesbian vampire in *Vampire Lovers* (1970), or even the late-capitalist, media-assimilated lesbian vampire in the independent film *Because the Dawn* (1988), her attraction is (in) her proscription. Only the proscription of the lesbian is literally portrayed – the occult becomes cult in the repression.

While the lesbian has become literalized in contemporary vampire films, the proscription against same-sex desire has also been reconfigured in a trope more consonant with late-twentieth century conditions. For one thing, nature isn't what it used to be, and likewise, the undead have altered with it. In the nineteenth century, the stable notion of nature as natural and of the natural as good made it possible to configure same-sex desire as unnatural – thus monster – thus vampire. Beginning with horror films in the fifties, the binarism of natural/unnatural gives way. Nature is contaminated – it is a site of the unnatural. Metaphors of Romantic organicism fail where technology has transformed. The agrarian dream gives way to the nuclear nightmare. The representation of nature, contaminated by nuclear testing in the desert, is a site for the production of monsters that transgress what was considered natural. Hollywood produced *Them* (1954), *Tarantula* (1955), *Crab Monsters* (1956), *Giant Grasshoppers* (1957), and *Killer Shrews* (1959). The urban replaces the agrarian as a haven. The humanist scientist, such as van Helsing, warring against the perverse isolated vampire gives way to the military–industrial complex warring against its own creations. The giant tarantula created by nuclear reaction is destroyed by napalm; another monster is killed by a shift in the ozone layer.

After the 50s, the lone vampire, or the family of vampires that threatened the human community, is replaced by a proliferation of the undead. Romero's trilogy illustrates the progression: in *Night of the Living Dead* (1968), a score of the undead threatens a family–unit–type group in a house; in the second film, *Dawn of the Dead* (1977), thousands of undead threaten a smaller, less-affiliated group in a shopping mall, one of the few places remaining; and in *Day of the Dead* (1985), the undead have successfully taken over the continent, finally threatening what dwindles down to the basic heterosexual-couple-unit in a military–industrial complex.[10] Successively, the undead have eliminated the family unit, claimed commodity reification for their own in the shopping mall, and defeated the military–industrial complex. One hope remains in a kind of Adam and Eve ending of the final film, although it seems unlikely. The undead overrun things, proliferate wildly, are like contamination, pollution, a virus, disease – AIDS. Not AIDS as just any disease, but AIDS as it is used socially as a metaphor for same-sex desire among men, AIDS as a construction that signifies the plague of their sexuality. But why is the taboo now lodged in proliferation? This is Freud's double gone wild, the square root of proximity. The continual displacements in the system have become like a cancer, spreading, devouring, and reproducing themselves. The oppressive politics of representation have cathected to displacement, settling their sites/sights there again and again and again. The taboo against same sex becomes like the Stepford wives when they break down, pouring coffee over and over and over again.

These neo-undead doubly configure away the lesbian position, since same-sex desire appears as gay male. The lesbian position is only the motor for multiple displacements. Where does this all leave the lesbian vampire, then? Outside of the mirror, collapsing subject/object relations into the proximate, double occupancy of the sign, abandoning the category of woman as heterosexist, and entering representation only in a guise that proscribes her. You still can only see her, in horror and fear, when you don't.

Finally, in tracking the vampire in representation in order to perceive how she counters blood myths of race and proper sexuality, I would like to turn to a text through which she moves – a lesbian choreopoem. This form particularly suits the vampire for several reasons, but specifically in its performance structures. The choreopoem is a theatrical form created by Chicanas and black women. These are performance pieces composed of loosely related poems and performed by ensembles. In this collection of poems, the performer is not a character, though she may, for a short time, suggest one. As the lyric voice moves among the several performers in the ensemble, they collectively enact the agency, or the lyric dynamic. Sometimes the performer inhabits the subjective "I" of the poet, sometimes she is the story itself, sometimes the storyteller.

In the choreopoem "No" by Alexis DeVeaux, the subject position is that of the desiring lesbian who is also active in black revolutionary politics. The title "No" itself functions to proscribe what the dominant discourse can articulate, while at the same time tracing a counterdiscourse. "No" consists of thirty poems: several are lesbian love poems to other black women, one is about a revolutionary woman who breaks away from the sexism of her male partner in the black movement, one is about the murder of children in Selma. The ground, then, the mise en scéne is the historical, social, economic, and emotional field of the black lesbian revolutionary subject. The agency, or subject position, is the itineration of that field through a collective of women, with its possibilities and impossibilities made dynamic by the lyric. In other words, the lesbian subject position is composed of this movement among performers and through the lyric "I" of the poet herself, whose desire flows through their mouths and their gestures and whose playing space is the historical and social borders of the possible and impossible for such a subject. She is both visible and invisible – visible in her lyric, collective movement and in the proximity of her politics and homosexual desire, and invisible as character or content. The poem celebrates the ethnic fashion of dreadlocks (the vampire's dread-lock) as seductive while also specifically coded as revolutionary, in proximity to a celebration of clitoral love-making between two women within their antiracist struggle; proximity/distance is marked as one. DeVeaux closes the space between women's economic and political struggles and lesbian desire.

Notes

1. I am indebted to Yvonne Yarbro-Bejarano for this analysis of sexual/racial honor, which appears in *Feminism and the Honor Plays of Lope de Vega* (West Lafayette, Ind.: Purdue University Press, 1994).
2. For a fuller discussion of this point, see the chapter on Spain in *Aryan* by Poliakov and the chapter on "Mystic Speech" in *Heterologies* by de Certeau, especially pp. 81–6.
3. The prejudice was so convincing that a fashion arose among middle-class women to visit the slaughterhouse and drink the blood of an ox to strengthen themselves. See Dijkstra, "Metamorphoses of the Vampire: Dracula and His Daughters," in *Idols*, particularly pp. 337–8.
4. Gallop suggested this in a discussion of the cover photo at the University of California, Riverside, on January 18, 1991.
5. Gallop, however, is one of the few authors to articulate issues between lesbians and heterosexual feminists within this kind of debate (107–8). Her discussion here, clearly written in solidarity with lesbians, is important and could be pursued at length.
6. I am indebted for this point to the work in progress of my colleagues George Haggerty and Gregory Bredbeck; to Bredbeck for his work on sodomy and the anus, and to Haggerty for his reconfiguration of the effeminate in the eighteenth century. See also Miller's reading of Hitchcock in "Anal *Rope*."
7. Both Silverman's and my positions are too complex to work out in this reduced form. A more complete development of them will appear in my book *The Domain-Matrix: Performing Lesbian at the End of Print Culture* (Bloomington: Indiana University Press, 1996), of which this essay is a fragment.
8. "Der Mutterschoss ist keine Einbahn-strasse" (Müller 91); translation mine.
9. Marjorie Garber suggested this in conversation at the 1990 Queer Theory conference in Santa Cruz, California.
10. I am indebted to Steve Shaviro for our discussions of the trilogy.

Works cited

Baudelaire, Charles. "Femmes Damnées Delphine et Hippolyte." *Les Fleurs du Mal*, trans. Richard Howard (Boston: Godine, 1983).

de Certeau, Michel. *Heterologies: Discourse on the Other*, trans. Brian Massumi (Minneapolis: University of Minnesota Press, 1986).

de Lauretis, Teresa. "Sexual Indifference and Lesbian Representation." *Performing Feminisms: Feminist Critical Theory and Theatre*, ed. Sue-Ellen Case (Baltimore: Johns Hopkins University Press, 1990), 17–39.

DeVeaux, Alexis. "No." Unpublished ms.

Dijkstra, Bram. *Idols of Perversity: Fantasies of Feminine Evil in Fin-de-siècle Culture* (Oxford: Oxford University Press, 1986).

Doane, Mary Ann. "Film and the Masquerade: Theorising the Female Spectator." *Screen* 23, no. 3–4 (1982): 74–87.

Freud, Sigmund. "The 'Uncanny'" (1919). *Collected Papers*, ed. Ernest Jones, vol. 4 (New York: Basic, 1959).

Gallop, Jane. *Thinking Through the Body* (New York: Columbia University Press, 1988).

Gomez, Jewelle. *The Gilda Stories* (Ithaca: Firebrand, 1991).

St John of the Cross. *Living Flame of Love*, trans. and ed. E. Allison Peers (Garden City, N.Y.: Image, 1962).

——. *The Poems of St John of the Cross*, trans. John Frederick Nims (New York: Grove, 1959).

Le Fanu, J., Sheridan. "Carmilla" (1872). *Vampires*, ed. Alan Ryan (Garden City, NY: Doubleday, 1987), 71–138.

Mayne, Judith. "Dracula in the Twilight: Murnau's *Nosferatu* (1922)." *German Film and Literature: Adaptations and Transformations*, ed. Eric Rentschler (New York: Methuen, 1986), 25–39.

Miller, D.A. "Anal *Rope*." *Representations* 32 (1990): 114–33.

Müller, Heiner. "Die Hamletmaschine." *Mauser* (Berlin: Rotbuch, 1978), 89–97.

Poliakov, Leon. *The Aryan Myth*, trans. Edmund Howard (New York: Basic, 1974).

Praz, Mario. *The Romantic Agony*, trans. Angus Davidson (London: Oxford University Press, 1954).

Rimbaud, Arthur. "Antique." *Illuminations*, trans. Louise Varèse (New York: New Directions, 1957).

——. *A Season in Hell*, trans. Bertrand Mathieu; Preface by Anaïs Nin (Cambridge: Pomegranate, 1976).

Silverman, Kaja. "Fassbinder and Lacan: a Reconsideration of Gaze, Look, and Image." *Camera Obscura* 19 (1989): 54–85.

Todorov, Tzvetan. *The Fantastic: A Structural Approach to a Literary Genre*, trans. Richard Howard (Ithaca: Cornell University Press, 1975).

Wilde, Oscar. *Salome*, trans. Lord Alfred Douglas; illustrations by Aubrey Beardsley (New York: Dover, 1967).

Williams, Linda. "When the Woman Looks." *Re-vision: Essays in Feminist Film Criticism*, ed. Mary Ann Doane, Patricia Mellencamp, and Linda Williams (Frederick, Md.: University Publications of America, 1984), 83–99.

5

The Queer Globe Itself

The concept of globalisation is most often understood as a gender-less, sexless phenomenon, signifying the processes of nation-states and transnational flows of capital as if they were purely self-referential dynamics. In spite of interventions into the critique by feminists and queers to personalise differences among those most affected by globalisation, the major discourses continue to inscribe the global and even the local as if abstracted, universalised categories. In fact, these authors take great pains not to "descend" to particulars, even when they insist that they are interested only in the materialist effects. Take Michael Hardt and Antonio Negri's influential work *Empire*, for example.[1] They write of "populations", "subjectivities" and "ethnic groups", in their so-called "Biopolitics" (*Empire*, pp. 31–7). Significantly, though, they treat "capital" as if it were an active subject, as in "capital does relate to and rely on its noncapitalist environment, but it does not necessarily internalize that environment" (*Empire*, p. 225). It is difficult, at least for this author, to imagine how capital could internalise anything. Nonetheless, economic processes, unmarked by gender and sexuality, are the dominant subject posed within their critique. Other familiar "big names" in the field, such as Fredric Jameson, move considerations of identity and difference into the misty regions of heady abstractions that operate as subjects: "As you begin to watch Identity turn into Difference and Difference back into identity, you grasp both as an inseparable Opposition. . . . At that point, you have approached the identity of non-identity."[2] Surely, the scene Jameson paints of a clash of philosophical Titans melting into one another registers some anxiety of specificity, but, beyond that, it is difficult to parse just what happened to differences in this collapse. More, David Harvey offers a seemingly activist role for "-isms" in his notion of "militant particularisms".[3] As for the local, it too appears as an active abstract term. The influential author Arif Dirlik defines it in this way: "The local as I use it here has meaning only inasmuch as it is a product of the conjuncture of structures located in the same temporality but with different spatialities."[4] We might hope that in one of those spatialities we would find something like a lesbian bar, but it is unclear whether or not the local actually signifies any populus.

From a feminist perspective, Carla Freeman argues that in these discourses the global operates as a masculinised concept.[5] Even though these authors seem to write critiques of the global, the agency and power they lend to it masculinise its role, if not their very discourse. Moreover, Freeman insists, since these accounts do not consider the role of gender in the global sphere, their seeming non-gendered space is, as usual, a masculinist space; for the unmarked has traditionally been construed as masculinist ("Local:Global", p. 1010). Freeman locates accounts of gendering processes within ethnographies, rather than within critiques of globalisation. Ethnographic accounts have recorded and understood gendered hierarchies as part of a specifically local scene ("Local:Global", p. 1011). This practice of situating gender within the local, argues Freeman, reinscribes the equivalencies among global/masculine and local/feminine (p. 1012). Finally, Freeman observes that in the macro-scenarios of global and local, the local is often construed as a rape victim of global capitalist domination. She argues that a feminist reconception of the global would understand local practices not merely as the effects of the global, or as a contradiction to it, but as constitutive of it (p. 1013). This means that gender would be a constituent of the global, rather than one part of its "other". The feminist shift to the discourse would install people as subjects, marked by differences of gender and class in contrast to the active "-isms" and economic processes of global critiques.

Apart from ethnographies, sexual practices and gender codes have been constituted as autonomous, discrete objects of study, carefully sorted out from global discourses and belonging only to critiques dedicated solely to them; thus queer and feminist writings are perceived to deal exclusively with sexuality and gender, respectively. In *Queer Globalizations*, Miranda Joseph notes how kinship and community have been constructed as part of the so-called "natural" and thus "extra-economic" realm.[6] If capital is perceived as an active agent of power that refers only to its own economic processes, sexual practices must belong to an order that is entirely self-reflexive.

As my students in feminist classes often ask, "How did this happen?" By way of an answer, Joseph offers a cursory consideration of the division of the economic from the embodied in the work of

Karl Marx as a kind of "origin" of influence for Leftist critiques. Joseph turns to Marx's use of the term "value" (as in "use value" and "surplus value") as establishing referents of economic value that are abstracted from embodied practices. These so-called "values", which actually define conditions of labour and consumption, serve only to refer to economic conditions, extracted from the values associated with embodied practices such as gender or heteronormativity (Joseph, "Discourse of Global/Localization", p. 86). Moreover, she argues, Marx's notion of capital, like that of "value", "depends on an abstract equivalence across cultures". She concludes that "this abstraction is what makes capitalism seem mobile and dynamic" (pp. 86–7). Ironically, Leftist abstractions of monetary operations and their values as culture/gender/body-free collude with those very operations and assumptions of global capital. Here is the actual battle of the Titans: one form of economics wrestles with another, abstracted from embodied processes.

So where, one might ask, does Marx situate the embodied practices of the subject? Unfortunately, for those outside the heteronormative order, he relegates all personal/social/kinship values to the family unit, for better or for worse. The family unit bears the weight of embodied production and kinship hierarchy. As Joseph notes, the family unit also serves as a compensatory site. It constitutes the private, personal realm imagined as supplemental to capitalist and market exploitation ("Discourse of Global/Localization", p. 88). The family is installed as the great keeper of the gender divide and hierarchy, the exclusive property-owner of the bedroom, and the single refuge from the arena of state and global economics. Here, the Left and the Right also seem to agree. The title of the volume in which Joseph's article appears, *Queer Globalizations*, reveals that any study that imagines large economic and state processes that would be marked by the social and particularly a social outside of the heteronormative zone must constitute a separate, autonomous critique of the local.

So first, what queer studies can bring to studies of globalisation is an understanding of the direct relation between economic forces and the social. Sexual practices and preferences can be seen to co-constitute not only local, but also global transactions. In other words, like feminist critiques, queer interventions can help to dissolve the autonomous sense of capital and economics upon which both critiques of the global and globalisation depend, infusing embodied practices in the root of these operations. Second, and most important, queer subjects can displace the self-referential discourse of the economic with an agent who is neither necessarily a resident of the local nor a normative citizen. Queer discourses can insist that there is a labouring/consuming subject within the global arena that is not defined by the family or kinship hierarchies. And the queer subject can be treated as a denizen of both the local and global arenas. In this way, queer studies of globalisation can alter the paradigm of the critique at its base.

The voyage out

A vast liner labours its way into the harbour. In many ports of the world this is a familiar sight. While the ship contaminates international waters with its waste, it also brings welcome tourist dollars to port regions. Street performers rush to the dockside, along with those who bring "local" foods and crafts in the hope of earning tourist dollars. When the passengers begin to disembark for their short visit to a "foreign land", the locals are shocked to see homosexual couples coming down the gangplank: men are holding hands with other men; women have their arms around each other. Performers who practise sexualised versions of local traditions on the docks, such as the hula, stop in their tracks, afraid that the gay men will respond to the male dancers and the lesbians to the female. Food vendors flee from imagined contamination. This scene could have happened anytime from the early 1990s to today, in many ports, but let's set it in the Cayman Islands, a British territory, where the islanders were, in fact, so offended by displays of same-sex affection that in December 1998 the local authorities denied docking privileges to an American gay cruise ship insisting that "gay vacationers could not be counted on to 'uphold standards of appropriate behaviour' ".[7] The public and national space, it seems, are imagined as heteronormative.

Gay and lesbian tourism creates a "visible and mobile homosexuality" in the world, challenging local behaviours (Puar, "Circuits", p. 102). Some queer theorists argue that creating a queer space is always a form of tourism, particularly in fleeing repressive societies at "home". From their perspective, the search for a safe habitat in which to express affection and desire in public, combined with a disposable income, launched a "golden age" of queer tourism in the 1990s. Today, "an estimated 5–25 million gays and lesbians . . . spend more than \$10–17 billion on travel products each year" (Puar, "Circuits", p. 105). The visibility of these tourists definitely challenges local prohibitions and seduces local market economies. A myriad of gay and lesbian travel organisations and publications now flourish, publishing descriptions of welcoming sites as well as homophobic ones for queer tourists. It is important to note that only certain queers are part of this venture, however. A marketing survey published in 2001 claims that 88 per cent of gay travellers are college-educated, most are white and many live in urban centres. Moreover, 94 per cent of gay and lesbian travellers are, in fact, gay; only 6 per cent are lesbians (Puar, "Circuits", p. 114).

However, critiques of queer travel perceive it as launching a form of globalism that reconstructs the imperial sense of travel, with its nostalgia for illicit, exotic encounters. In this way, queer travellers practise "the use of the exotic to transgress" (Puar, "Circuits", p. 104). Joseph Boone, in "The Homoerotics of Orientalism", traces this practice in the biographies and literatures of noted gay authors from André Gide to Roland Barthes.[8] The sex trade for boys in the Mediterranean and in Asian countries such as Thailand has financed new clubs and scenes, bringing a relaxation of local laws. Bangkok now houses numerous clubs, many featuring transgender or drag acts as entertainment, featuring *katoeys*, or ladyboys. Beach towns such a Phuket host many gay guesthouses and clubs. The majority of those who perform in these clubs and serve as sex-workers are young boys from poor homes, who have found economic success in plying their trade with gay tourists. The critique within feminism of the sex trade and the sexual use of poor women in the Third and Fourth Worlds has apparently not permeated the consciousness of these gay male travellers. So while queer tourists may bring a new, global visibility to alternative sexualities, they also exploit local conditions for a booming Orientalist sex trade that preys on poverty.

Queer women tourists have also financed numerous forays into the global. Their preferred method of travel, however, is less the occupation of cities and resorts than lesbian cruises. The earliest and most successful of these grew out of the feminist recording label Olivia Records, now known as Olivia Cruises. These are the lesbian specials, although not necessarily marketed that way by the cruises themselves. One needn't read the secret codes of the subculture to discover these are primarily lesbian cruises. Lesbian travel agencies advertise them as such. One lesbian travel agency, Flamingo Travel, notes:

> Olivia, serving the lesbian community since 1973, has worked to empower women through travel. It's different to say the list as lesbian

cruise travelers really feel free every minute of every day from the outside world. Olivia, like many other gay travel cruise companies, charters entire ships and resorts and they continually craft new vacation packages and unique experiences for the gay travel industry.[9]

Resources travel agency posts that "Olivia Gay Travel is up and coming and is one of the hottest gay and lesbian travel agencies in the world. Catering to the lesbian community, most if not all of Olivia's staff and customers are gay and lesbian."[10] These cruise ships feature musicians of feminist/lesbian note, travelling to Hawaii, the Caribbean, the Netherlands, the Greek islands, etc. The Netherlands may seem to stand out here as a different sort of port-of-call, but Amsterdam has long been recognised as a lesbian-friendly city, with several "hot spots" to enjoy. Along with Amsterdam, the cruises advertise "the buzzing social scene" of Key West, Florida – another known queer resort – as part of the "Caribbean Escape with Melissa Etheridge".[11] Etheridge, long a favourite in certain lesbian circles, provides what some describe as a "dreamy cruise", as she croons across the Caribbean. As this suggests, these cruises are more about romance on the far seas than sex in the port cities, while still offering short visits to various bars in the "buzzing social scene".

Prices for these cruises range from US$1,400 to $6,000. The Etheridge tour for 2006 sold out. This success indicates a flourishing class of lesbians who can afford such travel and leisure. To be fair, not all of these cruises are focused on romance: at least two evince an interest in "nature", one sailing to the Galapagos Islands, the other to Antarctica. While these cruises indicate a different sort of traveller and a different interest in the global, they also chart frightening incursions into fragile ecologies.

By the way, should heterosexual feminists feel left out of the portrait of global travellers, *Ms. Magazine* will be hosting its third all-women feminist cruise in 2007. On this cruise, speakers such as the activist Dolores Huerta, the actress Tyne Dailey and the president of the National Association for Women will (presumably) deliver feminist politics, while cruising the seas. In fact, our Women Studies programme at UCLA sent out e-flyers for this cruise. While the ship cuts through the Caribbean, stopping at familiar ports, it also hosts such events as a "meeting with Mexican feminists" and, more difficult to comprehend, a "feminist land excursion to the Guatemalan Mayan Ruins". While at sea, feminists can enjoy feminist gambling at the ship's casino and feminist facials at the spa. And all this for as little as $1,849 or as much as $5,800. The class of these feminists is fairly easy to deduce from these prices.[12]

However, the sight of independent women together, descending the gangplank, may have a liberating effect on those who find themselves in constrained social circumstances. At the same time, that capitalist independence might also produce a kind of cookie-cutter globalism in its image of feminist and queer women. One could imagine, too, that the sight of these upper-middle-class women on vacation might not inspire the working women in the ports, with their few vegetables and fruits.

Money does speak, in all these ways, with the growth of queer travel. Eng-Beng Lim, in his article "Glocalqueering in New Asia", describes the effect of "pink dollar politics" in Singapore – a nation-state long known for the persecution of homosexuals.[13] Recognising the economic benefits of luring queer tourists, Singapore reversed its policies to host "Asia's [queer] Mardi Gras" in 2003. A form of the Pride Parade, the event attracted tourists from many countries, including Germany, Malaysia, Thailand, Japan, Hong Kong and the US, along with more than 4,500 local participants. This enormous "coming-out party" eased restrictions on public displays of queer affections, including dancing. "Pink dollar tourism", then, motivated the nation-state to lift its prohibitions. Beyond state-instituted changes in legislation of non-normative sexual behaviour, the global visibility of queers has inspired the formation of more indigenous political organisations such as the Asian Lesbian Network, organised by the Thai group Anjaree in 1990; the first Indonesian Lesbian and Gay Congress in 1993; the Progressive Organisation of Gays in the Philippines in 1992, and the group Occur in Japan.[14]

Dubbing the queer voice

Adopting the globalised queer voice has become a strategy of resistance. In several countries, people have found it useful to "dub" the queer voice in order to mimic its association with transgender identification and same-sex desire. Some have found that mimicking these non-normative practices can offer protection within oppressive normative hierarchies; others have found a way to articulate their own set of identifications through this globalised paradigm. For example, Filipina domestic workers in Hong Kong, who suffer not only indentured servitude but also sexual exploitation, adopt a sexual identity called "tomboyism" to discourage the men for whom they work from making sexual advances and compromising their integrity (Freeman, Local:Global, p. 1016). They find that convincing these men that they are, in fact, masculinised women, interested only in other women, can successfully prevent their sexualisation. They appear less seductive and less available in their "tomboy" role. Some queer theorists posit this kind of strategy as a glocalised use of "lesbian" in contrast to a "global lesbian". In other words, local women appropriate the global signifier "lesbian" as a standpoint from which to resist oppressive practices: less a site of identification than a foil to traditional assumptions governing women's sexuality.[15]

These "glocal" adoptions of queer identities contrast sharply with the manner in which more official, seemingly feminist organisations in the international realm have eschewed any nominative association with lesbians. One need only recall what transpired at the UN-sponsored Fourth World Conference on Women in Beijing in 1995. As Katie King documents, a coalition of women's organisations from South Africa, Indonesia, the Netherlands, the US and Mexico drafted a document on sexual orientation and women's rights.[16] At the eleventh hour of drafting the Platform for Action of the World Conference, the term "sexual orientation" and its attendant issues were struck from the document (King, "There Are No Lesbians Here", p. 34). King points out how this process is tied to the human rights project of creating a "new global citizen", or, more specifically, the new global woman as citizen who signifies stable, normative identifications and social realities across cultural and national differences (p. 37). In so far as sexual orientation issues threaten the success of women's application for global citizenship, they are often considered dispensable. I have been asked by feminist representatives of three countries where I have delivered public addresses not to mention the term "lesbian", lest it impede the success of their feminist agenda there. So, ironically, while lesbian issues have been silenced in international feminist platforms, the voice or identity has been "dubbed" by other, local women as a strategy of resistance.

I have borrowed the term "dubbing" from Tom Boellstorff's notion of "dubbing culture".[17] Boellstorff coined the term to describe several local practices he discovered in his research on gay Indonesians. For example, he relates the case of "Darta", a Muslim man living in East Java, who adopted two English words to describe his sexual identity, first, "lesbi" and then "gay" as in *dapat gay juga* ("I Knew it Was Me", pp. 21–2). These words had travelled via gay literature and gay tourist contacts to his country and helped him to articulate his own practices and desires which had no name in his Javanese Muslim culture. Boellstorff records that 95 per cent of his informants from Java, Bali and Sulawesi cite the mass media as a source for understanding themselves as *lesbi* or *gay* (p. 33). Boellstorff also notes the widespread use of the term "tomboi" in Indonesia as signifying various forms of transgender identification (p. 31).

Surprisingly, the term "tomboy" has been adopted across cultures as a strategy of resistance and self-definition. Not only have Hong Kong domestic workers and Javanese Muslim men "dubbed" the term, but Taiwanese butch lesbians have adopted it to signify their social identity. Apparently, in the 1960s, gay men in Taipei began referring to women who wore ties and trousers and sported short haircuts as T boys. By the 1980s, the women themselves were using the term, hanging out in what came to be known as "T bars". Antonia Chao reports that more than 30 such bars have opened in Taipei, Taichung and Kaohsung since the 1980s.[18] These are globalised environments, specialising in karaoke and global music videos, so the identity of "T" could be perceived as a purely global phenomenon. Yet, notes Chao, while these women seem to participate fully in a global commodity culture, their T identification plays on traditional Confucian gender codes of the masculine, including Chinese beliefs in sexual potency, etc. So, while their nomenclature and social space are globalised, their codes of transgender identification are derived from the local Chinese traditions.

The process of "dubbing culture" describes how globalised queer identities can be used to "animate a sexual self felt to be fully modern and authentic, yet a disjuncture from the local" (Boellstorff, "I Knew it Was Me", p. 22). As a dubbed soundtrack is shaped by images originating elsewhere, so a "dubbed" identity is something one cannot originate, but only receive. The "dubbed" identity mimics the original in order to disrupt the naturalised cultural referents that are determined by the traditional. Thus, the term is neither strictly globalised, nor strictly localised, but oscillates between the two, in offering, through the global, a local identity. Boellstorff argues that beyond this dubbing, queer identities are positioned in a similarly oscillating manner within global critiques. They are perceived as either autochthonous bearers of "traditional identities masked by Western terms, or as traitors to tradition, partaking in global gay imperialism" ("I Knew it Was Me", p. 27). "Dubbing" negotiates between the practice of globalised assimilation and local tradition. What Boellstorff has termed "dubbing" others have called "glocalisation": or "the localization and indigenization of globally mobile understandings of sexuality" (Berry, Martin and Yue, *Mobile Cultures*, p. 7). Thus, the queer subject is both local and global, assimilated and resistant.

Electrifying global sex

In their introduction to *Mobile Cultures: New Media in Queer Asia*, Chris Berry, Fran Martin and Audrey Yue periodise the global transmission of queer sexualities, citing *Time* magazine's assertion in 2001 that "the Internet had done to Asia's gay and lesbian communities what Stonewall enabled in the West . . ." (p. 2). The new millennium; it seems, ushered in an electronic network of sexual and political contacts for queers. High-speed technology and the "ephemerality of the commodity" form a network of what these authors perceive as mobile and transient cultures' (p. 2). As the Web provided online possibilities for assignations and even actual sex around the globe, it also created opportunities to share strategies for political organisation. Websites and chatrooms enabled a new meshing of the public and private – the twilight zone where queer identities and practices form. At the same time, new forms of surveillance have been put in place to monitor and punish these contacts. As usual, sexual practices prompt censorship and moral outrage. Globalising sex also globalises morality.

The case of Josephine Chuen-juei Ho, a prominent academician in Taiwan, chair of the English Department at the National Central University and president of the Cultural Studies Association, illustrates how both radical intervention and surveillance can meet on the Web. In June 2003, 14 Taiwanese conservative NGOs filed charges against Ho for two bestiality hyperlinks located on the zoophilia webpage in her Sexuality Studies databank. Ho has been researching sexuality and supporting freedom for marginalised sexual minorities for ten years. She has published 17 books in the area of sexuality studies and feminism. These groups, which had been hounding her for the duration, used the website as an issue to insist that Ho be dismissed from her teaching post. The conservative coalition included a censorship group, Christian groups and a parents' group.

Ho described the hyperlinks in this way:

> In my case, the hyperlink in question is situated at the bottom of our 'animal love' webpage, one among more than 50 webpages on sexuality studies that we are building, preceded by a collection of essays on zoophilia, literary pieces on zoophilia, topical news about cases of bestiality. The hyperlink, when clicked, would reveal a warning message that

says, 'The following are photos of alternative bestiality sexual acts. Those
who may feel offended should refrain from entering.' The hyperlink itself
leads to a string of a dozen or so zoophilia photos that I found on one of
the bestiality sites in the US. This collection was chosen mainly because
it illustrates not only the various types of animals involved but also the
cliché scenarios portrayed. BTW, I have never used the databank in my
teaching; it was merely a research reserve for like-minded researchers.[19]

The study and representation of queer sexual practices, it seems,
must be omitted in favour of the normative. Even research implies
unhealthy participation, and the global sharing of research pollutes
the new, emerging global citizenry. Ho's response to the censoring of
her website clearly articulates the issues:

> Imposing a law on cyberspace that decrees that 'the mere provision of
> hyperlinks' to the so-called obscenity sites is criminal is simply absurd. For
> hyperlinks are not direct avenues to fantasyland, but moments of choice-
> making. A person has to initiate the click to effect his decision to enter.
> That is something totally different from the passive situation in which you
> are handed a flyer of obscene images on the street corner. If providing a
> hyperlink to difficult knowledge is a crime, then search engines from
> Yahoo to Google would all have to be shut down for they all can lead
> us to numerous unspeakable terrains.   ('The Chronicle: Colloquy Live
> Transcript')

The charge inspired a response by local scholars and activists and a
transnational internet petition of over 1,000 signatures from 35 countries and areas, including formal letters from the AAUP, [American
Association of University Professors] the Hong Kong Association of
Sex Education and others. Ultimately, two investigative hearings were
held concerning the structure and content of Ho's sexuality databank. Apparently, the Taiwanese legal system considers all explicit
sex-related information to be an obscenity and not scholarly material.
In the trial, the prosecution could not distinguish between a hyperlink and a holding in a databank, claiming that Ho had violated the
criminal code in making graphic and obscene materials easily available. The court proceedings became a site for activist education – a
50 foot-long petition with signatures was unfurled outside the courtroom, the building and plaza were jammed with protestors, etc. Ho
was found not guilty, but the case focuses internet issues around the
internet representation of alternative sexualities, rights and processes
of access, new definitions of the public space, and local, juridical holds
on global databanks.

Ho's case challenges the location of the moral choice. She argues that morality is not located in the databank of knowledge, but in the decision of the user. Moreover, she illustrates how search engines of online materials are successfully opening doors to knowledge and contacts across cultures and national laws in a way that is impossible to censor. Sexual practices reveal how the global space is one of extreme anxiety in terms of censorship or security. As the private becomes the public in sexual politics and liaisons, codes of the normative seem even more difficult to presume and enforce.

In response to such acts of surveillance and censure, the Taiwanese filmmaker Shu Lea Cheang produced a digital sci-fi porn film, *I.K.U.: A Japanese Cyber-porn Adventure*, to provide what she deemed a feminist intervention into the mainstream production and reception of digital images considered to constitute a moral outrage. Her film satirises corporate-linked digital-cyber-porn, with porn stars portrayed as mobile flows of the transnational corporation Genom.[20] The fictional corporation sends collected sexual pleasure signals directly to the brain of consumers, without any "physical friction". I.K.U. orgasm decoder chips, in different colours for different sexualities, provide access to the Genom server. Thus, Cheang's film sidesteps all issues of identity and even sexual practice, as the process uploads entirely into the digital realm. Katrien Jacobs claims a "queerscape" for Cheang's work, which projects a mythologised site, animated in many cases, and projected into the future.[21] The digital realm, then, challenges the notion of the sexual as embodied. The global sexual subject may be formed in the future as a collection of digital effects.

The few strategies offered above may begin to suggest ways in which queer studies can intervene in normative global critiques and discourses. They prompt the visibility of untested normative assumptions that are built into the global and local, suggesting ways to imagine a more nuanced and varied global subject. Queers studies can intervene in the bipolar opposition of the global and the local, offering an oscillating position from which to perceive economic and social effects.

Notes

1. Michael Hardt and Antonio Negri, *Empire* (Cambridge, MA and London: Harvard University Press, 2000).
2. Fredric Jameson, "Notes on Globalization as a Philosophical Issue", in Fredric Jameson and Masao Miyoshi (eds), *The Cultures of Globalization* (Durham, NC and London: Duke University Press, 1998), pp. 54–77, p. 76.

3. Quoted in Matthew Hyland, "In Place of a Conclusion", in Jameson and Miyoshi (eds), *The Cultures of Globalization*, pp. 378–9.
4. Arif Dirlik, "The Global in the Local", in Rob Wilson and Wimal Dissanayake (eds), *Global/Local* (Durham, NC and London: Duke University Press, 2000), pp. 21–45, p. 39.
5. Carla Freeman, "Is Local: Global as Feminine:Masculine? Rethinking the Gender of Globalization", *Signs*, 26:4 (Summer 2001): 1007–37.
6. Miranda Joseph, "The Discourse of Global/Localization", in Arnaldo Cruz-Malavé and Martin F. Manalansan (eds), *Queer Globalizations* (New York: New York University Press, 2002), pp. 71–99.
7. Jasbir Kaur Puar, "Circuits of Queer Mobility: Tourism. Travel, and Globalization", *GLO*, 8:1–2 (2002): 101–37, p. 101.
8. Joseph Boone, "Vacation Cruises; or The Homoerotics of Orientalism", *PMLA*, 110 (1995): 89–110.
9. Flamingo Travel Group, www.flamingo-travel.com. Accessed 29 September 2006.
10. Gay Resources Online, www.gay-resources-online.com. Accessed 29 September 2006.
11. Olivia Cruises, www.olivia.com/cruises. Accessed 29 September 2006.
12. Ms. Magazine Cruise, www.msmagazinecruise.com. Accessed 29 September 2006.
13. Eng-Beng Lim, "Glocalqueering in New Asia: the Politics of Performing Gay in Singapore", *Theatre Journal*, 57:3 (2005): 383–405.
14. See Dennis Altman, "Rupture or Continuity? The Internationalization of Gay Identities", *Social Text*, 14:3 (Fall 1996): 77–94, p. 79.
15. See Chris Berry, Fran Martin and Audrey Yue (eds), "Introduction", *Mobile Cultures: New Media in Queer Asia* (Durham, NC: Duke University Press, 2003), pp. 1–18, p. 8.
16. Katie King, " 'There are no Lesbians here': Lesbianisms, Feminisms, and Global Gay Formation", in Cruz-Malavé and Manalansan (eds), *Queer Globalizations*, pp. 33–45.
17. Tom Boellstorff, "I Knew it Was Me: Mass Media, 'Globalization', and Lesbian and Gay Indonesians", in Berry, Martin and Yue (eds), *Mobile Cultures: New Media in Queer Asia*, pp. 21–51.
18. Antonia Chao, "Drink, Stories, Penis and Breasts: Lesbian Tomboys in Taiwan from the 1960s to the 1990s", *Journal of Homosexuality*, 40:3/4 (2001): 185–209, p. 186.
19. The Chronicle: Colloquy Live Transcript, http://chronicle.com/colloquylive/2003/10/controversial.
20. I.K.U.–com, www.i-k-u.com.
21. Katrien Jacobs, "Queer Voyeurism and the Pussy-Matrix in Shu Lean Cheang's Japanese Pornography", in Berry, Martin and Yue (eds), *Mobile Cultures: New Media in Queer Asia*, pp. 202–1, p. 211.

Part II

Feminist Performance

6

Feminism and Performance: a Post-Disciplinary Couple

Feminist studies do not imagine their base as situated within a particular scholarly tradition of reading and writing. They did not develop from within disciplines, or even across disciplines. Instead, feminist studies resulted from activist challenges to the very institutionalization of knowledge. They made their way onto campus, or, rather re-made curricular, pedagogical, and scholarly practices in order to accommodate their goals. Thus, springing from activism, feminist studies, like studies of performance imagine their ground in embodied actions performed, somehow, socially. The "deed done", as Elin Diamond has termed it,[1] or "blooded thought", as Herbert Blau puts it,[2] absorbs disciplines of the body as well as of the intellect in its articulation. Material practice and intellectual pursuits are fused into a complementary compound.

Embodied knowledge is positioned differently, though centrally, in the institutional practices of both feminism and theatre. In performance, training practices represent the footprint of the body in the institution, while in feminism, the activist, or social wing of the project informs the creation of the scholarship. Social codes of/on the body inform both institutional inquiries. Training practices, once imagined as aesthetically insulated from social critique, now self-consciously represent gendered gestures as traditionally performed, or teach strategies for "crossing" gender roles. Moreover, the social relationship between performance and the public has altered drastically in the past few decades, from the formal relationship that obtains in the theatre, to site-specific, improvisatory social relations within the public sphere. Within feminism, the relationship to the activist movement significantly altered the object and structure of scholarly discourse. Although this relationship no longer pertains in the same way as it did in the 1970s, there is still an intermingling of these projects. What is deemed "social", once understood to be clearly different from the scholarly, is now caught up in the production of discourse. Ever-expanding market forces and commodity fetishism fuse systems of representation to those of social organization. The traditional Marxian equation between base and superstructure dissolves, as the cultural sphere absorbs the material base. Thus, scholarship, or writing, and activism are caught up in a complex, interactive paradigm of production.[3]

The absorption of the social and the focus on the body, shared by feminist studies and theatre studies, has brought them into a more proximate relation to one another. Rather than imagine the interplay between feminism and performance from within a disciplinary axis, such as that of theatre, I want to invent a kind of mytho-historical account of how these two studies, enmeshed in considerations of the body and the embodied, have interacted across a social and intellectual field during the past few decades. More than interdisciplinarity, the ever-more proximate relations between gender and performance yield both a new philosophical inquiry and a more encompassing sense of what might constitute performance.

Shouting theatre in a fire

The political ferment that took place in the United States in the late 1960s through the 1970s used the academy as the site for direct action, often bringing about the complete shutdown of the institution. The bifurcation between doing and studying could no longer hold, with sit-ins in classrooms and administration buildings, riots in the hallways and outside the windows, and police in riot-gear guarding the periphery of the institution. All aspects of the institutionalization of knowledge were challenged: admittance practices, curricula, pedagogical assumptions about learning, forms of administration, the civic responsibility of academia, and the political nature of university investment policies. Although that time of social disruption has past, those events forged a connection between the social and the scholarly that remains. The study of theatre, once focused primarily upon the work of individual (male) playwrights or their periods, producing dissertations on, say, Harold Pinter (Elin Diamond), or Heiner Müller (Sue-Ellen Case). The permeation of the ivory tower by the social movement began to yield such areas of inquiry as Jill Dolan's *Feminist Spectator as Critic*.[4] Dolan's organizing principle, that there is a spectatorial position organized through feminism, was characteristic of a new perspective on the critical interpretation of productions. The social affixed itself to the theatrical event, affecting not only its interpretation, but also its production. Dolan's feminist spectator could attend new forms of feminist performance. The rise of performance art in the late 1970s offered gestural and scenographic portrayals of the socially disciplined body, opening skills' acquisition and discursive disquisition alike to politically invested projects.

Even the protests themselves were theatrical. As Abbie Hoffman, one of the leaders of the Free Speech Movement, put it: "Free speech is the right to shout theatre in a crowded fire."[5] Campus protests joined other protests in the streets to represent rebellion against dominant codes of citizenship, national policy, and oppressive morality through activism and acting. Costumes visualized issues: the bathing suit composed of slabs of raw meat, which was worn in protest against the Miss California beauty contest, literalized the sense of the display of women's bodies as meat. The burning of bras staged a revolt against restrictive fashion. A woman in an evening dress sitting in the midst of a garbage heap imaged the discounting of her body through the fashion of objectifying gowns. These political events were not functional so much as theatrical in their efficacy. "Demonstration" came to mean a performance of oppression and liberation through gesture and deed, forming both political action, through disruption, and a pedagogical device. As the institutionalization of theatre studies became perforated by the social critique, so the realm of political action became self-consciously performative. In one sense, it could be interpreted as taking the Brechtian *Gestus* into the streets, only to have it return to the training for the stage.

Some of the student strikes, and here I am thinking specifically of those at San Francisco State College, insisted that the issues of the streets become part of the formal curriculum of the campus. These strikes brought the invention of new programmes: first, Ethnic Studies, followed by Women's Studies. Established as programmes, rather than disciplines, they brought a new cross-disciplinary organization onto the campus. Their very composition defied departmental boundaries by housing a faculty, often adjunct, or part-time, from across disciplines. The notion of Women's Studies not only challenged disciplinary boundaries within the Humanities, but also brought together the Humanities, Social Sciences, and even the so-called "hard" sciences. Sociologists, using complex empirical studies and providing large databases and statistical results, gave hard evidence of women's social conditions and practices. Likewise, psychologists, using databases of sexual studies and other important profiles of behaviour, added to the composition of what "woman" had come to mean in social practices. These scholars found themselves at work with those who produced literary history and theory, where women's autobiographies and lyrical poetry composed traces of a consciousness of gender-specificity. Invited speakers in any one of these disciplines brought scholars from across the campus to hear the latest developments in what seemed to be the unified field of women's studies. Feminist scholars began reading journals and anthologies from within several disciplines. New journals and anthologies combined articles from various fields. *Signs*, founded in 1975, was to become one of the most prominent journals in the field. The journal typically pairs two co-editors, one from the field of the Social Sciences and one from the Humanities to assemble a variety of approaches to feminist scholarship. Readers in a range of different critiques of feminism, identified as those by women of colour, lesbians, third-world women, and others, were published by feminist presses, which included poetry, first-person narratives, sociological studies, or essays in critical theory, all together under one umbrella term. Such newly formed interdisciplinary programmes and publications would later ferment the field for a wide variety of interdisciplinary studies such as cultural studies, critical theory, and studies of sexualities.

At the same time, a diaspora of the feminist critique began to move out into the traditional departments of literature, anthropology, sociology, psychology, music, art history, and theatre. The pull towards an interdisciplinary centre in Women's Studies also produced the counter-phenomenon of the spread of these studies into the departments themselves. Yet the works were still not defined narrowly by discipline. While they might have been composed to intervene in the history of a disciplinary production of knowledge, they did so by reading across disciplines. In theatre studies, early feminist work cobbled together strategies from semiotics and film, early French feminist theory, current social issues, and literary history in order to respond as "feminist spectators" to the history of performance. This intervention in the traditional study of theatre relied upon interdisciplinary studies for its scholarly ground.

The notion of a field of study challenged organization by discipline. Social issues could magnetize a field of different orders of things. For example, the issue of rape organized a field of action and study, from the writing of new city ordinances to demonstrations like "Take Back the Night",[6] performance art pieces, such as those by Suzanne Lacy,[7] and courses in the university. In order to understand any one of these elements, the others were required. For example, to understand the representation of rape in a play, one needed to know the statistics, the laws, the redefinition of intent, and the way such an action fits into the broader patriarchal society. Social issues thus informed specific reading practices, or interpretations, as well as incited social action.

As a performer, or spectator, the feminist scholar might also belong to subcultural and activist groups outside the university, participating in a broad sense of feminist "consciousness". Indeed, "consciousness" became a key concept in the early feminist movement. More radical than the crossing of departmental lines within the university, the formation of "consciousness raising" groups sought to bring together women from all classes and professions to "break the silence" of history by etching out a collective consciousness of the forces of gender oppression and the possibilities for change. The notion of "consciousness" became historical, in its practice of remembering; sociological, in its organization of data; psychological, within the group processing of fear, suffering and hope; and even theatrical, as groups passed on their discoveries to other women, founding feminist theatre. "Consciousness raising" ignored the basic institutional proviso: the organization of formal requirements for knowing. In these groups, the notion of "experience" replaced "training" as the basic essential for knowing.

This conjunction of experience and knowing created one of the basic tenets of early feminist thought: *the personal is political*. Calls to lay down what Audrey Lorde termed the "master's tools", meaning patriarchal conventions of knowing, urged women to invent a new language, or more broadly, a grammar of representation.[8] Within the radical feminist movement, Mary Daly invented her new design for expression in *GynEcology*, using newly minted terms as well as new definitions of those already in existence.[9] A lexicon of new words and spellings appeared in daily feminist usage, such as "womyn", and "herstory". Adrienne Rich put into poetry *The Dream of A Common Language,*[10] while feminist critical theorists discussed Hélène Cixous's "The Laugh of the Medusa".[11] Cixous's Medusa prompted the question: what relationship, if any, obtains between women's bodies and their writing? The "objective" voice in scholarly writing betrayed, said the feminist critics, a patriarchal remove – a privilege – a distance from material conditions and a masculinist shunning of the feminized personal.[12] How to change the very style of dissertations, learned tomes, and so-called his-stories in print, or otherwise disseminate knowledge of the body and the archive of the emotions? Lest these inventions of a feminist script were to become too arcane, the activist movement insisted that scholars compose their thoughts and their evidence in a language accessible to those outside institutional training.

Along with scripting, bodily practices and modes of self-representation were perceived as coded: how one dressed, from within or without the regime of fashion; how one moved, walked, and gestured; even how one situated oneself within social spaces (proxemics) constituted either a patriarchal inheritance, or a new feminist "consciousness". Sexual practices were particularly at issue, from the insistence, within heterosexual practices, on women's pleasure, redefining the role of vaginal and clitoral orgasms, to the new visibility of lesbian sexuality. Common to both feminist and theatrical creation was a renewed sense of the body. The body–particularly the nude body–became a site for political and representational change. In the hippie subculture, the grass-roots women's culture, performance practices, and women's studies, the naked body offered up, in the costume of a "moment of truth", both a demand for change and a portrait of a given condition of social oppression. The Living Theatre called it *Paradise Now* as they yelled, "I can't take my clothes off in public", and proceeded to do just that (1968). In *Hair,* naked bodies presumably signalled the "dawning of the age of Aquarius", and the Performance Group resurrected the god in *Dionysus in '69* through naked improvisations with the audience (1969). Women's performance art, as in the work of Carolee Schneemann, staged the nude female body as exhibiting a specifically female agency, freed from the fetters of patriarchal signification, in productions familiar to feminist audiences, such as *Meat Joy* (1964) and *Interior Scroll* (1975). The nude body was a utopic site, where oppression was stripped away, sometimes gleefully cavorting in a new, wild jumble of proximate, pleasurable social relations. The sense of the liberated, civic body became a form of both social and theatrical imagery. Looking back at these naked bodies from the perspective of the "new millennium", we can understand the hyperbolic proclamations of the body's significance as a kind of last hurrah of the capabilities of the flesh to establish public and civic powers as well as sovereign semiotic ones.

From pillage to post

A jubilant coupling of partitioned territories signalled the creation of a new field of theory and practice in the heyday of the feminist and student movement. As the decade of the 1980s wore on, these early, somewhat utopian presumptions about the collective creation of a unified field of knowing and doing became severely fractured. Yet, in a new mode that emphasizes difference rather than similarity many of the elements of the early experiments continue to inform performance and the study of it. Even though the nude body is not what it used to be, it continues to appear in performance practices aimed at disrupting dominant codes of gender and sexuality, such as in pieces by Karen Finley and Tim Miller.[13] Suzan Lori-Parks stages the African woman's nude body in *Venus* (1977). Annie Sprinkle even provides a speculum for the audience to peer further into her female parts.[14] However, these performances problematize rather than heroicize the body as a sign of social agency. They aim at producing the effect of social differences, juridical inscriptions, or binary oppositions rather than signalling some sense of an alternative, unified potential for the body to "mean" and do. Finley hystericizes the revelation of the body; Miller calls for it to manifest its desire in spite of the threat of AIDS; Parks presents a complete deconstruction of the reception of the "Hottentot Venus", staging the collusion of anthropology and medical research with colonialism and racism.

The notion of the body as a site where contesting discourses converge, rather than as a site for a shared identification as "women", operates as a nodal point for a variety of "post-disciplinary" works central to critical theory. *Deviant Bodies* (1995) edited by Jennifer Terry and Jacqueline Urla brings together articles about colonialism, anthropology, homosexual studies, popular culture (Barbie), epidemiology, and race.[15] *Volatile Bodies* (1994) by Elizabeth Grosz reviews phenomenology and the work of Deleuze and Guattari in the service of a feminist corporeality,[16] while *BodySpace* (1996) edited by Nancy Duncan includes articles on new technologies, nationalism, heterosexuality, and urban planning, to name only a few.[17] These collections cannot be subsumed under any field, such as feminist theory, or Ethnic Studies. They share only the sense that some use of the sign "body" has inspired contradictory and competing discourses, which they trace through various traditions, or institutions.

The term "post-disciplinary", now in current usage, announces a different relationship to fields of study than the earlier term "inter-disciplinary" might connote. We can imagine "interdisciplinary" as a term that signals a sense of a unified field, produced through the historical convergence of subcultures, social structures, and training practices, as described earlier in this article. "Post-disciplinary" retains nothing of the notion of a shared consciousness, or of a shared objective that brings together a broad range of discrete studies. Instead, it suggests that the organizing structures of disciplines themselves will not hold. Only conditional conjunctions of social and intellectual forces exist, at which scholarship and performance may be produced. Scholars do not work within fields, but at intersections of materials and theories. Several developments have proceeded from this new practice. English Departments, which once focused exclusively on literature written in English, now regularly offer courses in film, bi-lingual Chicano literature, and feminist, postcolonial and psychoanalytic critiques, among other things. With faculties numbering sixty or more in the large universities they are, in fact, like small colleges and are able to absorb scholars working in the newer fields. Ironically, the expansion of departments of English has been promoted by the dissolution of disciplines. New undergraduate and graduate programmes in American Studies, Critical Theory, Liberal Studies, and Cultural Studies signal a future of a greater proliferation of scholarship that does not conform to any traditional notion of field.

Performances, located along a spectrum of the performative, may be more difficult to identify as discrete occurrences. Some performances, which are informed by these theories, cross the boundary of intellectual and performance production by complicating the notion of the body with the thing itself. Susan Leigh Foster's "danced" lectures defy separation between scholarly and choreographic performance. Dancing while delivering a paper at, say, the Modern Language Association conference, confuses the borders of scholarship and performance. In theatre, Einar Schleef's *Verratenes Volk* (*A Betrayed People*) (2000) begins with the director himself reading aloud from Nietzsche's philosophical text *Ecce Homo*. The play contains no dialogue and is composed from historical and critical texts rather than from those understood as theatrical. The clear boundary between theory and practice breaks down as discourse becomes performative and performance discursive. Activists have also broadened the parameters of performance. After years of interventions by the coalition known as ACT UP!,[18] performance may be perceived as a social injunction. Augusto Boal proffers a form of "invisible theatre" as one of his practices.

We can perceive this post-disciplinarity as part of the legacy of early feminist activism and theory. As the critique of gender insisted upon the fusion of activism and scholarship, a new grammar of representation, and a sense of "feminist consciousness", formed a contingent, complex field. The urgency of the need for change assailed the remove of contemplation, yielding a more improvisatory, responsive approach to training, or experience. This lively, socially connected environment of knowing and performing is surely more inviting than the emphasis on "disciplines". Perhaps it is here, within this contested and promising site, that feminism most breaks free of patriarchal traditions.

Notes

1. Elin Diamond, *Unmaking Mimesis* (London and New York: Routledge, 1997).
2. Herbert Blau, *Blooded Thought: Occasions of Theatre* (New York: Performing Arts Journal, 1982).
3. For the full argument, from commodity to discourse, see "Bringing Home the Meat" in Sue-Ellen Case, *The Domain-Matrix: Performing Lesbianism at the End of Print Culture* (Bloomington, IN: Indiana University Press, 1996), pp. 127–89.
4. Jill Dolan, *The Feminist Spectator as Critic* (Ann Arbor, MI: UMI Research Press, 1988).
5. The Free Speech Movement (FSM) was a large student organization that began on the campus of the University of California/Berkeley in 1964. In the Fall of 1964, the UC Berkeley Administration tried to enforce new resolutions that would move political groups off campus if they were soliciting members, or distributing information around off-campus issues. The students perceived these resolutions as impinging upon their right of free speech, secured by the First Amendment to the US constitution. Since many of the students were already active in the Civil Rights movement, organizing sit-ins and other demonstrations, they began to use those tactics on campus to assure their rights to political organization as students. The FSM, along with the Students for a Democratic Society (SDS), became the core groups for organizing students on a nationwide basis during the 1960s and 1970s. Ultimately, the student movement became successful in organizing protests against the war in Vietnam.
6. Take Back the Night rallies have been held throughout the United States since 1978. The first Take Back the Night originated in Germany in 1973 in response to a series of sexual assaults, rapes, and murders. Today, marches are held in numerous cities in the United States, Canada, Latin America, India, and Europe. While different organizations and agencies may sponsor this event, the Take Back the Night Rally is designed to bring awareness and empowerment to individuals and to inspire action that will bring an end to violence against women. Violence against women is associated with forms and representations of sexual violence,

from actual rape, battery, and murder to industries that capitalize on representing that violence, such as certain forms of pornography.

7. For example, Suzanne Lacy and Leslie Labowitz created *Three Weeks in May* (1977). In a gallery, a lamb's carcass hung in a dimly lit storefront, which people entered. Four nude women, painted red, sat quietly on a ledge. A graphic depiction of sexual assault was scrawled on the floor below. Tapes of women talking about their experiences of rape and assault ran in the background. Giant maps pinpointed locations where rapes had occurred in the city.

8. Audrey Lorde, "The Master's Tools Will Never Dismantle the Master's House", *Sister Outside* (Freedom, CA: The Crossing Press, 1984), pp. 110–13.

9. Mary Daly, *GynEcology: The Metaethics of Radical Feminism* (Boston: Beacon Press, 1978).

10. Adrienne Rich, *The Dream of A Common Language: Poems, 1974–1977* (New York: W. W. Norton, 1978).

11. Hélène Cixous, "The Laugh of the Medusa" in Elaine Marks and Isabelle de Courtivron (eds), *New French Feminisms* (New York: Schocken Books, 1980), pp. 245–64.

12. For a collection of essays concerning this topic, see Deborah Cameron (ed.), *The Feminist Critique of Language: A Reader* (New York and London: Routledge, 1998).

13. Karen Finley's most successful piece was *The Constant State of Desire*, performed first in 1986 and published in *OUT FROM UNDER*, edited by Lenora Champagne (New York: Theatre Communications Group, 1990), pp. 59–70. Tim Miller performed *My Queer Body*, 1982.

14. Although Annie Sprinkle began revealing her cervix in live performances around the country, she has now made it available online. If interested, you can check out her website for her cervix-viewing page at www.heck.com/annie/gallery/cervixmain.html.

15. Jennifer Terry and Jacqueline Urla (eds), *Deviant Bodies* (Bloomington, IN: Indiana University Press, 1995).

16. Elizabeth Grosz, *Volatile Bodies* (Bloomington, IN: Indiana University Press, 1994).

17. Nancy Duncan (ed.), *BodySpace: Destabilizing Geographies of Gender and Sexuality* (London and New York: Routledge, 1996).

18. ACT UP! was an activist group that created performances in public places to intervene in medical, social, and legal restrictions around AIDS. ACT UP! is an acronym for AIDS Coalition to.Unleash Power, which began in 1987 in New York. This performative form of protest encouraged local chapters to be founded in cities around the world, including Seattle, London and San Francisco.

7

The Masked Activist: Greek Strategies for the Streets

Decades ago, I wrote about Greek tragedy from within the feminist notion of the construction of Woman.[1] At that time, the concern was to establish that there might not have been any relationship between the depiction of Woman onstage and the lives of women. Along with later work by Elin Diamond, the study constituted the feminist critique of mimesis, within historical models.[2] Today, after two decades of feminist practice concerning classical theatre and its repertoire, I would like to return to the model in relation to activism. I would like to explore how feminist scholars have constituted the classical period as one in which women's civic performances were appropriated by the tragedy and then see how some contemporary revisions of the plays relate to current activist notions.

Feminist scholars have argued that the function of the tragedy was to serve as a social mechanism to appropriate the civic participation of women and their rites into a masculinist state structure. In *Dangerous Voices: Women's Laments and Greek Literature*, Gail Holst-Warhaft argues that the form of the tragedy was an appropriation of women's only condoned public performance – the lament.[3] Laments consisted not only of wailing, but also of public expressions of anger and blame for wrongful deaths. Through the lament, then, public figures could actually be characterized through a women's chorus, which responded to the closure of a sequence of public events perceived as a "life". Women's laments were a potential form of political activism in the streets. Improvised and uncontrolled by form or censure, these laments gave women a public forum of responses to civic actions. Solon severely restricted women's laments by deeming them "wild and disorderly", an inappropriate form of public behaviour. Apparently, for Solon, a chorus that improvised its own responses to the actions of public figures needed to be somehow controlled. Along with the proscription of the laments, the Athenian state invented an apparatus of control, tightly prescribed in form and performed only by men: the tragedy. As the discipline of Greek theatre literally masked activism in a move to clean up the streets, contemporary performances of the Greek plays deploy that masking effect to repoliticize the form. For Heiner Müller, playing the Greek tragedy sounded a dirge of activism, foregrounding the success of the imperialist project for political effect; for the Lysistrata Project, the Greek mask served as an international figure for organizing activist cells against the Gulf War; and for certain Arab productions, the notions of the Greek plays were found wanting when applied to current warfare.

Tragedy as street cleaner

Masculinist anxieties concerning the disruptive laments of women haunted the Greek cultural imaginary for centuries, always adjacent to the practice of theatre and to the construction of gender codes. Either these lament-able practices were disciplined by the apparatus of the tragedy, or they were censored completely, adjacent to the anti-theatrical impulse. In both cases, the egregious public practice of improvised emotional responses to the lives of men was associated with the gender role of women. In Book III of *The Republic*, Socrates laments laments. How, he asks, in one of his edicts masked as a question, could you train political leadership in the perfect state, if these young men were to witness and, worse, emulate the lament? Would that womanly, public display of uncontrolled emotion be an appropriate action in the disciplinary regime of the perfect state? (Evidently, Socrates learned much from the practice of masking, while condemning it; for the masked question, just like the masked chorus, only seems to debate an ethical action, whose final, moral outcome has been predetermined by the narrative structure.) After the young man to whom Socrates poses these questions acquiesces to his argument against laments (masked seduction?), Socrates preaches his penetrating commandment:

> Then we should be right in doing away with the lamentations of men of note and in attributing them to women, and not to the most worthy of them either, and to inferior men, in order that those whom we say we are breeding for the guardianship of the land may disdain to act like these.[4]

The "hardening" of the line, from appropriating the lament to excising it, may have accompanied the degradation of the participatory practices of Athenian democracy, reflected in Plato's own one-sided form of the dialogue. Nonetheless, his imagined future of the Greek state would be one of orderly public places, where no crowds of womanly people would express, emotionally, their reactions to the events in the lives of their leaders. Perhaps the only disruptions would be older men, stopping young men to ask them a series of penetrating questions that masked their final intent.

Later, Plutarch once more rehearses Solon's edicts against laments, recalling their censure against the "weak and unmanly behavior" of the women.[5] Ironic as it may seem to condemn women for "unmanly behavior", this seeming contradiction helps to reveal gender operations in the Athenian cultural imaginary: "manly" behaviour, or the masculine, had become abstracted into a kind of moral state, while "womanly" behaviour had become abstracted into a representation of the "base". These gendered attributes constituted part of the disciplinary state apparatus: the citizen must be masculine. Gender coding helped to tie propriety to civic order, but more, seeming to separate gender from sex, "manly" from men and "womanly" from women, representations of gender could take on ethical transcendence. Its semiotic "floating" was a key device for cleaning up the streets. Not only did Solon pass a law to keep women off the streets, confined to the home, but men must have their disruptive tendencies incarcerated for their "womanly" attributes. The solution was the tragedy.

The tragedy incarcerated unruly lamenting on the streets in the physical boundaries of the theatre, where a few might lament, while the majority watched, seated and still. Womens' improvised laments were fashioned, finally, into scripted actions, that at least one philosopher deemed as proceeding through a "beginning, middle, and end". Consider, for example, how Electra's laments in *The Libation Bearers* are fashioned into set dirges that lead to a predetermined narrative closure. Political action could be morphed into civic theatre, where direct political responses would become deflected into fictions and made into mythical morality rather than history. The chorus learned its part and was, presumably, made somehow to speak and dance in unison. This strict control of the image of citizens banding together staged an extreme response to the wild laments of women – particularly, we might imagine, when the chorus was composed of a group of masked men representing women slaves.

The mask of tragedy froze the corporeal practices of lament, abstracting the lacerations of the flesh, as in *Oedipus*, or the results of violent civic revolt, as in *The Bacchae*. What had been an improvised public action morphed into a static visual representation that obscured the face. But more, the tragic mask abstracted and appropriated public performances by women by affixing the mask, the face of the lament, exclusively onto the face of the male actor. Only the textualization of women's presence remained, issuing through the gaping hole in the tragic mask, filled by the manly voice. The mask secured a haunting displacement of sex by gender – only a ghostly (read mythical) apparition of unruly women remained.

The question remains, then, how these male performers actually represented the female characters. Who knows how the female roles were danced and what constituted their gestures? Considering proscriptions against the "unmanly", one might reason that perhaps there was no strictly mimetic performance of women's gestural systems. For, if women represented the "unmanly", surely, for the sake of civic health, the playing of female characters would need to abandon those gestures. Although we often imagine these performances through contemporary practices of drag roles, or even through other living classical traditions, such as Japanese Kabuki, perhaps in the Greek tragedy there was no imitation, in that sense, of female gestures and carriage. If the bodies were strictly excluded, one might ask, then why would they be mimetically reproduced? If the civic strategy was to abstract the role of the woman into moral principles, then what would be the forms of that abstraction?

Playing women as men

The playing of women as principles of a masculinized morality can help us to reconsider the playing style in which some of the major heroines were represented. Consider, say, playing Medea. Would she be performed through some physicalization of the female body and gestures? Helene Foley, in her discussion of the tragedy in *Female Acts in Greek Tragedy*, argues that when the mask of Medea slips, we actually see an archaic hero behind it.[6] In other words, what appears to be a female character on the all-male stage is, in essence, a representation of an earlier form of masculine heroism. Following Foley, we can see the construction of Medea as a hero derived from the epics and oral traditions of heroic men. The womanly character provides the dramatic potential for representing a disruptive – and therefore, seemingly, base – civic act, while filling a heroic role. The female mask was both the licence and the historical remnant of a civil disobedience, not a mimetic representation of a woman.

Although Medea is disruptive, she actually refuses to lament – even the death of her own children. Finally, Medea transcends. But does the actor portray the gestural system of an embodied woman who transcends? In a chariot? After all, manly men drove the chariots in classical Greek culture. In fact, the chariot race constituted one of the central agons of manly strength. (By the way, men have continued to insist that driving somehow requires the manly body for centuries to come.) So how was such transcendence physicalized? Was it not, as Foley suggests, heroic? Can we imagine, then, the playing of Medea in her chariot as a civically disobedient hero, rather than as a woman? Or let us consider, for a moment, the playing of Clytemnestra. Clytemnestra, that character who is accused by the chorus of having appropriated the male role in the state, was surely not played with the gestures of the modest, home-bound, head-covered Athenian wife. Once again, the female mask, haunted by the disruptive activism of lamenting women, serves to represent egregious actions, while still secured, or warranted, by the male actor – the image of masculinized state order. Both Medea and Clytemnestra required strength for their murders and decisiveness in their discourse. Surely these qualities were not performed by feminizing gestures. And, finally, consider Athena herself, at the end of the *Oresteia*. Of course, she is literally a manly woman, in appearance and genealogy, bearing the fashions of war, and eschewing even an origin in a womb. How could she be portrayed by imitating feminine gestures, when attired in a helmet and bearing a shield? So we could conclude, then, that women were not mimetically represented on the Athenian stage, but that their gender was used to signify disorder, while safely controlled by the apparatus of the civic tragedy.

Perhaps in the comedy there was more of a mimetic playing of feminized gestures, in a bawdy burlesque style, since the moral was more perverted and less abstracted than in the tragedies. If the feminine signified the base, perhaps its mimetic production was appropriate to comedy. Perhaps all of those strapped-on phalloi mark the increased anxiety surrounding the more mimetic playing of women and a call to ranks around their disruptions. For example, Lysistrata, even when playing a threat to state practices, illicitly occupying state architectures, is completely surrounded by a plenitude of erections.

Perhaps the more mimetic portrayal of Lysistrata accompanies a more directly mimetic representation of civil disobedience, particular to the Aristophanic comedies. Yet the masking of political activism remains in place. Even in Aristophanes, the activism is not in the streets, but in *The Clouds*. Theatre still works to contain improvised, collective street action through its gendered masks.

For actual women, the very performance of the theatre may have seemed a frightening, literally distant experience, somewhat like battle. Perhaps, from their distance in their homes, they could hear the powerful chanting voices of the male choruses, followed by the thunderous applause and shouts from the ten thousand men gathered on the hill to watch. The men were up there taking a tragic tonic, as it were, celebrated by Aristotle as a healing catharsis and prescribed in the proximate Asclepian pharmacies for the healing of the citizen soul. Through gender displacement, the men were cleansing and gathering strength in large numbers, dancing and singing the physical and moral fitness of their manly citizen bodies and souls, cleansed by narrative of the womanly mask of disobedience.

Later: women like-ing women

If these female characters are the representations of the displacement of women's public performances, icons of formal abstractions of direct political actions and beacons of masculinized morality, why, then, in the late twentieth century and early twenty-first have *Medea* and *Lysistrata* enjoyed such popularity, when played by women rather than men? Many productions seem to specifically stage the embodiment of these female roles with scant costumes and broad, seductive gestures. In fact, after the successes of the feminist movement, both *Medea* and *Lysistrata* have often been interpreted as feminist texts that reveal the civic strategies of strong women. I would argue, and hope that my examples might reveal, that it is precisely the abstraction of gender from sex that actually continues to inform these stagings rather than the embodiment of it. Even though many productions stage gender as the sole issue of the play, in so doing they actually deploy the abstracted distance of gender from sex for their political intervention. The plays actually script gender codes rather than roles for women, staging the formal conditions Judith Butler describes in her now-familiar notion of performativity, in which it is the codes that act and not the subject. As Butler argues, rather than "a prior and volitional subject", the performative "constitutes as an *effect* the very subject it appears to express".[7] Butler describes a "reiterated acting that is power in its persistence and instability... a nexus of power and discourse that repeats or mimes the discursive gestures of power".[8] In other words, it is gender that acts and not the woman.

Two kinds of revision, one of *Medea* and others of *Lysistrata*, illustrate how the contemporary reception of these texts focuses on the playing of gender as a moral or political principle, extractable from a "sexed" actor. The signifiers of Medea and Lysistrata semiotically float, playing the discourses of power rather than powerful characters. The first example is Heiner Müller's *Medea*, which represents Medea as historical and political material; the second is the *Lysistrata Project*, which disseminates the nexus of power in the play over multiple sites of resistance to the Iraq war, and, finally, productions which question the basic premises of *Lysistrata*.

Medeamaterial

In English, the full title of Heiner Müller's play is *WASTED SHORE MEDEA MATERIAL LANDSCAPE WITH ARGONAUTS* (1982). In German, Medea and material are agglutinated to produce the term *Medeamaterial*. As the title nomination suggests, Medea is something other than a character, she is "material", in the Marxist sense of the term: a particular, gendered condition of economic and social production. As in many of his later plays, Müller scripts the lines of the text as proximate to a character's name, but not assigned to one as dialogue. The extended body of verse floats free of the speaker, inspiring productions that assign the lines in various ways to actors and even voiceovers. Medea, then, represents a particular condition of production and consumption, rather than an individual woman.

In the title, as in the play, Medea is a material condition situated between a wasted shore and the landscape of Argonauts. Müller stressed that the play takes place on "the threshold where myth turns into history" – the myths of the classical Greeks.[9] The wasted shore thus represents the threshold where the Greek project of forming imperialism into an enduring myth became an origin for the ideological development of European history. Müller invokes the Greek myths as inscriptions of the originary practices of imperialism within the history of Europe: "European history began with colonization."[10] The Argonauts are the agents of that imperialism, landing on multiple shores, grounding their colonial ownership.

For Müller, then, the figure of Medea is one that inscribes the material base of colonization. Medea and the wasted shore are both literally and figuratively the grounds of colonial territorialization. Insofar as Medea is emotionally and sexually wasted by Jason the Argonaut, she represents the colonized. This reading or revision of Medea as an effect of colonization is a familiar one in the twentieth century, but Müller's particular donation resides in how he stages the woman's body as a figure, a principle, a structure of colonization, rather than a mimetic image of a so-called "real" woman. As both an archive of the originary mythology of imperialism and the strategy for the abstraction of woman, Greek classical tragedy becomes the apparatus that Müller seeks to deploy.

First, Müller draws critical attention to how familiar terms link-ing land and woman (think of "motherland", for instance) reveal the way in which oppressive colonial practices concerning the assimi-lation of land and women's bodies have been inextricably linked. In the first section of the play, entitled WASTED SHORE, famil-iar sexist, slang terms for women's bodies are fused with terms of a wasted land. For example, he invents the term SCHLAMMFOTZE, which combines two slang words: one of the wasted environment, *Schlamm* or "sludge", and the other *Fotze*, or "cunt", a sexist deroga-tion of women's sexual organs. The term thus combines a derogation of earth as garbage and woman's body as obscene sexual organ in one agglutinated term. Müller suggests how this derogation works in the full poetic line, translated by Carl Weber as "Garbagecunt I say to her / This is my man / Poke me Come here, Sweetie".[11] Here Müller runs a sexist derogation, "cunt", into a familiar term of marriage, "my man" (German: *mein Mann*) often meaning "husband", and continues to run marital phrases into the language of a sex worker: "poke me", "come here, sweetie". The derogated body of the colonized subject is a common trope in colonial dramas, as Gilbert and Tompkins point out in their study *Post-colonial Drama: Theory, Practice, Politics*, but here the derogation of the body runs through the obscene discourses that inscribe it into the social, political economy.[12] The body is the body of usage, across several symbolic systems.

As the story of Medea clarifies, the owner relationship expressed in the term "my man" is actually the reverse. It is the woman who is owned and not the man. Müller makes the violence of sexual economics clear by running the line on to "Poke me Come here, Sweetie". The occasional sale of sex and the long-term ownership of marriage are proximate to one another. Prostitution and connubial relations are both conditions of the ownership of women's bodies. Müller has scripted a familiar Marxist critique, central to much of his dramaturgy. From the time of Marx and Engel's essay "The Holy Family", through early revolutionary practices, the ownership implied in the family unit was critiqued by Marxists as the ground of the state and private property. In Müller's *Medea*, getting "poked" and getting a husband are being "taken", in more ways than one.

In the long verse passage in the play that is adjacent to Medea, the only property remaining is described as the "images of the beaten", and "the screams of the abused".[13] As a representation of the material conditions of colonization, Medea is a figure composed of the images and screams of imperialist violence and waste. She is the whirlpool effect of waste, where these images and screams revolve. Medea is not a character, but the sum effect of the discourses, images and screams distributed across the text. For Müller, this abstraction of the woman's body or subjecthood has been accomplished not by the playwright, but by the appropriative historical and political practices that he stages through his representation of this originary myth. In the first production of the piece, directed by Manfred Karge and Matthias Langhoff in Bochum in 1983, Medea was played by a woman. But closer to Müller's concept was the casting of Medea's children as cans of dog food. This directorial concept comes closest to the abstract signification of the text. No "real" actor's bodies should be made to signify these individuals; instead, the children are represented as commodified waste products scattered across the stage.

For Müller the wasted shore is not only the ground of colonization, but also the originary ground of representation – the classical tragedy. The structures of representation, as I have argued here, create the representational production of the wasting of the woman's body. In the third section of the play Müller's dialogue describes the conditions of performance as consonant with the conditions of the imperialists. The structures of the theatrical enterprise belong to Jason, the waster of Medea. Jason: "Our harbor was a dead movie house".[14] It is a dead system of representation, one wasted through the centuries until its richness of meaning is entirely depleted. The actors are "zombies perforated by commercials".[15] If there is a body that can signify, it is also a dead one, emptied by the processes of reification and market fetishism. And what remains of scenery? "The forests burn in Eastman color".[16] The scenery is Eastman color, already a corporate, Technicolor wasting of "burning forests". Medea agglutinates these depleted abstractions of the human and nature. Like them, she is a signification, wasted by the material and semiotic practices of imperialism.

For the Greeks, the city state projected its political and social discipline through masks, a technology of "live performance" that signalled the abstraction of the material through the exclusion of women, and the displacement of the body. The tragedy uploaded the politics of the city state into formal abstractions. In Müller's version of late twentieth-century performance, the corporate screen of "dead movie houses" projects the mode of ownership and social relations out through its electronic technologies, abstracting material relations and any notion of the live into the recursive loop of film, in which all action is already past. Actual women, basically excluded from the all-male stage of corporate and software technologies, are still foreign and still shut away, but this time in special economic zones, where they work overtime hours making the electronic components. If they do appear in this new cyberspace, it is as sexualized, violent avatars, contemporary forms of archaic heroes, as, say, behind the mask of Lara Croft.

The Lysistrata Project

The Lysistrata Project offers a different strategy of abstraction of woman. Rather than abstracting away from direct political action, it abstracts towards it. In the classical tradition of Aristophanes, the comedies frolicked on the borders of the formal, often poking their fun directly at personages and events active in the political scenery of Athens. Joining that tradition, the Lysistrata Project brings the cycle of abstraction full circle, using the masked abstractions to point directly back to the improvised, unruly practice of the laments.

The Lysistrata Project consisted of 1,029 readings of *Lysistrata*, performed in fifty-nine countries on the day of Monday 3 March 2003, in order to protest the Bush administration's unilateral war on Iraq. More than 300,000 people attended the readings organized by what were called the "spearheads". Some productions were hosted by large regional theatres like Berkeley Repertory Theater, others by experimental companies like London's KAOS Theatre. Some occurred in living rooms, high schools and hospitals. In New York alone, forty roving bands of players presented the play in public spaces. Most illustrious, the BAM Harvey theater hosted a major reading, directed by Ellen McLaughlin and starring Mercedes Ruehl and Kevin Bacon. Altogether, the readings raised an estimated $125,000 for non-profit organizations working for peace and humanitarian aid. Some readings did not raise money, but the fact that they occurred at all resonated as a powerful symbol of world citizens united for peace. For example, a secret reading in northern Iraq was organized by members of the international press corps; a reading in Patras, Greece was held by Greeks and Kurdish refugees in an abandoned factory; and secret readings took place in such places as China, Israel and Mindanao. These readings were perceived as acts of civil disobedience, directly related to protesting against the war in Iraq.[17]

The official poster for the project shows a thinly veiled woman's body, clearly visible through a diaphanous garment, rejecting the helmet of war. Here the female sex, not the abstraction of gender, is invoked by the representation. Essentially, the Greek classical female body is deployed here as a sign for an anti-war protest held through the reading, not the playing, of a text. Choosing a text so filled with descriptions of women's anatomy, and so full of sexual referents would seem to inspire the kind of bawdy, burlesque performance the Greeks might have enjoyed. The corporeal emphasis in the text might indicate that an embodied protest is the most desirable intervention against the practice of war. Yet the activist project was to organize readings of the text – the least embodied form of theatre. Most did not act out or physically represent the women's gestural systems at the core of the play's action.

Of course, the play itself is a cynical representation of sexuality in the original Greek context, since men were often not monogamous and therefore would suffer little from such refusals from their wives. After all, numerous concubines are represented in the tragedies, such as Cassandra in *Agamemnon*, or Andromache and Tecmessa in *Ajax*. Helene Foley cites this passage from a fourth-century BCE Athenian text that describes the range of different liaisons available to men: "We have *hetairai* for pleasure, *palakai* to care for our bodily needs, and *gunaikes* to bear us legitimate children."[18] Of course, this passage does not even mention the man–boy sexual relations also practised by men. This full range of sexual availability would seem to enfeeble the strategy Lysistrata deployed. Perhaps that, too, was part of the comic effect. With the leather *phalloi* and the play of seduction, it is likely that the performance more clearly resembled a drag show than, say, the tragedies, in which feminizing gestures supported the effect of the comic. In general, the action available to women was simply to resist rather than to initiate and *Lysistrata* reveals even their resistance as comic. Nonetheless, something in this play continues to inform our own anti-war demonstrations. Perhaps it is the individual manner of the protest at a time when the majority governments seem so deaf to large, public protests. Perhaps it offers a striking return of the body amidst the technologies of war. Yet the adoption of the play was not for embodied performance, but for a reading. The abstraction of the classical Greek stage was further enhanced by simply reading rather than performing. Moreover, the technology of distribution was not the festival, or the physical theatre, but the Internet. The Lysis-trata Project website managed the distribution by uploading the text itself, offering a model publicity packet and organizing details, and effectively interacting transnationally in a way that other media could not. The overall project, as composed of a thousand readings, came together through the virtual, disembodied technology of the internet. The woman's body, then, was abstracted at its Internet core, dis-tributed electronically, through printed text, to groups of people who wanted to protest against the Bush war machine. Finally, Lysistrata was not a female character, but a collective, transgender identification through readings against the war. The classical Greek female body was uploaded into cyberspace, where it served to hail anti-war protestors.

However utopic this reconnection of the Greek model to activism might seem within the basically US-led project, the model of *Lysis-trata* changes dramatically when imagined on the Arabic stage. Marina Kotzamani reported on a project she led to explore how the play might work as an anti-war play on the Arabic stage. The basic assump-tions of the model fail to translate in several ways. Kotzamani notes, to begin, that "participants point out that the Peloponnesian War was a conflict between parties of equal power, who also shared common culture and values".[19] The model does not work when applied to a superpower deployed against relatively small, guerilla actions, nor to competing social and ideological cultures. The idea of militat-ing for peace itself is problematic within certain conditions, as one Egyptian playwright responded: "To preach a message of peace of today's Arab audiences is tantamount to instructing the victims to accept sheepishly the dictates of their arrogant oppressors."[20] As for sex and gender, Kotzamani notes, "Participants are intent on show-ing that higher powers, such as autocratic states, U.S. imperialism, the media, and patriarchy control individual desire."[21] In other words, sexual desire is distributed by the state and other social institutions. It is not an individual matter. Thus using it as a tool brings one into collusion with those institutions, rather than creating a subversion of them. One Egyptian play, *The Peace of Women* by Lenin El Ramly, provides a complete revision of the original model that reveals some of the specific conditions that work against its application.[22] The play begins with women in a park in Baghdad, before a statue of Saddam Hussein, organizing against the coming American invasion. They agree to abstain from sex for peace. Some women are European and some Iraqi, as in the original set-up with Athenian and Spartan women. However, one character, Madonna, is a male American spy disguised as a woman. As the women demonstrate in front of CNN and Al-Jazeera for peace, their coalition falls apart. A Frenchwoman berates the Iraqi women for wearing the veil and remaining quiet. The Iraqi women become irate, accusing the European women of immorality and heresy. One woman decides to become a suicide bomber, Madonna escapes, some of the veiled women are raped, and the war begins.

Thus we can see that the basic categories of the play, so secure in Athens and even in some Euro-American revisions, become contested when brought to specific activist situations outside of the European legacy. The category of "peace" is not necessarily a positive one; gender roles are at issue between warring cultures; the effects of activism take different forms; and war, rather than the deterrence of war, becomes the consequence. Perhaps these differences are closer to those originary public laments by women than to the state apparatus of theatre. Lacerations, self-inflicted wounds, contestations, improvised actions and disruptive behaviour win out over predetermined happy endings, applauded by a disciplined audience. The apparatus of the state, the media and the patriarchy drive the women back into the streets, where the outcome of their behaviour is unknown.

Notes

1. Sue-Ellen Case, "Classic Drag: the Greek Creation of Female Parts", *Theatre Journal*, 37:3 (1985), pp. 317–27.
2. Elin Diamond, *Unmaking Mimesis* (London and New York: Routledge, 1997).
3. Gail Holst-Warhaft, *Dangerous Voices: Women's Laments and Greek Literature* (London and New York: Routledge, 1992).
4. Plato, *The Republic*, trans. Paul Shorey, in Edith Hamilton and Huntington Cairns (eds), *Plato: The Collected Dialogues* (New York: Random House, 1961), p. 632, lines 386–90.
5. Quoted in Holst-Warhaft, *Dangerous Voices*, p. 99.
6. Helene Foley, *Female Acts in Greek Tragedy* (Princeton: Princeton University Press, 2001), p. 261.
7. Judith Butler, "Critically Queer", *Glq: A Journal of Lesbian and Gay Studies*, I: 1 (1993), pp. 17–32, here p. 24; italics mine.

8. Ibid., p. 17.
9. See p. 124.
10. Cited in Carl Weber's notes to *DESPOILED SHORE MEDEAMATERIAL LANDSCAPE WITH ARGONAUTS*, in Carl Weber, trans., *Hamletmachine and Other Texts for the Stage* (New York: Performing Arts Publications, 1984), pp. 124–5, here p. 124.
11. Heiner Müller, *WASTED SHORE MEDEAMATERIAL LANDSCAPE WITH ARGONAUTS*, in Weber, *Hamletmachine and Other Texts for the Stage*, pp. 126–135, here p. 127.
12. Helen Gilbert and Joanne Tompkins, *Post-colonial Drama: Theory, Practice, Politics* (London and New York: Routledge, 1996), pp. 203–54.
13. Heiner Müller, *WASTED SHORE MEDEA MATERIAL*, p. 94.
14. Trans. mine.
15. Trans. mine.
16. Trans. mine.
17. *The Lysistrata Project* (www.lysistrataproject.com) (12/06/06)
18. Foley, *Female Acts*, p. 89.
19. Marina Kotzamani, "Lysistrata on the Arabic Stage", *PAJ*, 83 (2006), p. 14.
20. Ibid., p. 15.
21. Ibid., p. 16.
22. In Kotzamani, pp. 24–6.

8

Performing Feminism on the International Stage

Feminist research and performance have both nurtured and critiqued the project of uniting women across national and cultural differences. Virginia Woolf registered the sentiment to unite in 1938 in *Three Guineas*, when she wrote: "As a woman I have no country, as a woman I want no country, as a woman, my country is the whole world." As a woman, Woolf had been exempted from state and institutional practices, so she could imagine herself as outside the state, and once out there, able to reach out to other disenfranchised women in the world. Even before Woolf's literary experiments around gender, *ur*feminists, such as Alexandra Kollentai, linked women's interests to anti-nationalist, or inter-nationalist politics. As part of the international Communist movement, Kollentai wrote *Sexual Relations and the Class Struggle* in 1918, calling for women to extricate their sexual practices from property-based sexual institutions, such as monogamy and the family.[1] Kollentai understood the legislation of women's sexual practices as constituting a fundamental repression necessary for the formation of national identities.

More recently, the Latina feminist, Gloria Anzaldúa, combined Woolf's sense of being a "woman in the world" with Kollentai's call for sexual freedom to create a new political subject. Anzaldúa locates the agents for political change in *Los atravesados* in what she identifies as "the squint-eyed, the perverse, and the queer". Anzaldúa combines gender with ethnicity, and alternative sexual practices to imagine, as Woolf had done, a position outside of the state-imposed identities, where women may effect change. Anzaldúa situates these outsiders as straddling borders, living upon them and through them, rather than being contained by them. She identifies, as activists, "the mongrel, the mulatto, the half-breed, and the half dead".[2]

125

This call to the international runs through feminist writings, from its aggressive sound, as in Anzaldúa, to its more plaintive. The African American author, bell hooks, writes of a "yearning" for a "common affective and political sensibility which cuts across the boundaries of class, gender, and sexual practice", while Rosi Braidotti, writing from the Netherlands, seeks to traverse a "fertile ground for the construction of empathy", creating an "emphatic proximity" or "intensive interconnectedness".[3] Braidotti's emphasis on a political construction of "proximity" echoes one of the early key strategies in feminist theory. Critically imagined by Hélène Cixous and Luce Irigaray, the practice of proximity closed the removed, all-knowing distance of the so-called "objective" methodologies. Within theatre, one might see proximity as a contradiction to Brecht's patriarchal, scientistic distanciation. For feminists, the *"Verfremdungseffekt"* or "Alienation effect" might be exchanged for an *"Ernäherungseffekt"* – a critical staging of "coming closer", to be situated among the hierarchies of power, intersected daily through emotional, sexual, and material practices. For example, in the 1976 play *Sonntagskinder* (Sunday's Children), the German playwright, Gerlind Reinshagen, portrays the structures of a Fascist mentality in the kitchen, in the power relations between a mother and daughter in the making of jam, rather than in the public, spectacular, official operations of the state. Thus, as feminists understood their politics as up-close and personal, they extended this anti-patriarchal proximity to a kind of global imaginary, as if an empathy for the conditions of women around the world might cut across cultural differences.

Certain issues have travelled well, such as the work against the global traffic in women, begun at the Global Feminist Workshop in 1983 and still carried on today. From the international sexual slavery of young girls, to mail-order brides, which today is a multi-million dollar business, issues of selling women and girls as sexual chattel are still sites of stringent watchdogging and organizing in the politics and performances of feminism. Performances and plays find commonalities in portraying these issues, sometimes enjoying almost uncanny consonances. For example, the issue of rape has been treated in many performances around the world, but Tomson Highway's *The Rez Sisters* and Cherríe Moraga's *Giving Up the Ghost* also stage an eerie consonance of detail in their portrayals. *The Rez Sisters* tells the story of a Zhaboonigan woman whose vagina is penetrated by a screwdriver by a gang of white boys. In *Giving Up the Ghost*, the Chicana protagonist narrates an incident in which, as a child, she was violated by a janitor, who also used a screwdriver to, as she says, "make me a hole".

Yet, as the feminist movement matured, what had once seemed an obvious impulse, even a mandate toward the global, became a site of self-criticism and struggle. To certain key audiences, the feminist stage began to resemble the isolated white figure of Anne-Marie Stretter in Marguerite Duras's *India Song* (1973). Duras's play sets the white, colonial woman character on stage as the mute object of male desire. In this way, Duras reveals the emotional and sexual objectification of woman. At the same time, the staging of that unmarked white woman upstages the indigenous beggar woman, a colonial subject, who is represented only by the song she sings on the streets – "The India Song" – a song which wafts through the walls of the British colonial compound, where Stretter stands a prisoner of the gaze. To some, Stretter on stage, could be made to represent the image of First-World feminism, unmarked as white, importing issues that invited indigenous women to the stage, only to upstage them with imported values that remained ignorant of local conditions.

Within this critique, the Ghanaian playwright Ama Ata Aidoo provides a succinct portrait of European feminists, as "a new wave of imperialists eager to invade the African continent brandishing a particular political doctrine while remaining blissfully ignorant of the culture, history, and needs of individual groups of African women".[4] One of the starkest dramatic representations of this critique may be found in Tess Onwueme's play *Tell It To Women*. Two characters, Daisy and Ruth, identified as Western-educated, urban feminists and probably lesbians as well, first recruit rural women into the movement, raising their hopes for betterment, then cruelly mistreat one of their leaders, whose local practices and rites become objects of their educated, Westernized disdain. These two feminist characters display a class privilege and disdain for rural women that is breathtakingly cruel. Worse, the language of feminism is represented as so limited by Western, academic traditions, that the local women to whom it is addressed cannot understand it. In the following extract Ruth, the feminist, is addressing the village women:

> RUTH.   We are the bearers of global sisterhood. Our mission is to break boundaries of confinements and compartmentalization of our potentialities in the oppressive, despotic and tyrannical hegemony of patriarchy imposed on women these many years . . .
> CHORUS OF WOMEN.   Eeih!
> SHERIFAT.   Go on! Fly, our daughter! Fly our eagle Lutu!

ADAKU.   What do you mean? Can you understand what she is saying?
SHERIFAT.   Well, I cannot. But eh . . . can't you feel the way she rolls
the words on her tongue like yam in oil?[5]

As these two village leaders raise their voices in a debate over the
power and problems of the adoption of Western ways, the feminist speaker repeatedly blows through her microphone to attempt to
regain their attention. The play eventually shifts the power of organization to the rural women, who organize themselves through their
own traditions and social structures, to better their conditions. Feminism, then, begins to resemble other political and cultural exports
from the "First World".

Appended to this form of cultural imperialism, in Onwueme's play,
is the suggestion that the two feminists are enjoying a lesbian relationship. The insinuation that lesbian practices are a Western import is a
familiar charge in the international feminist arena. Certainly, nam-
ing sexual practices across cultures is a complex task, where the
structures of sexual relations are caught up in the different forms
of social and economic relationships. But something else is at work
here. As recent as the International Conference for Women in Beijing in 1995, the majority of representatives voted to exclude lesbian
issues from the report. Although this problem requires much study
and greater specificity, I would conjecture here, something derived
from Alexandra Kollentai's thesis in 1918: that this alternative sexual practice challenges the formation of national identity and in such
conferences as the one in Beijing, where Hillary Clinton appeared
at the podium, national agendas insist upon a relation to gender that
does not threaten the structures of heteronormativity that support the
construction of citizenship. Later, when we turn to the transnational
critique, we will see how the practice of alternative sexualities, along
with economic practices, may be consolidated with gender issues in
deconstructing national agendas.

At this point in the argument, however, we are observing how
lesbian practices are appended to feminism understood as a form of
cultural imperialism. As in Onwueme's play, feminism is understood
as partaking in the dynamics of importation and exportation, tied
to the critique of the feminist movement as a First-World project.
Now, these debates derive from a presumed model of production and
reception, with the First World as producer and the so-called Third
World as the receiver. In performance, the issues of production and
reception hinge upon the relation between staging and the spectator.

The feminist spectator finds herself situated within the contradictions raised in these critical theories. On the one hand, she may feel the "emphatic proximity" to events which Braidotti suggested, as she watches plays with familiar themes for women in many cultures. For example, issues of rape, or the economic determinants of prostitution may seem familiar and moving to her when she sees them depicted on the stage, allowing her to partake in a kind of cross-cultural empathy. On the other hand, she may find herself alienated from the performance, as she becomes aware of the exportation of First-World feminism, particularly where unequal trade practices seem most exaggerated. In fact, her feminist response to gender issues in the performance may cause her to be charged with an invasive politics that violates the local structures of performance. Diana Taylor records this dilemma in her book on state and theatrical spectacle in Argentina. Taylor recounts how, at a public forum in Argentina, she rose to critique a performance she had witnessed for its sexism, noting how it eroticized, in its staging practice, the state violence it set out to critique. "Someone from the audience called me a Fascist for trying to restrict or censor what could be shown . . . [another] refused to speak to me, except to point out that I wasn't Argentinian, hadn't lived in Argentina during the Dirty War, hadn't experienced torture and therefore knew nothing about it and should keep quiet. . . . She dismissed me as a 'Yanqui feminist'."[6] In spite of such criticism, however, Taylor proceeded to write a book which combines a gender critique with one of state politics, regarding performance representations of torture as answerable to the politics of gender as well as to an anti-Fascist critique.

The feminist spectator, then, is challenged to forge an appropriate connection between her gender identifications, or dis-identifications, and her role within ethnic or national structures. Rey Chow, in *Woman and Chinese Modernity*, notes that it is specifically the images of women, as well as the condition of the feminist spectator that evoke the intersection of China with the West, or more broadly, the intersection between tradition and the modern.[7] As in Onwueme's African play, women represent the place where the Westernized, urban, or transnational forces must confront the local, traditional ones. As they are made to bear the domestic and moral remove from commerce and the marketplace, women's situation stages the force of the confrontation between the two cultural factions. For example, David Henry Hwang's new play about China, *Golden Child* (1998), focuses on the wives of a rich merchant, who must wrestle with the incursion of his new Westernized ideas into the domestic realm, where the gods are worshipped, the moral values are tested, and where children are educated. Through their sexual and familial bonds to the man of commerce, these women must manage the modern within the traditional domestic sphere.

While wives may translate the modern to the traditional in the home, the Mexican tradition offers a darker vision of the consort as the site of intercultural betrayal. The woman known as "La Malinche" – the Mexican woman who became the translator and mistress of Cortez – represents the "sexual traitor to the race".[8] For the Mexicans, and through the diasporic cultures of the Chicanas, La Malinche has come to represent the traditional image of woman who knows the language and culture of the invading forces and of the local people, but who, through sexual "intercourse" (here a precise term for one form of cultural exchange), sells out her people. La Malinche is a central image within the Chicana feminist movement to be recuperated by women from its traitorous past, into a revised understanding of how women may become the radical edge between the modern and the traditional.

Thus, as Rey Chow argues, it is specifically woman who is situated at the crossroads of the traditional and the modern, the indigenous and the imported as both an image and a spectator. Chow revises this condition which women have inherited, as wives or consorts, into a site for a new productivity, in her construction of the "ethnic spectator". Chow sets it up this way: as the Chinese woman watches a dramatization of her condition, she is caught in a cross-cultural context "between the gaze that represents her and the image that is supposed to be her".[9] In other words, how can she constitute her gaze at "herself" on stage? Chow seeks to understand a spectator who might gaze at "herself" in a shared space, which she calls a "coeval" space among cultures. In other words, the woman ethnic spectator maintains the structures of several cultures in her gaze and in her recognition of the Chinese woman on the stage. She looks through the lens of feminist theory, as Chow employs it, from the Anglo-American tradition, while also bearing the values of the Chinese culture.

Chow goes on to imagine how that shared space might continue into the writing about performance. The feminist critic, then, who watches a performance that images the Chinese woman, would attempt to organize a writing time and space that was not withdrawn from the culture it intersects. The Chinese woman, employing feminist theories from the so-called West, would write within a time and space where the Chinese and the Western cultures were equally present and evocative. Likewise, the Western feminist would not take "field notes" of sorts, at the Chinese performance and then withdraw to her Western library to write her review. Instead, she would seek to remain in the space and time where the Chinese culture insisted upon its own operations, as she brought her Western critical strategies to bear on what she saw on stage.

Chow's ethnic spectator begins to amalgamate the binaries of modern and traditional, indigenous and imported in a single gaze. The prior sense of "First" and "Third-World" feminisms mutates into a more interdependent, complex relation among cultures. Chow's vision here is in line with new corrections to earlier feminist theories, which were based on notions of "margin and centre", First and Third World, and which are now perceived as retaining colonial structures in their order. In the very terminology of "First" and "Third World" the model continues to duplicate the uneven distribution of power it sought to repair. The "Third World", after all, is located on the margins and women living in the Third World are made to bear the greater signification of "difference".[10] The more recent concept, termed "transnational feminism", is designed to knit feminisms across national boundaries in a more evenly distributed sense.

Transnational feminism charts the movement of capital among and within nations as a constitutive part of any gender analysis, recognizing its local inventions as well as the kind of hyper-nationality created by its operations. In *Feminist Genealogies, Colonial Legacies, Democratic Futures*, Jacqui Alexander and Chandra Mohanty add something new to this critique. They call for the study of the state enforcement of heterosexuality through its "citizenship machinery, which makes lesbians into the disloyal citizen and thereby suspect".[11] They have linked state practices and lesbian identities in ways that allow a combined perspective on colonial and heteronormative practices.

As we have seen, since its inception, the feminist critique has sought to bring together women in the world and to interrogate that project critically, constantly adapting to changing conditions in notions of the world. If, at one point in history, it was progressive to think in terms of international organization, the current climate of transnational "worlding" has turned the notion of the global into a form of commodity marketing. How, then, to situate issues and performances around gender politics in this new configuration?

A few simple alterations come to mind in terms of our pursuits in studying performance. We cannot assume equal conditions around performance practices or gender representation, as expressed through terms like "intercultural". The easy comparison, or association across cultures, suggested by terms such as "intercultural" obfuscates the dynamics of capital and gender hierarchies at work in cultural trade. The question for us, as feminists, is how to convene within a global arena? What is the proper relation between our objects of study and conditions in the world? How do we remain aware of our own unconscious participation in national agendas? How do we, as feminist spectators, find a relation to performances across cultures? How do we construct empathy, if that is a useful concept, participate in mimesis, if that is one, or reap the benefits of mimicry, when they are arranged through site-specific conditions? These are a few of the questions that guide our pursuits within our IFTR/FIRT [the International Federation for Theatre Research]/Feminist working group.

Notes

1. Alexandra Kollentai, *Sexual Relations and the Class Struggle and Love and the New Morality*, translated by Alix Holt (Bristol: Falling Wall Press, 1972).
2. Gloria Anzaldúa, *Borderlands/La Frontera* (San Francisco: Spinsters/Aunt Lute, 1987), p. 3.
3. Rosi Braidotti, *Nomadic Subjects* (New York: Columbia University Press, 1994), pp. 2, 5.
4. Helen Gilbert and Joanne Tompkins, *Postcolonial Drama* (London and New York: Routledge, 1996), p. 118.
5. Tess Onwueme, *Tell It To Women* (Detroit: Wayne State University Press, 1997), p. 30.
6. Diana Taylor, *Disappearing Acts: Spectacles of Gender and Nationalism in Argentina's "Dirty War"* (Durham: Duke University Press, 1997), p. 17.
7. See Rey Chow, *Woman and Chinese Modernity* (Minneapolis: University of Minnesota Press, 1991).
8. See Yvonne Yarbro-Bejarano, "The Female Subject in Chicano Theatre: Sexuality, 'Race', and Class", in Sue-Ellen Case (ed.), *Performing Feminisms: Feminist Critical Theory and Theatre* (Baltimore: Johns Hopkins University Press, 1990), pp. 131–49.
9. Rey Chow, *Woman and Chinese Modernity*, p. 32.
10. See Inderpal Grewel and Caren Kaplan (eds), *Scattered Hegemonies* (Minneapolis: University of Minnesota Press, 1994).
11. M. Jacqui Alexander and Chandra Talpede Mohanty/(eds), *Feminist Genealogies, Colonial Legacies, Democratic Futures* (London and New York: Routledge, 1997), p. xxiii.

9

The Screens of Time: Feminist Memories and Hopes

At first, it seemed that feminist futures were to be found in feminist pasts. The beginning swells of the second wave deliriously projected images of a feminist past onto the bifurcated screen of time, reimagining matriarchies, amazons and goddesses along with the secret lives, the so-called untold histories of those few women history had managed to recognize. Feminist historians, literary critics, and artists filled pages and stages with these mythical creatures whose lust, power, love and accomplishment stunned and seduced the gray tired so-called "male" histories. The story telling of the grandmothers and their ghostly performances in the passing flesh, displaced the notion of history with that of cultural memory. However termed, these projections logged images and events on to the screen of time, establishing an account of cultural capital for the present movement. The feminist present and the feminist future were animated by these figures, these actions, these settings deemed as remembered. In one sense, many were imagined utopias, hopes for the future, embedded in the past. The bipolar screen of time, the past and the future was a form of collective dreaming through temporal tropes.

Yet, growing up alongside and within these temporal twins, a slip-stream of time, a wormhole of time, imagined through the notion of palimpsests complicated the strict division of past, present and future. In the artifact itself, in the present performance, one could perceive the layering of memories, image painted upon image, the erasures, the re-engravings, the gestural remains and even the traces of the future. Although these traces are located within a circumscribed material such as a canvas, or a square where performances had taken place, the strict chronology of those figures could not be ascertained. No development or progression could be marked. Uncertainty haunts the image, where erasures have occurred, or where images overcome the traces beneath them. Synchronicities appear there and it is difficult to separate out projections of the future from memories of the past.

Semiotic slippage put time on a banana peel, prat-falling on to the stage of representation. These time slippages can be hopeful and bright, in the tradition of early feminist imaginings, but they can also be dark reminders of exclusion. In specific, the very representation of "woman" both set things in motion and determined their end-point. As Teresa de Lauretis put it, in her 1984 book, *Alice Doesn't*, the representation of "woman" serves as "the source of the drive to represent and its ultimate, unattainable goal".[1] "Woman", then, a cultural myth made to stand in for women's experiences, catalyses both the past and the future – the beginning and the end of representation. Gender codes are, in fact, time codes, complicit with the structuring of the desire and the dream into partitioned, policed zones.

On a happier note, in performance studies, Joseph Roach, in his book *Cities of the Dead*, launched the notion of "surrogation", in which contemporary performances could be seen as embodying the past in present performances. Now one could view "expressive movements as mnemonic reserves, including patterned movements made and remembered by bodies, residual movements retained implicitly in images or words (or in the silences between them), and imaginary movements dreamed in minds not prior to language but constitutive of it".[2] The present is perforated by the past in this new form of understanding embodied histories. Even improvisation, the form meant to signal the present in its momentary invention, is a process of remembering and forgetting in its gesticulations. Somatic memories propel the body through space, making the performer a time traveller. Performances are both portals into an unknown future and kinesthetic and oral reserves of the past.[3]

The closet of time

If de Lauretis marked an exclusion as temporal ground and future, queer scholars began to identify other forms of exclusion that they could liberate – semiotically bringing past works "out of the closet" into the brighter present and future of queer epistemologies. Returning to the notorious old queen – of the novel *Remembrance of Things Past* – who opened the twentieth century with the discovery that memory could be embedded in the body, Proust could now be queered. Proust had narrated how eating the Madeleine, or stumbling

on the pavement were kinesthetic sites of memory that could invoke
the past in a more complete and vivid fashion than any voluntary
memory could perform. These episodes were kinesthetic theatres of
memory, in fact, replete with characters and a detailed *mise-en-scène*.
But his own voluntary writing could also be brought out of the closet
through new readings of its involuntary inscriptions. Proust's epic
novel bound his queer body to an intricate interweaving of cultural
and personal memory, performed through transgender identifications,
inextricably binding sensual and sexual escapades with spectacles of
class difference and cultural production. *The Remembrance of Things
Past* mapped out the critical topography of the twentieth century at its
inception. However, as Freud and Lacan have pointed out, each thing
that is remembered is another forgotten. Proust's closet of memory,
formed by cultural restrictions against his transgender identifications
and his sexual proclivities displaced his homosexualized liaisons and
longings on to phobic images of queers such as Albertine, who is portrayed as performing seemingly condemnatory acts, such as cavorting
with another woman in front of her mother's portrait; while his intimate portraits of social circles were bound tightly to the "right"
bloodlines. Rereading phobic images as desires, the past of Proust
and his world can be liberated into the present queer moment as a
monument to the trans-world of the early twentieth century.

Such semiotic slippage can be made to serve its own master, as
D. A. Miller wittily and elegantly configures in his book *Bringing
Out Roland Barthes*. Miller asserts that "With increasing visibility
after *S/Z*, Barthes is engaged in the ambiguously twinned projects
of at once sublimating gay content and undoing the sublimation in
the practice of what he himself refers to – in the case of Proust's
inversion – as *form*."[4] By form, here Miller means Barthes's own
semiosis. Miller organizes a way to read Barthes's play of sign and
referent, by referring to his own experiences with the discourse of
the sub-culture, thereby recognizing how the specifically gay codes
are deployed through slippage, and other devices designed to create
an esoteric homosexual semiosis. Thus, Miller's knowledge of gay dis-
tricts in Tokyo allows him to read, say, Barthes's *The Empire of Signs*,
to reveal a different register of referents that mark a gay Tokyo and
offers another, more seductive way to read how Barthes may have
been looking into the eyes he discusses there.

Such "outing" processes, slipping through transgender inversions
and tortuous, complex projects of sublimation and inscription,
have brought to the stage a space for utopic projections of future

possibilities into past dreams. Split Britches and Bloolips, in their production of *Belle Reprieve*,[5] "out" Tennessee Williams through transgender casting and the development of the sexual subtext within *A Streetcar Named Desire*. The laughter and the cheap jokes demonstrate how the present possibilities for sociosexual identifications and relations are free from the repressive coding in the text. Yet it is precisely that past which shapes the joke. They perform a present and promise a future in their songs that are "outside" the Williams text, addressed directly to an audience bound to the history of the theatre of repression and despair. When the suffering, tortured character of Blanche Dubois is transformed into a "critical fairy" (a postmodern drag queen) whose rival is a woman playing Stanley Kowalski (Peggy Shaw), the sub-cultural queer semiosis overcomes, through slippage and gender inversion, the fixed, determinist codes of the 1940s. Moreover, as Miller could find the gay Tokyo beyond Barthes's *Empire of Signs*, the *mise-en-scène* of *Belle Reprieve* literally flattens out Williams's seemingly realist referent into painted drops that signify psychic processes of identification. The light bulb Blanche seeks to cover with her veil of illusion is bared on a painted flat, isolated in its signification, no longer part of the "realistic" setting of a bedroom. The play slips, semiotically, into the symbolic and imaginary registers of sexual and gendered identifications, surrogating, as Roach would have it, the past, while also stepping out of its hold. Time becomes, as it is in dreams, Freud argues, simply an imagined structure of the negotiations of power and desire. Memory is embodied as Peggy Shaw's Stanley cries out the mantra of sado-masochistic pain/pleasure in the by-now famous "STELLLLA"! Yet her self-reflexive play on the passage safely ossifies that past, while still invoking it in the present, and also promises release from its determinism. The theatrical past and the historical fixing of the author are everywhere present and abandoned.

Queer scholar José Esteban Muñoz identifies what he terms "the future in the present" outside of the heteronormative sense of it. Muñoz notes that heterosexual culture "depends on a notion of the future: as the song goes, "the children are our future".[6] Seeking to establish a different tradition for a future in the present in "cultures of sexual dissidence", Muñoz argues for an "anticipatory illumination of a queer world" ("The Future in the Present", p. 93). In a sense, the performance of *Belle Reprieve* can be understood through this critical lens as performing that anticipatory gesture in Williams's play.

The subject of time

Although feminists began to have their way with time, reflexively participating in its screening effects and, like Alice, sliding happily across its semiotic fields and wriggling through its wormholes, its deterministic dynamic still took hold. While the shape of time could be fashioned, its power to produce meaning could not. The agent, or the subject, became a kind of side-effect, rather than operator of the time machine. Those earlier feminists who were animating the past with matriarchs and mermaids were doing it alongside the feminist project of recuperating a subject position for women. Some feminists took the motto "the personal is the political" of the activist movement into their cultural work, seeking to abandon the then-termed patriarchal voice and procedures of the objective historian or critic. The personal "I" figured woman's empowered standpoint, in locating a site of negotiation among issues of class, sexual practices, racialized codes and, of course, gender, while also retaining the power to alter them. However, the great cleansing of the "I" through attacks against essentialism encouraged another form of slip-streaming, or wormholing. Applications of psychoanalytic theory both created the interrogation of the subject and swapped the personal for the cultural. Displacement through multiple objects, or Lacan's familiar "*objet petite à*" creates an ego that is an archive of the approaching and discarded objects of identification. Thus, the "I" is an archive of the past and a site of possible identificatory streaming.

But looking back from the now-more-varied readings in critical theory, we can see that even the so-called objective tradition of writing theory was only one form of philosophical inquiry, which had been remembered in order to displace another. Another notorious homosexual, Ludwig Wittgenstein, whose *Tractatus Logico-Philosophicus* was lionized by, of all things, logical positivism, considers the operations of the subject in this painful passage marked by sublimation and inscription in *Culture and Value*, or *Vermischte Bemerkungun*: *Nobody can truthfully say of himself that he is filth.* Because if I do say it, though it can be true in a sense, this is not the truth by which I myself can be penetrated: otherwise I should either have to go mad or change myself."[7] One might say, given the status of the notion of "shame" in Sedgwick's theories of queer performativity,[8] that Wittgenstein launched the queer performative voice in his consideration of Kierkegaard and Christianity in 1937. But with this important difference: Wittgenstein's "self" was only partially the performative one, completely constructed or hailed by the dominant ideology that would "shame" him. Instead, he remains truly split in his shaming of himself, for the subject who shames cannot be the one who is shamed – for Wittgenstein, that would be a logical and grammatical impossibility, implying madness. Unlike Althusser, for whom the subject is interpellated, "hailed" by ideology, always already in an object position,[9] Wittgenstein implies that in order to mobilize the system of shaming, or ideology, the subject must retain its power to initiate. If the subject has been displaced by a functionalist or structuralist kind of objecthood, for Wittgenstein, it can logically and grammatically only inhabit that object status by retaining its bipolar relationship to the status of the subject. Interestingly, for Wittgenstein the only way the subject could be understood as pure object would be as one who goes mad, which means that one cannot operate within linguistic or logical systems.

Sarah Kane's play *4:48 Psychosis* scripts the mad roles that the "I" as subject and object may play – particularly through the process of shaming.[10] In this play, psychosis is both a psychological and a social condition, rather than an aspect of a character, for the play has no characters in the traditional sense of the term. Psychosis is the state of mind and the mind of state that fractures social affiliations, as well as any lasting cohesion of the subject position. The personal and the political play across the interior and social field of the play. The remains of character are occlusions of shame and shaming, stopping and being stopped. They act either as restrictions, as in the deployment of therapy-ese, or as refusals, stopping desire, change and identity formation on the part of the subject/object patient position. Much of the agency in the play is stoppage at the site of interpellation: "I can't eat"/"I can't sleep"/"I can't think"/"I cannot love"/"I cannot fuck"/"I cannot be alone"/"I cannot be with others" and "I do not want to live" (*4:48 Psychosis*, pp. 206–7). Pronouns substitute for nouns in much of the text, with purposefully indistinct referents, so the "I" hangs (itself) as a position in the psychotic social space. Take, for instance, the following use of the "I":

> I gassed the Jews, I killed the Kurds, I bombed the Arabs, I fucked small children while they begged for mercy, the killing fields are mine... and when I die I'm going to be reincarnated as your child only fifty times worse and as mad as all fuck I'm going to make your life a living fucking hell I REFUSE I REFUSE I REFUSE LOOK AWAY FROM ME.   (Kane, *4.48 Psychosis*, p. 227)

This is both the personal "I" of early feminism, with its desire and its social positioning marked, but it is also the "I" of the state. It is the speaking of self through the past of its violent oppressions and of its future in reincarnations of violence. But the refusal stops the determinism of both time and repetition. Although only a stoppage, it is powerful in halting the run of revenge.

With nothing like a characterological position, a subject in reserve articulates its actions in a string of unmoored repetitions: "Slash wring punch burn flicker dab float". These strings are followed by groups of three nouns. One group is particularly vibrant for the condition of the theater as locked to the social: "Victim. Perpetrator. Bystander" (Kane, *Psychosis*, p. 231). Here is a key to the dark scene – one cannot pretend not to witness, not to see, and thus not to partake. Sometimes collecting itself into the "I" of the storm, Kane installs the subject of time as psychotic, mad in Wittgenstein's terms. The social past of that subject, in killing Kurds and bombing Arabs, is its future, in reincarnation. Her madness is in opting out of the system altogether – the violence of her escape is like the violence of the system itself – the madness of a war zone, the loss of the subject position that could control the verb, the action, wrested from her by the authority of doctors and the state.

Kane's "anticipatory" gestures, as Muñoz would term them, reside in what could be termed a "negative utopia". Borrowing from Ernst Bloch, one could find a wish, a "residue" "that is not fulfilled and made banal through fulfillment...".[11] Or as Adorno, in conversation with Bloch, imagines, "the contradiction between the evident possibility of fulfillment and the just as evident impossibility of fulfillment" which compels the spectators to "identify themselves with this impossibility and to make this impossibility their own affair" (Bloch, *Utopian Function*, p. 4). The longing for change inscribed in the play, seeking semiotic and social liberation through the reception of its performance is its negative utopia. The future must be activated in a present so determined by its past. Of course, ascribing the resolution of this contradiction to Kane's suicide would release the spectators from this obligation – deny them the utopic promise in the piece. Melancholy would delimit the response, invoking Kane's own death as the final resolution of this anticipatory gesture.

Wrapped in the American flag, Holly Hughes acts out the address Kane impounds in the performance of her play, *Preaching to the Perverted*. Hughes scripts her journey up the steps of the Supreme Court in 1998 to hear their decision on the appeals the "NEA four" made against censorship of the arts in the case *Finley* v. *NEA*. Four artists, with queer performance materials, had their grants revoked by NEA (the National Endowment for the Arts) in 1990 for offending "standards of decency". Staging the dark forces of state power as a comedy, in contrast to Kane's tragedy, Hughes appropriates the flag that waved against her and the others who were "stripped" of their NEA funding. The Supreme Court justices appear as nine yellow rubber ducks who hear the arguments.

Hughes:
> But the obvious question doesn't get asked:
> How does the government decide someone is decent?
> . . . .
> Perhaps they used my mother's method:
> They check your underwear.
> First, it has to exist; no drip-dry advocates need apply
> It must be all natural fibers, preferably white
> No holes, stains, sagging waistband, safety pins!
> Maybe a simple pattern but no slogans please!
> No "I can't believe I ate the whole thing"
> And it's got to be appropriate:
> No boxer shorts on women
> No lacey thongs on men.[12]

Richard Meyer observes that "rather than countering these attacks by defending her work as respectable or decent, Hughes insists upon the symbolic power of the unrespectable and indecent" (Meyer, "Have you Heard", p. 552). Hughes mobilizes the juridical past to argue her case, in her own constituted queer performance court, by soliciting an identification with the perverted and their cause against the puritanical prudery in the Supreme Court decision. She invokes, then, a virtual court that could reverse this decision, changing the future for the queer arts within the state.

Hughes's performance piece was more prescient, more pregnant with the future than we could imagine. Now, some few years later, the Bush administration has been re-elected on the grounds of so-called decency in its civil struggle against gay marriage. Conflating "homeland security" with the exclusive right to marriage by heterosexuals, the Bush administration hopes to mount the steps to the Supreme Court in order to pass a new amendment to the federal constitution, denying the rights of marriage to any but the heterosexual couple. The future was definitely embedded in the past, in this performance by Hughes. Only the laughter, the cutting courage of Hughes's humour can securely wrap the queer body in state protection and privilege. Hughes installs an agency in the citizen subject increasingly at risk.

Hughes discharges what Ernst Bloch imagined as the "*undischarged, underdeveloped, in short, utopian*..." gesture.[13] The future and the past are fully installed in her performance present. Indeed, much promise has been laid at the feet of performance art, from Josette Féral's early essay,[14] to Peggy Phelan's description of its ontology,[15] to Diana Taylor's utopic transdisciplinary claims for it in her recent book on Archive and Repertoire.[16] Most recently, some feminist scholars, in considering the work of Hughes and other performance artists, have located utopic effects in the conditions of performance itself, installing future promise in present conditions. Live performance, argues Jill Dolan, can produce the "feel" of a utopic future/present in a collective setting. Dolan terms this the "utopian performative", that offers, in its practice, a sense of "what utopia would feel like rather than how it would be organized. It works at the level of sensibility, by which I mean an affective code...".[17] Dolan regards the space of performance as a "space apart" in which "Staying together in that space can be a time of shared subjectivity" ("Performance, Utopia, and the 'Utopian Performative'", p. 468). Dolan ultimately moves to a discussion of the "Messianic" in Deborah Margolin's performance work, finding what she terms "messianic moments" in works "that herald the arrival of a new and better world" ("Performance, Utopia, and the 'Utopian Performative'", p. 476).

Rather than a content, then, that can be semiotically liberated, or a negative dialectic embedded in the cultural artifact, Dolan would offer the experience of certain performances, the affective charge they produce in those present, as the discharge of the hope, the coming of the messianic moment that "heralds" a better future. Dolan posits the collective moment that has been confounded by state practices, corporate immersions and technological isolation in the conditions of live performance, where its utopic potential may be realized by certain kinds of performance.

But returning to Bloch, who was attacked by other Marxists for a kind of "messianic" subtext in his "principles of hope", we can see just why he configures the utopic or the present as specifically "unfulfilled". Unlike Dolan, or perhaps even Augusto Boal, who would have people imagine the better world and realize its image or affect, Bloch wants to hold it within a kind of "negative dialectic". When utopia is "cast into a picture", as he puts it "there is a reification of ephemeral and non-ephemeral tendencies". For Bloch, the utopic resides in the "it-should-not-be" of the longing for a "coming in order". "The function of utopia", for Bloch, "it a critique of what is present" (Bloch, *Utopian Function*, pp. 11–12). To actually discharge it would be to reify it.

Elfriede Jelinek, who won the Nobel Prize for Literature in 2004, inscribed such negative subjects-of-promise in her play *Illness or Modern Women (Krankheit oder Moderne Frauen)*.[18] In this play, the men speak only in hyperbolic platitudes of health, strength, efficiency, success, competition, sports and so on. Dr Heathcliffe is both a dentist and a gynaecologist. His nurse, Emily (Brontë) is a lesbian vampire. Emily falls in love with a patient, Camilla (Le Fanu), a housewife/mother and wife of a tax collector. Camilla dies in child-birth in the gynaecological chair as Emily sucks her blood. Brought back to life by vampiric means, Camilla returns Emily's affection and celebrates her new status of "undead". As the women bond through blood, the men continue their mutual backslapping, congratulating themselves on their various successes. Their narcissism and sexism blind them to the vampiric satiety the women achieve with one another. Act II opens on a 1950s style bedroom with twin beds, actu-ally twin coffins, in which Camilla and Emily lounge as Emily writes on her protable typewriter. A negative utopia is staged with great irony, as the women find fulfilment in their negative status, dripping with blood, haunting graveyards and drinking from medical beakers of blood. Finally, the women are able to merge into a double-headed single creature that feasts on all flesh and blood. The women have successfully removed themselves from social functions as well as any romantic attachment to nature through their undead condition. The lesbian vampires are both deconstructive figures evacuating by their presence the dominant social logic.

However, their very fulfilment, the "fleshing out" of their promise also brings, as Bloch would predict, their demise. The double-headed creature is destroyed. Its representational fulfilment brings its demise. To come out of the closet, in this play, is to depreciate future promise. And yet, the fact that Jelinek, a feminist author despised in her home country of Austria for her critical works, could be awarded the Nobel Prize for literature does seem somewhat fulfilling. Perhaps, as Bloch would have it, the contradiction is what promises hope.

At this point in history, it seems difficult to imagine any kind of a promising or feminist future. The re-election of the Bush regime in the United States seems to promise nothing but suffering to people and to the environment. The rights and privileges of citizenship are being restricted by immigration laws, the lawless incarceration of terrorist suspects, moral censorship of the arts, and homophobic amendments to the constitution. In spite of Jill Dolan's enthusiasm for the realm of radical performance, it seems more and more divorced from social conditions. In fact, performances focused on singularly human concerns seem more and more untied from the crisis in the environment, with increasing numbers of animals becoming extinct, whales and other fish beaching themselves and dying in record numbers, the arctic poles melting, and the future of a sustainable environment more and more unlikely as water reserves begin to disappear.

With crises of domination of nature and other humans forming on every front, the title of a performance piece by the lesbian artist Reno seems evocative: *Rebel Without a Pause*. In the past, queer scholarship revealed the relations between formations of citizenship and minoritarian sexual practices. Sarah Schulman's *My American History*,[19] the Parker/Rousseau/Sommer/Yeager anthology entitled *Nationalisms and Sexualities*,[20] and David Evans's *Sexual Citizenship*,[21] all traced, in various ways, the formation of sexual citizenship as an effect of national and juridical processes. But after the traumatic pressure the events of 9/11 unleashed on national and juridical identificatory processes, the lesbian performance artist Reno crafted a piece in which she reversed the equation: the events of 9/11 are not made to reveal the citizen status of the lesbian, but the lesbian performer reveals the militaristic isolationist violence of the state.[22] If, in the past, the practice was to reveal the status of one who identified with a sexual minority within the processes of citizenship and legislation, this performance stages the lesbian performer as one who speaks about the nation as a citizen – looking out from that vantage rather than playing out issues surrounding her unique identity. This point was made to me by David Román who invited Reno to perform this work at the University of Southern California precisely because he wanted to foreground the importance of gay/lesbian performers dedicating their work to a rebellion against national processes.

It seems ironic to conclude an article on feminist futures, once located in an autonomous movement, a separatist culture, an identitarian sub-culture, with a consideration of the nation-state. This is not to suggest that the nation-state is the effective form of organization, as in the modernist, bourgeois tradition; nor would I like to pose a non-gendered kind of politic that returns to the unmarked status of "citizen". The promise I can hold here, in *Rebel Without A Pause*, is in the residue, the contradiction between rebellion and take-over, the negative dialectic of aggression and expenditure, which makes the audience responsible for change. This residue exceeds the gesture of response and responsibility in the rebel as subject, tied to activist performers in Seattle, say, with giant puppets performing against the WTO, or those garbed as tomatoes and other vegetables demonstrating against the genetic alteration of "frankenfoods", or the marching masks of Bush in the anti-war marches, or the masked women at sewing machines in front of the Acropolis, staging the sweatshop production of athletic clothing during the Olympics. As old as Medea (to slipstream back into the past), the woman terrorist who poisoned the state and murdered its future, who escaped by chariot into the utopic heavens, while the rebellion brims, stirred in large cauldrons by witches and vampires, visible, like those secret signs of the underground movements, agitating, remaining behind masks, in the dark holes of aporias, never really to actualize, be recognized, punished or tamed.

Notes

1. Teresa de Lauretis, *Alice Doesn't: Feminism, Semiotics, Cinema* (Bloomington: Indiana University Press, 1984), p. 13.
2. Joseph Roach, *Cities of the Dead: Circum-Atlantic Performance* (New York: Columbia University Press, 1996), p. 26.
3. Joseph Roach, "Deep Skin: Reconstructing Congo Square", in Harry J. Elam, Jr. and David Krasern (eds), *African American Performance and Theater History: A Critical Reader* (Oxford and New York: Oxford University Press, 2001), pp. 101–13.
4. D. A. Miller, *Bringing Out Roland Barthes* (Berkeley: University of California Press, 1992), p. 27.
5. See Bette Bourne, Paul Shaw, Peggy Shaw and Lois Weaver, *"Belle Reprieve"*, in Sue-Ellen Case (ed.), *Split Britches: Lesbian Practice/Feminist Performance* (London and New York: Routledge, 1996), pp. 149–83.
6. José Esteban Muñoz, "The Future in the Present: Sexual Avant-Gardes and the Performance of Utopia", in Donald Pease and Robyn Weigman (eds), *The Future of American Studies* (Durham, NC, and London: Duke University Press, 2002), pp. 77–93.
7. Ludwig Wittgenstein, *Culture and Value*, G. H. Von Wright, ed., trans. Peter Winch (Cambridge, MA, and Oxford: Blackwell, 1980), p. 32e.
8. See Eve Kosofsky Sedgwick, *Touching Feeling: Affect, Pedagogy, Performativity* (Durham, NC, and London: Duke University Press, 2003).

9. Louis Althusser, "Ideology and Ideological State Apparatuses (Notes Towards an Investigation)", in *Lenin and Philosophy and Other Essays*, trans. Ben Brewster (New York: Monthly Review Press, 1971), pp. 127–88.
10. Sarah Kane, *4.48 Psychosis*, in *Sarah Kane: Complete Plays* (London: Methuen Drama, 2001), pp. 203–45.
11. Ernst Bloch, *The Utopian Function of Art and Literature: Selected Essays*, trans. Jack Zipes and Frank Mecklenburg (Cambridge, MA: MIT Press, 1988), p. 2.
12. Quoted in Richard Meyer, "Have you heard the one about the lesbian who goes to the Supreme Court: Holly Hughes and the case against censorship", *Theatre Journal*, 52 (2000): 543–52, p. 551.
13. Ernst Bloch, *The Principle of Hope*, trans. Neville Plaice, Stephen Plaice and Paul Knight (Oxford: Blackwell, 1985), p. 102.
14. Josette Féral, "Performance and Theatricality: the Subject Demystified", *Modern Drama*, 25 (1983): 170–81.
15. Peggy Phelan, "The Ontology of Performance: Representation without Reproduction", in *Unmarked: The Politics of Performance* (London and New York: Routledge, 1993), pp. 146–66.
16. Diana Taylor, *Archive and the Repertoire: Performing Cultural Memory in the Americas* (Durham, NC: Duke University Press, 2003).
17. Jill Dolan, "Performance, Utopia, and the 'Utopian Performative' ", *Theatre Journal*, 53 (2001): 455–79, p. 460.
18. Elfriede Jelinek, *Krankheit oder Moderne Frauen* (Cologne: Prometh Verlag, 1987).
19. Sarah Schulman, *My American History: Lesbian and Gay Life During the Reagan/Bush Years* (New York: Routledge, 1994).
20. Parker, Rousseau et al. (eds), *Nationalisms and Sexualities* (New York: Routledge, 1992).
21. David T. Evans, *Sexual Citizenship: The Material Construction of Sexualities* (London and New York: Routledge, 1993).
22. See Reno, "Reno: Rebel without a Pause: Unrestrained Reflections on September 11th", www.citizenreno.com/indexrebel.html, viewed 6 December 2004.

Part III

Gendered Performance and New Technologies

10

Performing the Cyberbody on the Transnational Stage

Familiar terms such as "being connected," "linked-up," "plugged-in," "interfacing," "projecting," and "making contact" share referents between social processes and computer technologies. As technologies have borrowed images from social behavior to describe electronic functions, such as the "handshake" to represent a recognition between systems, human interactions are currently being described by terms borrowed from computer functions. We have become accustomed to the use of the term "interface," a description of a connection made between systems, to include human interactions – as if they were electronic systems. The human mind no longer enjoys terms of transcendence to describe its place among systems, but has become, in the words of science fiction, "wetware," a water-based version of software. Deep in quotidian usage, lie buried the perceived notions that bonds between people are forged through and across technologies. *Contact*, as Jody Foster plays it, happens through giant, deep-dish ears, and in outer space.

These terms for meetings and unions suggest new forms of hybridity between people and "machines" (as they were once called) – cyborgean fusions, crossings between species in transplants, genetic forms of reproduction, and the crossing between sexes, through trans-sexual technologies. Our ethical terror of these new forms plays out in films like *Alien Resurrection*, whose heroine is a clone created to provide a womb for a monstrous alien, while our hopeful outreach toward global expansion and immigration is imagined through narratives like *ET* and his desire for his distant home.

These computer terms and science fiction tropes represent not only our anxieties and pleasures in confronting the effects new technologies are having upon our bodily and social organization, but also serve as tropes for the economic and social processes which accompany the global growth of new technologies. As Connie Samaras argues, in her article "Is It Tomorrow or Just the End of Time," the current craze around alien abductions and UFOs, with their narratives of abduction from the domestic space, sexual experiment, and insemination, reveal contemporary anxieties around the collapse of privacy, the end of traditional forms of insemination, and the contestation of traditional gender roles and sex assignment (210–11).

The world wide web describes not only an electronic, virtual space, but also the new transnational practices of labor and capital that accompany it. The role of technology in forming new unemployment and employment practices has been a key player in creating transnational patterns of immigrant labor and capital. The current craze for flying saucers and alien abductions serves to both represent and mask these new forms of labor and capital transport. As virtual systems displace certain sectors of labor, the drive to relocate within their exclusive boundaries has even encouraged one cult of website designers known as Heaven's Gate to commit mass suicide. With Nikes on their feet (a sure symbol of First World success through oppressive Third World economic practices), wearing identical clothing (to signify they were "beyond" gender), with some male bodies having been surgically altered to make sexual practice impossible, and with a little change in their pockets, the Heaven's Gate web designers killed themselves in the hope of finding permanent employment somewhere behind the fleeting material body of the Hale-Bopp comet. They were the first interstellar immigrants seeking work. Their example illustrates one deadly way in which changing fantasies around gender, sexuality, and technology are combining to transform lives. (Archived as www.heavensgate.com)

Theatres of the flesh

Growing up alongside this formation of a science fiction imaginary, is a new cultural imaginary of the body, which we might call "theatres of the flesh." Flesh, once perceived as the given envelope of nature, has now become a theater of operations.

In so-called "live" theater, traditional acting regards the body as an expressive tool for inner, psychological processes, as in Method acting. Gestural systems are devised to reveal the emotional impact of memory or desire as perceived through the body. The carefully-lit face of the actor operates as a register of internal processes. Today, this tradition of theater seems somehow dated. In the new technoculture, the body's own fleshly status serves to reveal how it is altered by, or operates in consonance with new technologies. An array of new performance techniques illustrates the widespread sense of the body as its own theater of change, through technology, rather than as a register of unseen, internal motivations.

Perhaps one telling example may be found in the work of the French performance artist, Orlan. Her work consists of a series of cosmetic surgeries designed to reconstruct her facial features to resemble so-called "beautiful" women in the history of art. Orlan's seventh surgery took place in New York in 1993. It was relayed by satellite to galleries around the world, where people gathered to communicate with the performer by phone, fax, and video satellite. During the piece, Orlan is dressed in a costume, as are the doctors and attendants. She reads from a psychoanalytic study on the body, while the doctors prepare. She entertains questions from those watching the satellite hook-up. Although the actual operation is not broadcast, photos of her bruised and healing face later record the progress of the change. These photos are then installed in the galleries. Orlan is staging technology's power to alter the body as a performance. "Live" performance, in this instance, means performing the technologized body, both through medical intervention and through telecommunication. The localized body is medicalized through reconstructions of the regime of beauty. Orlan performs the sense of the "medical gaze." Yet she also uses telecommunications as prostheses of the body to beam it out into sites of spectatorship and exhibition.

Linked to the performance of surgeries of the flesh, or these new theatres of the body, studies of the transsexual, or transgendered body insist upon the medical reassignment of gender as one of the most structurally definitive practices of our time. Susan Stryker, in her article "Christine Jorgensen's Atom Bomb," situates "transsexuality as a site of technological innovation in the mid-twentieth century, [which] foregrounds the question of how technological change, particularly in the biomedical realm, impacts the conditions of embodied subjectivity."[1] Stryker goes on to define the transsexual body as "an operationalized surface effect achieved through performative means." In other words, the flesh serves as the threshold upon which subjectivity is produced through its interaction with technology. Subjectivity is external, then, rather than internal. The flesh does not reflect or translate subjectivity as an internal process, as in Method acting, or other traditional forms, but flesh actually produces a performative register of subjectivity as it is changed through technological interventions. The transsexual body replaces what Stryker calls "inner secrets," or the psychological, mental processes of internality with "internal secretions," proffering "estrogen and testosterone as deep truths of the body," rather than Freudian paradigms. There is a biochemical reconstruction of gender, here, through the ingestion of hormones, which displaces the internalized, subjective construction of gender that Freud would map in his developmental notions of the Oedipal process.

Now, one might say that theater and performance have been working to stage this encounter between body and technology since the early decades of the century. Marinetti, one of the founders of the Futurist movement, exalted the machine, as it was then known, in relation to the flesh, finally culminating in what he regarded as the transcendent arena of war. For the Futurists, the body was poised at the threshold of its celebratory destruction. The excitement and speed they so admired, were rushing toward that explosive effect. At the same time, the Expressionists set up the agonies of interiority, as caught in the spotlight of authoritarian regimes of objectivity. Science was the operating room in which subjectivity was tortured by objectivist structures. The diagonal lines that cut across their stage sets mark the twisted state of the subjective, cut through by the machinic remove of the new technologies. In the film *Metropolis*, we see humans relegated to servitude to the machine. Bertolt Brecht, informed by these two movements, founded a theater that would assimilate science and technology back into human processes. Brecht eventually found, in the Marxist sense of materialism, a way to compound the opposing regimes of subjectivity and objectivity through the paradigms of labor and learning. For Brecht, the working body produced a social, perhaps collective subjectivity, as well as an agency for technology. His theater, then, moved not from the inside reality to the external, through expression, but from the outside condition, into an internal one. The body performed its social relations, emphasizing their incarnation in the fleshly materiality of the body. Nevertheless, the body remained intact. It performed its relation to technology, with technology still imagined as a machine or a tool. The body was not a theater of operations, but an agency for operations.

These are but a few of the performance strategies from the earlier part of the century which situated performance in relation to the rise of technology, up through its deadly transcendence in World War II.

Susan Stryker's transsexual critique takes up where these performances leave off – in the decade of the 1950s. Stryker situates the publicity around the transsexual operation of Christine Jorgensen alongside the reception of the atomic bomb. Earlier performances wrestled with machines as externalizing effects, produced against a backdrop of the internal as human: humans have feeling, while machines do not. Stryker insists that Christine Jorgensen's transsexual body revealed how medical technologies could redesign sex assignment, blurring the borders between social, interior processes, and technological ones. The body as exemplum of organicist ideals and humanistic values, which the Expressionists could stage in its agonized encounter with new technologies, had been tampered with all the way down into its interiority – its hormones, and of course later, its genetic structure. Understood in this context, the transsexual body and transgender politics organize a body that is already deeply intermingled with virtual systems in its composition. If Brecht understood the body as a register of the social through its proximate relations on stage and its gestures, the new transgendered body imploded the social codes of sex and gender into its very hormonal structure. Performance resides in the testosterone-induced growing of the beard, or estrogen-induced growing of the breasts. The body performs itself, its capacities in its tissues. Jordy Jones, one of the cyber-leaders of the transgender movement, has created a performance around his change from female to male entitled the "Injectable Man." In one sense, he performs his achievement by simply putting his bearded body on stage. In this way, the body performs itself as a theatre of change.

Kate Bornstein, another transsexual performer has produced a new piece, *Virtually Yours*, which places her body in front of the computer screen. She becomes involved with a computer game as a form of self-discovery. Her problem: her girlfriend is becoming her boyfriend. Thus, Bornstein, a male-to-female transsexual finds herself in a relationship with a female-to-male transsexual. What worries the couple, is the fact that their homosexual, lesbian relationship is turning into an inversion of a heterosexual relationship. The one-time girlfriend begins to perform the sex of male to Bornstein's performance of female. The sex assignment determines the sexual definition of heterosexuality. Now, in the midst of this crisis of sexual performance, Bornstein finds guidance and solace through the computer screen. An interactive computer game provides an opportunity to analyze the emotional responses to the effect medical reassignment surgery has upon sexual practices.

Reviewing these performances, from Orlan's cosmetic surgeries through Bornstein's inter-transsexual relationship problems, we might imagine something like an axis of technology, running deep into the body as well as out through the internet. Following this axis, how might we reconfigure what we consider to be the body? And how does one perform that body?

In order to pursue these queries, I would like to consider a website that organizes a new interaction among the elements of body, gender, and performance.

The Brandon website (Brandon.Guggenheim.org)

The Brandon website offers a virtual space, where virtual bodies "trans" gender and technology. This website has been designed to somehow perform the representations of transgender bodies as well as the social violence against those bodies. Moreover, the Brandon website, as Jordy Jones explains it, creates "cyber Brandons."[2]

The name for the website is derived from the life and death of Teena Brandon, known in transgender circles as Brandon Teena. Brandon Teena was a twenty-one-year-old who had lived his adolescent life as a man, making a spectacle out of his success in dating good-looking girls in small towns in the Midwest. In 1993, he was brutally raped and murdered by two men who had discovered "he was a girl," as they put it. His murder prompted a national move for protection rights by several agencies, such as the National Gay and Lesbian Task Force. The name of the agency suggests some of the identity issues surrounding the case: was Brandon to be perceived as a lesbian who lived as a butch, or as a transgendered person who lived as a man? The debate hinges upon the relevance of the biological body, in considering the signs of gender.

While the website alludes to the historical evidence surrounding Brandon Teena's death, it is not a website dedicated to Brandon Teena; rather it is a site where "multiple cyber-Brandons" appear, both in the site, and in the traversal of the site. The web designer, Shu Lea Cheang, a noted underground filmmaker, created a very complex website, that links discovery, rape, murder, transsexuality and gender through difficult navigation devices. It is neither obvious nor easy to traverse the site, nor are its significations direct in their referents. Each navigation is unique – foming a cyber-Brandon along its path.

Big Doll

One image within the site is identified as the Big Doll. The Big Doll, itself a secondary term of reference, provides a flashing glimpse of the techno-body of the late twentieth century, constructed through the lens of transgender discourse. Here we see fragments of a subcultural body marked by the practices of alternative sexualities; gendering inscriptions through tattoos, scarification, and piercings; newspaper headlines around Brandon Teena's violent death and legal proceedings; anatomical sketches, suggesting a scientistic discourse from an earlier era, and even trans-species genitals – pistils, and stamens. The cyber-Brandon animates along framed spaces like comix[3] – those underground books of images that inform much of the visual composition on the web. However, the frames do not delineate narrative moments, but appear as fields which situate morphing. Each frame provides several orders of images that, together, constitute multiple "dolls," or compositions of identification. What makes these images cohere is a field of allusions organized by several different kinds of codes – a cyber-Brandon is composed by the user who can traverse these codes and the flickering signifier the doll represents. Traversal by the mouse animates these image morphings, and, as the user begins to put together a field of identification, through a recognition of how these body practices, this trial, and medical technologies inter-relate, a cyber-Brandon is formed, or rather, is performed.

Roadkill

There is a locational referent in this website, signified by the image of a highway. The mouse moves up the screen, following the yellow line, as if following a road. This section is known as "Brandon's Roadtrip." The title of the section hints at the formation of the cyber-Brandon, who "trips" through this part of the site. The travelling cyber-Brandons encounter historical transgender figures, whose images lie splattered across the highway. History as roadkill.

When clicked upon, these figures reveal, for example, Herculine Barbin, a 19th-century French hermaphrodite, discussed in the work of Foucault; Jack Garland, born the daughter of the first Mexican consul to San Francisco, in the early 20th century, who lived his life as a man; and the cross–dressed Venus Extravaganza from the film *Paris Is Burning*. As Peggy Shaw put it, when playing a trans-gendered Stanley

Kowalski in the play *Belle Reprieve*: "I'm so queer I don't even have to talk about it. I'm just . . . parts of other people all mashed into one body . . . I take all these pieces . . . and I manufacture myself. When I'm saying I fall to pieces, I'm saying Marlon Brando was not there for me, James Dean failed to come through . . ." (Case 1996: 177). Like Shaw, the cyber-Brandon "trans" body is constructed through traversing the images of Herculine, Jack, and Venus. To reverse Shaw's phrase, this is a process of "coming to pieces."

In this case, the performance is in the animation of these images through the movement of the mouse, while the user actively constructs identificatory processes across the images. While the identification is formed through allusion and metonymy, both social and eccentric processes, the movement of the mouse might be perceived as a disciplined motion, controlled by the design of the images as well as that of the mouse itself. The mouse both glides freely among images, and is also choreographed by the placement of those images.

The cyber-Brandon performs, then, through a kind of disassociation between manual gesture and psychological identificatory processes. Unlike the earlier performance techniques that sought some kind of consonance between bodily gesture and internal state, the cyber-Brandon is composed by the disciplined, repetitive motion of the mouse in relation to the metonymic and indirect floating, if you will, of the sign for self.

Now, this cyber-Brandon may also "play" these images in the flesh. S/he may be a practitioner of one of the bodily rites, such as piercing, or scarification, or more, inject his or her body with hormones, or more, have had a double lateral mastectomy performed on the body. (One part of the website has actual images of such an operation.) If so, a certain mimesis might occur here, in the morphings. The person before the computer screen may experience something like a mirror effect, although even so, these images are nestled among other, more distant ones. Mimesis, if it occurs, is accidental, in the process of electronic representation.

As we have seen, the Brandon website creates a cyber-body through the lens of transgender identifications. In consonance with medical technology and gender play, this body traverses the axis in its own "trans" way. As Jordy Jones observed, "new cultural life forms are beginning to appear out there." His notion of a "cultural life form" is a brilliant composite of biology, culture, and technology.

"Out there," to Jones, is on the world wide web – a new world-ing device in this sense – a sense the web encourages. By referent and production, the Brandon website is international. The referent, Brandon Teena, was from the Midwestern US. The site was first housed at the Banff Centre, an influential Canadian centre of new projects which combine virtual systems and art. The website designer, Shu Lea Cheang, is a Taiwanese educated in the States, well-known for her inter-ethnic films. But more, the site is now linked to several other institutions that arrange for it to become a performance site, or rather a magnet site for performances of cultural issues linked to transgender politics. The Brandon website is now situated at the Guggenheim museum in New York, which announced Brandon as "a one year narrative project in installments." It is also linked to events located on a Dutch site, the Society for Old and New Media. It is also linked to the Harvard Institute on the Arts and Civic Dialogue, directed by the playwright and performer, Anna Deavere Smith. Smith's organization focused on the Brandon site in its first summer of creating a dialogue between the arts and the social by organizing a multi-site public event, as it was called, on August 5, 1998 at 8 pm. The event was called "Brandon's Virtual Court System," taking place at the Harvard Law School. Using documents based on real and cyber sexual assault cases, Shu Lea Cheang and the theatre director Liz Diamond created a courtroom drama. Five actors from the American Repertory Theatre played the roles of the victims, with legal scholars playing the jurors. In May 1999 the Dutch site provided the second such performance.

In other words, a performance of an international virtual "court of law" sits in session through a website. The liberative elements of such an event are breathtaking. First-rate legal scholars will perform as a jury, while actors perform, as characters, the facts of actual cases concerning sexual assault. This virtual court may offer what the actual courts do not, in equity and understanding. It may rehearse a change in the system.

However, beyond "democratic futures," what such events illustrate is the increasing sexualization of the civic and the social, both in courts and as traversed on the web. New transnational spaces are formed through emulations, or evocations of gender and sex. The web performs itself to the body through an interface organized by the discourses of sex and gender. While Smith's virtual court illustrates the founding of a liberative public space, it is a space built by and through the worlding devices of transnational capital.

The world wide web is both a colonizing and deterritorializing space, which often boasts that it "transcends" geographical boundaries, in a new, enthusiastically-embraced formation of community apart from traditional forms of territorial ownership. To some degree, as we have seen, this can be effective. However, the local is evacuated for citizenship in this "webworld," serving as what Lacan calls the "pound of flesh" that one must pay in order to enter this new form of the Symbolic. If, in Lacanian terms, castration is the price one pays in order to enter speaking and writing, this new form of the Symbolic requires "place" to be evacuated, in order to become a citizen of the "new world."

As "place" is evacuated, marked bodies perform the residual effects of territory and citizenship. As we will see, tropes of sexuality and gender are organized within transnational spaces to make the locations of new transnational capital seem familiar while they displace traditional national and local geographies. The reorganization of the "East" or Asian-Pacific territories through new globalizing practices offers one of the more vivid examples of how sex and gender are deployed to reconfigure and make familiar globalized space.

Transnational uses of sex and gender

Mitsuhiro Yoshimoto, in his article "Real Virtuality," argues that this "dissociation of space from place . . . of time replaced by speed" make "image and spectacle . . . [into] commodities, which can be consumed and disappear immediately . . ." In turn, their digital reproduction renders "the material base increasingly ephemeral" (115). Yoshimoto concludes that the digital image is becoming the basic commodity in the global economy (116).

What is important to our consideration here is how this transnational space organizes around the discourses of gender and sex for its representation. In its most liberative sense, it creates cyber-bodies who "trans" restrictive social boundaries in their very composition. But this deployment of the discourse of sex is also of use to the formation of transnational corporations, who must invent a new sense of territory and identity for their labor and commercial profits.

Neferti Tadiar, in her article "Sexual Economies in the Asia-Pacific Community," argues that new labor and commodity markets are being formed through what she terms a global sexual fantasy. Tadiar explains that new transnational "economies and political relations of nations are libidinally configured, that is, they are grasped in terms of sexuality" (183). This desire is specifically heterosexual in its mode, enacted according to what Tadiar refers to as the "prevailing mode of heterosexual relations" (186). Therefore, in its composition, it creates both licit and illicit relations. Since heterosexuality has historically claimed the privilege of marriage, it must bear the burden of the licit, and the potential of the illicit (as Clinton has embodied). Moreover, hetero relations have always depended on the "kindness" of the stable binary of gender.[4]

Turning specifically to the Asian-Pacific region, Tadiar notes that this region once signified a threat to the global power of the US. The struggles of the Vietnam War, followed by economic growth and practices that threatened to make the region more independent and powerful, made South-East Asia a signifier of irreconcilable differences. Thus, a new dream of the region was required to transform it into a part of the transnational pool of capital. The new region dropped out national names to become "the Asian-Pacific community." Tadiar argues that the new region was imagined through a sexualized representation of a "marriage" brokered between the United States and Japan, with, in the licit relations, Japan as wife, and the US as husband (185–6). Yet within the Asian-Pacific region, asserts Tadiar, Japan encouraged a performance of illicit relations, in which Japan plays male John (emulating some occupational practices of American soldiers in the region) to the poorer countries. The relations play through the image and the reality of the prostitute. As evidence, Tadiar lists the 100,000 Asian migrant women who enter Japan each year to work as "entertainers in the booming sex industry." Ninety percent of them come from the Philippines, Thailand, and Taiwan (198).[5]

Alongside this material practice, which sexualizes economic power and makes underdeveloped nations into "hostesses," the labor conditions of women in free trade zones are constructed as a sexual masquerade. The work camps in the economic zones emulate the conditions of a brothel, where women (and only women) are forced to live where they work, putting in 60–80 hour weeks for little money. Tadiar concludes that the transnational zone is formed "not so much [by] nations acting like people, but [by] people embodying nations" (204). Deterritorialization finds a new ground in gendered bodies, which offers them up to transnational uses through scenarios of seduction and sexual practice.

The painter Masami Teraoka offers a brilliant and witty artistic vision of the penetration of a feminized Japan by Western transnational capital. Teraoka uses traditional Japanese painting styles and scenes to ironize the penetration of transnational capital into that historical imaginary. In 1974, his series "McDonald's Hamburgers Invading Japan" placed french fries in the midst of a traditional Japanese woodblock. Teraoka then moved on to depict something more sexualized and gendered than the invasion of commodities.

Using images from ghost tales and Kabuki theater, Teraoka places condoms, the issue of safe sex, in the hands of a bathing geisha (see Figure 2). This one, entitled "Geisha in Bath" paints the fear of AIDS, which even a thousand condoms can't quell. The geisha, the hostess in the "pleasure quarter" as Teraoka puts it, both feminizes and

Figure 2 Masami Teraoka, AIDS Series/*Geisha in Bath* (1988), watercolor on unstretched canvas, 274.3 × 205.7 cm

sexualizes the image of Japan here, with a fear of a deadly penetration, situated within its own traditional imaginary. Without trivializing the AIDS pandemic, these images may also be read, particularly in the light of his earlier work, as a form of revealing the sexualized nature of the transnational contact. In his notes to one of the paintings, Teraoka makes this sense even more viable, as he wryly attributes this thought to the geisha: "Hmmm. These condoms are so big – they must be for foreign visitors, they are too big for my lover."

Teraoka's next series, in the '90s, moves to the computer. In these images, the danger of sexualized transnational contact becomes a wounding of the gendered body (Figure 3). This watercolor, entitled "Eve with Three Blind Mice" situates the nude female body, hooked up to mice and keyboard, standing in front of the ruins of European culture. Japanese calligraphy, a form of writing, joins the architecture of the Coliseum, to frame the body. Wounded and green, the body stands in for material culture, ruined by new systems of virtuality. The nudity emphasizes the body as gendered, feminized, as a receiver – a receptor – of the systems.

Another piece, entitled "Adam and Eve/Mousetrap" (1995), likens the computer mouse to the vulture, strapping the mythological figures, Adam and Eve, our figures of the origins of gender and sexuality, to a tree (Figure 4). The mouse replaces the snake in the garden of Eden, wounding the bodies of original sin. With Japanese script in the painting, the world wide web is made to seem more like the world-wide carnage of the body, but particularly the gendered, sexualized body. The blank, bloodied computer screen hanging darkly as a fruit of the tree, is, perhaps, the apple. In other words, transnational, virtual systems strike at the very origins of the bipolar organization of gender and sex.

Together, Tadiar's article and Teraoka's paintings visualize the body as a transnational zone composed by a heterosexualized version of the body as a transnational zone composed by a heterosexualized version of its elements. "Trans" remains outside the body of stable gender, preying upon it, or using it to embody the sexualization of nations. The heterosexualized body differs in its effect from the trans-gendered body, in which the "trans" lies deep in the hormonal structuring, with virtual or cyber deterritorialization both within the body and the body within it. Using the trope of heterosexual relations, the transnational zone is organized through licit or illicit relations across the bipolar gender divide. If this is so, then what of its counterpart – the organization of transnational territories through representations of the homosexual?

Figure 3   Masami Teraoka, *Eve with Three Blind Mice*

Figure 4 Masami Teraoka, *Adam and Eve/Mousetrap*

Figures of homosexuality in the transnational zone

In a dissertation on Taiwanese Lesbian Identities, Yengning Chao describes how the formation of lesbian identities was intricately interwoven with the building of a Taiwanese national identity. Taiwan was set up to create a new China, one that would distinguish itself from the "other" China – the communist China. Chao establishes

Taiwanese identity as inventing itself within colonial occupations, from its status as an early colony of Japan to the place where Chiang Kai-Shek set up his exiled government, noting that Chinese culture, since the 19th century, has "been a product of transnational negotiations" (14).

Homosexual identities were made to play a dangerous role within these national conflicts. In 1947, the troubles between the various factions brought the imposition of Martial Law, which remained in effect until 1987. The Bureau of Journalism censored the media, while public gatherings were curtailed. Chao contends that lesbian identity could not be fully formed until the lifting of Martial Law, for in the anti-communist era overt gender crossing, associated with homosexual activity, fell into the category of "anti-social acts" (39). "Tomboys" were recognized as "Communist spies" (fei–tieh) by the police and mass media (39). Chao recounts a complex incident in which a woman wearing drag was arrested on the charge of treason. In other words, lesbian sexuality, accompanied by a transgender identification was considered "communist" – the bad binary opposite to the new Taiwanese identity.

Conversely, Katrin Sieg, writing about "Sexual Subjects of the Cold War" traces the construction of the notion of homosexuality between the divided Germanies: along the socialist/capitalist wall. Sieg notes that an early communist acceptance of "free love," including homosexual love, in 1879, changed to its condemnation by the German Communist Party (KPD). Within the identity formation of the German Democratic Republic, homosexuality was denounced as a "symptom of the degeneration of the fascist bourgeoisie" (Stümke, qtd. in Sieg, 93). Thus, the gay and lesbian struggle for visibility and representation in the GDR was considered unfaithful to the socialist state – a form of treason.

In both of these examples, we can see how homosexuality was made to play a role in national identity formation along the binary of communism and capitalism. Ironically, it was considered treasonous within Taiwanese democracy as well as within communist East Germany. The borders of national identity shored themselves up through the abhorrence of illicit homosexual identities that crossed gender, when walls of state were being erected through binary opposites.

Now, if once trans-gender identification lent itself to the melodrama of the Cold War, Chao goes on to illustrate how, in today's Taiwan, such identification may be considered part of a progressive, liberatory process associated with democratisation. The emerging homosexual identity is not constructed as "lesbian," but rather, as a version of "butch-femme" role playing, that is, through the masquerade of the production of gender. At present, Chao identifies the terms "T" and "P'o" as representing the two lesbian sexual identities as performative (17). "T" originally derives from the English word "tomboy," a word gay men used in gay bars to refer to masculine-dressed lesbians and "P'o" literally means "wife," understood, within U.S. discourse, as "femme." Moreover, contemporary T-bars are located within urban environments, often with Karaoke and TV screens in the bars (58). Thus, the origin of the term "T" is transnational, in its referent to the English "tomboy," while the bars, the performative sites for that identification, are also the site of the importation of several screens, from the Japanese Karaoke, to the TV window on the world. The liberatory identification is composed through a conjunction of national histories and transnational contacts.

Similarly, Took Took Thongthiraj finds that in Thailand, emerging homosexual identities are also not formed through any referent to "lesbian," but through what is called the "tom and dy scene" which is analogous to butch-femme (46). In both Taiwan and Thailand, then, we can observe the spread and resistance to the U.S. discourse for homosexual issues across nations. The transnational nature of the discourse of homosexual visibility is received as both liberatory and as a mark of U.S. cultural imperialism. This is a complex system of assimilation and resistance, in which sexual practices and gender identifications are put to use in the formation of national identities and profiles of the "citizen."

We might find a representation of this paradigm in the play *M. Butterfly*, by David Henry Hwang. Hwang navigates the space between French colonizing forces and the Chinese Cultural Revolution through a homosexual relationship, in which a cross-dressed Chinese man seduces a member of the French consulate. Hwang is clear in his play that the East is feminized in relation to the masculinized Western colonial forces. China is a woman, even as a cross-dressed woman, in the imaginary of the West, and the West's masculinity depends upon the masquerade for its power. But the portrait is even more complex. In Hwang's play, later made into a film, a Chinese man in drag stands in front of the Cultural Revolution, which sought to equalize gender roles. He plays the hyper-feminine woman to the colonial forces obscuring, or upstaging the experiment in gender equality that accompanied the cultural revolution.

Moreover, this cross-dressed man represents the allure of traditional and imported forms of performance, from Chinese opera to *Madame Butterfly*. When the French consul stumbles in to one of those performances sanctioned by the cultural revolution, he is revolted to see a "real" woman on the stage, displacing the transgender casting of traditional Beijing Opera. This revolutionary female subject of the cultural revolution fails to offer the colonial consul the seductive promise of more traditional Chinese inequities of power. Traditional gender and performance practices are made to appear more sympathetic than the revolutionary experiments. The character of Comrade Chin – a woman dressed in gender-neutral Mao fashion, constitutes the antagonist to this cross-dressed Beijing Opera performer in a dress. The communist Chinese woman, Comrade Chin, appears as masculinized, unsympathetic, cruel, and, as desexualized, dull.

Homosexuality is portrayed here as associated with the colonial and the decadent – with the West. By now, this is a familiar trope (that homosexuality is not an indigenous practice outside of the European context), but here this trope serves a complex interest. The international zone, even if colonial, is narrativized as more seductive than the national, communist one of the cultural revolution. Further, homosexual relations are made to reinforce traditional gender roles, set up against more progressive roles for women in the social sphere. Gender and sexuality are organized as the alluring interface with a transnational identification.

Thus, while celebrating the liberatory uses of new homosexual identifications, we may also wonder if they can be made to serve the formation of new transnational zones. They may be used to further cultural imperialism, as illustrated in the examples of discourses of emancipation derived from the US. They may also be used to promote a sense that a seductive, alluring assimilation of traditional gender roles can organize a new form of identification that resists local movements for change and identifies instead with a new so-called community of transnational interests.

Nevertheless, these same homosexual identifications may serve to alienate one from nationalist projects aimed at forming around strictly heteronormative values, as in the cultural climate organized by the Bush administration in the US. For example, in 2002, there is a drive to make welfare funds available only to married individuals. While other countries, such as Sweden, recognize homosexual unions, they may also find ways to organize the relationship between homosexuality and citizenship as a basis for the production of the normative middle-class.

Conclusion

Using strategies derived from the production and analysis of performance, I have proposed several examples to illustrate how new technologies and transnational interests are being received and promoted in the system of representation. Science fiction tropes can be understood as both masking and revealing our anxieties and understandings of new technological and employment practices. However, primary among the elements forming the new cultural imaginary, are those which organize the tension between representations of the body and virtual spaces. The cyborgean interface requires the adaptation of several discourses surrounding the body to be deployed toward soliciting identificatory processes within digital compositions. I have proposed that the discourses of gender and technology now construct the interface between people and these new spaces. Sexualizing and genderizing effects may produce a creative, even playful space where identifications may be explored. In this paper, the discourse of gender solicits identifications through two forms: transgender identification through the Brandon website and bipolar, normative gender production in new transnational territories, even if produced through homosexual unions. The Brandon website is a magnet site for the performance of transgender identification. It also offers a forum for testing the formation of civil and legal procedures through such identifications. In this way, the website presents a liberatory, playful space that can invite the performance of de-regulated gender crossings. Conversely, the bipolar gender effect that accompanies normative gender regimes, is seen to mark transnational incursions into national traditions, displacing the effect of the local with a new, transcendent, immaterial zone.

The discourse of sexuality takes two forms here: the heteronormative and the homosexual. As licit and illicit, the heteronormative paradigm can be used to transport economic alliances between nations that, in the end, produce a new territory defined solely by the movement of capital. The emergence of a homosexual discourse has been treated variously in different projects toward organizing a national identity. Used punitively in the era of the Cold War, a homosexual identification was seen as treasonous. Today, a new liberatory visibility may be gained through gender masquerade, while at the same time, serving the cause of cultural imperialism.

It is a very complex world wide web of associations that encourages a new global economic fantasy as sexual. Yet the critiques we have at hand do not intertwine these elements. Within the movement and theory of alternative sexualities, the study of transnational capital has not become part of the critique. Likewise, in postcolonial and transnational critiques, heterosexuality and tropes of the family unit are often presumed, with little sense of transgender identifications, or sexual practices outside the heteronormative ones.

Given these conditions of representation and deterritorialization, I would argue that only through a combination of the sexual critique and the transnational can we begin to perceive just how this new global fantasy is being constructed. The World Wide Web is a concept used to seduce nations into transnational cooperation with the First World as well as an internet composition. Through the above analysis, we can see how the address, WWW, creates an electronic universe that mirrors the imaginary of the transnational one. We are able to operate on the web because of the cultural imaginary already formed across various media and business transactions. Corporate in structure, the WWW offers representations of personal and social relations that encourage identificatory processes on the part of the user. Most of the figures of the web simply reproduce stereotypical notions of gender and sexuality to seduce users into collusion with transnational capital through these identificatory modes. The conflation of commodity fetishism with the codes of gender and sexuality promote a subject/object status for the web figures that seems familiar and available for the users. Elsewhere, I have argued that these are actually interfetish relations, posing as identificatory ones within web uses of the avatar. In fact, the WWW could be perceived as an animation of logos, who are portrayed as gendered and sexual in order to seduce users into interacting with them. Still, some uses of the web continue to trace alternative spaces. The question remains, how will people be able to imagine an alternative to the status quo, given the prevalence and persistence of the corporate imaginary.

Notes

1. These citations are from an unpublished MS. See 'Works cited' section below.
2. Today, the Brandon website has been archived in an altered form.
3. Term used for underground Comics.

4. "Kindness" is a send-up of Blanche's line from *A Streetcar Named Desire*: "I've always depended on the kindness of strangers." It is a campy line, very familiar in some circles.

5. I must say now that Tadiar's article was written before what is known as the "Asian financial crisis."

Works cited

Bornstein, Kate. "Virtually Yours." In *O Solo Homo,* ed. Holly Hughes and David Román (New York: Grove Press, 1998), pp. 229–78.

Case, Sue-Ellen. "Digital Divas: Sex and Gender in Cyberspace." *Critical Theory and Performance*. Revised edition, ed. Janelle Reinelt and Joseph Roach (Ann Arbor: University of Michigan Press, 2007), pp. 547–6.

Chao, Antonia. "Embodying the Invisible: Body Politics in Constructing Contemporary Taiwanese Lesbian Identities." Dissertation, Cornell University, 1996.

Jones, Jordy. Unpublished talk. University of California, Davis, 1996.

Samaras, Connie. "Is It Tomorrow or Just the End of Time." *Processed Lives: Gender and Technology in Everyday Life*. Eds Jennifer Terry and Melodie Calvert (London: Routledge, 1997), 200–13.

Sieg, Katrin. "Deviance and Dissidence: Sexual Subjects of the Cold War." *Cruising the Performative: Interventions into the Representation of Ethnicity, Nationality and Sexuality*. Eds Sue-Ellen Case, Philip Brett and Susan Leigh Foster (Bloomington and Indianapolis: Indiana University Press, 1995), 93–109.

Split Britches. *Belle Reprieve. Split Britches: Lesbian Practice/Feminist Performance*. Ed. Sue-Ellen Case (New York and London: Routledge, 1996), 149–83.

Stryker, Susan. "Christine Jorgensen's Atom Bomb." Unpublished ms. This manuscript was later published in an altered form in *Playing Dolly*, ed. E. Ann Kaplan and Susan Squier (New Brunswick: Rutgers University Press, 1999), pp. 157–71.

Tadiar, Neferti Xina M. "Sexual Economies in the Asia-Pacific Community." *What is in a Rim?* Ed. Arif Dirlik (Boulder: Westview Press, 1993), 183–210.

Teraoka, Masami. *Paintings by Masami Teraoka* (Washington, DC: Smithsonian Institution, 1996).

Thongthiraj, Took Took. "Toward a Struggle Against Invisibility: Love Between Women in Thailand." *Amerasia Journal* 20.1 (1994): 45–58.

Yoshimoto, Mitsuhiro. "Real Virtuality." *Global/Local*. Eds Rob Wilson and Wimal Dissanayake (Durham and London: Duke University Press, 1996), 107–18.

11

Dracula's Daughters: In-Corporating Avatars in Cyberspace

In *Dracula's Legacy* (*Draculas Vermächtnis*), Friedrich Kittler wittily deploys the elements in Bram Stoker's *Dracula* to image the new relations between women and technology.[1] For Kittler, *Dracula* illustrates the anxieties, possibilities, and repressive strategies that accompany women's emerging role in the use of new technologies. Two characters represent a simple bifurcation of women's roles: Mina Murray, who knows stenography and the ways of the typewriter, and her friend Lucy Westenra, who is bitten by the vampire and thus confined by doctors and other men, who scrutinize her "hysterical" behavior.

Mina Murray figures the secretaries who will transcribe patriarchal discourse throughout much of the century, transforming the individual writing or speaking of men into an objective script that can bind together the transactions of business and nation.[2] She will enter the office, the work force, as an adjunct of men, in an unequal relation to their labor, social standing, and salary. Mina will operate what Kittler, in a German agglutinate, terms the "discoursemachineweapon" (*Diskursmaschinengewehr*), the Remington typewriter, developed and capitalized by the company that made weapons for the Civil War (29). In the later twentieth century, Mina would represent not only the women at the keyboard, but also those women in Third World Special Economic Zones whose labor on the machine produces its internal parts. They produce the "discourse machine" that bears the load of First World software designers, who are, for the most part, men.[3] In sum, Mina signifies the gendered production of uneven power between men and women in the new techno-economy. While women enable the transmission of the discourse, they do not create it.

Meanwhile, back in the bedroom, Lucy Westenra has been suffering, or enjoying, nightly visits from Count Dracula. Her perforated body, exhibiting the tracks of his bites, along with her wanderings, "delusions," and illicit lust bring her under the scrutiny of doctors and other "rational" men. They attempt to confine her to the bed, or the divan, where she will serve as the object of psychoanalytic "truths" of the time concerning hysteria.[4] The rational men huddle around her body, which is clothed in a revealing and suggestive peignoir. Her misbehaving, induced by illicit penetration, provides a rationale for the men to murder the "foreign" Count Dracula.[5] Although it is important to bind these two roles together in order to fully understand how women have been situated in the world of emerging technologies, it is Lucy's role that I would like to develop here as the precursor of the construction of the sign "woman," within the new technologies. Her perforated body signifies the drive toward increasing interactive relations between machinic devices and corporeality. She represents how images of women's bodies are put to the uses of virtual penetration.

Between the user and the various machines of communication, analysis, and production, the screen stages their interactivity through images that have historically represented notions of identity, desire, and anxiety.[6] Software design enables the play of images as functions of interactivity (the GUI, or Graphical User Interface). In order to do so, it necessarily borrows from the lexicon of familiar signs to represent the user and his or her actions in the cybersphere. As the user finds her/himself more and more imbricated in the web of new technologies, an increasing need for some sign of location, or identity, is needed to locate her/his functions. The sign for "woman" serves to manage this interaction, lending appeal and allure to the functions. As Kittler reminds us, this woman was first perceived as that sexy stenotypist, who first replicated men's discourse on the machine. Soon, her image began to be produced within the cultural imaginary to figure the interactive functions with machines as both seductive and threatening. She appeared as a robot in films like *Metropolis*, or *The Stepford Wives*, which narrativized how her seductive qualities still required disciplining by the men she would serve. The sign system was up and running in its traditional semiotic production of the sign "woman," but still required new management of her referents. "Woman" was securely in the machine, but her referents were not yet fully absorbed by the new synergies of scientific, corporate, and social technologies.[7] "Woman" would need to exit, completely, her referents to the "real" world in order to successfully marry into cybersociety.

A variety of performance practices stage these relations between gender codes and the virtual spaces of new media. I have selected a few examples that trace a trajectory of signification, from the staging of the sign for woman and machine as a corporeal encounter, to the screening of the completely virtualized avatar of gender. Hopefully, these few examples can function as signposts of semiotic switching between the machinic and the social. As we will see, the referents of gender coding undergo a complete alteration as the corporate virtual composes its new cyberspace.

Virtually Yours

The title of Kate Bornstein's performance piece, *Virtually Yours*, wittily captures the inscription of ownership and desire in relations with the virtual.[8] Discovered in the light of her computer screen, Bornstein narrates how she, a transgendered male–to–female lesbian, is struggling with her girlfriend's decision to become a female-to-male heterosexual (see Figure 5). Bornstein processes how her girlfriend's impending sex reassignment surgery confuses her own identity, based upon gendered sexual practices. She listens to a phone message from her girl-soon-to-be-boy-friend, telling her that she should play the new computer game *Virtually Yours*. Thus, Bornstein's body, already perforated by medical technologies as a reconstructed sex, sits before the terminal, where she will play the game of identity, prompted by the voice on an answering machine. The (stored) object of Bornstein's desire catalyzes her search for a locational identity in the new virtual space.

The telephone, after all, was the first instrument of virtual interaction to really penetrate domestic spaces. In "The Telephone and its Queerness," Ellis Hanson considers various erotic uses of the telephone, insisting that phone communication is "a mechanism of fantasy and pleasure," a site of perversions, and erotic behaviors, from the private cooing of couples, to the completely commercialized performance of phone sex (37). Hanson insists that through the telephone, "desire makes brazen its age-old love affair with capital," where these phone-borgs are "chips in the integrated circuit," which confuse "the conventional distinctions between human and machine, desire and commerce" (35). In Bornstein's piece, the phone messages are played on the answering machine, which, like the computer, was

Figure 5 Kate Bornstein, *Virtually Yours*; photograph credit: Dona McAdams

designed to store data. The phone voice, then, is the site of both the object of desire and the anxiety of being "cut-off." The lover is already a virtual one, whose absent body is being perforated by surgical operations and hormonal injections.

Following her girlfriend's advice, and in hopes of assuaging her grief and anxiety, Bornstein engages with the computer game, which promises to act as a kind of cybertherapist. She relates and performs scenarios of desire as her input into the game and, simultaneously, as her "live" performance. She entices her audience to interact with one of her s/m rituals, which once offered her both erotic pleasure and an identification that placed her in proximity to her lover. As her scenarios increasingly complicate the relations among identification, sexual practice, desire, and loss, the game becomes unable to sort out the symptoms. Unlike Lucy's rational doctors, who could restrain her through analysis and cure the symptom by killing the count, the cybertherapist ultimately suffers a breakdown of its own identity, asking: "Who am I, when you don't play the game?"

In one sense, Bornstein performs the triumph of the bodily regime, something she also displays through her revealing costumes and seductive play with the audience. Although she performs her location as somewhere between medical technologies and two virtual systems, the "live/corporeal" performer still runs the show. In effect, Bornstein "channels" technology, rather than the reverse. In the terms of s/m, she "tops" the process of interactivity, suggesting that the corporeal representation of identificatory processes is still too complex to be entirely situated within virtual technologies. The "live" still animates the technological, even though it suffers loss and confusion in the process. Yet, to stress only her triumph over loss would not do service to the delicate balance Bornstein's piece achieves. She is, quite literally, as well as figuratively, illuminated by the computer screen – the postmodern Lucy – perforated, but not perishing from it.

While Bornstein performs the corporeal/virtual splits, uses of "woman" appear within cyberspace, made to signify its own processes. In the simplest form, "women" appear as avatars on the computer screen. For those less familiar with online activity, avatars are images on the screen that seem to represent the user. Often, avatars can be selected at a particular website, where a variety of images are stored. The more practiced user might create her own avatar, using a photo, a photomontage, or a cartoon character as her representative on the screen. Some avatars can even perform limited movements, while others remain stationary, but nearly all can be moved around the space of the screen, in varying degrees of proximity to other avatars. Users may imagine their own participation within cybersocieties in the form of these avatars.

The term "avatar" is borrowed from Hindu texts, becoming generally familiar through the text of the *Bhagavad-Gita* – the first epic story of avatars (Parrinder 19). In Sanskrit, the term means descent, or a "downcoming." Etymologically, the term *Avatara* is formed by the verb *tri*, meaning to cross over, or save, with the prefix *ava*, which means down. Hindu theological discussions of the term raised similar issues around the appearance of avatars to those that surround the uses of cyber-avatars today. For example, the eighth-century philosopher Sankara raised the problem of dualism in the notion of the avatar. Sankara argues that if Brahma is only One, how can he be two – both Brahma and his incarnation, or avatar? Sankara solved this seeming contradiction by insisting that the manifestation of the god is not a "real" incarnation, but merely another image within *Maya* – the veil of illusion (50). The online avatar raises a similar question: is the online avatar a mask of a "real" user, whose "presence" is, somehow, acting online, or is it simply a part of a complete simulation – merely another empty cipher in the veil of cyber-maya?

Jennifer Gonzalez, in her article "The Appended Subject," offers a useful mediating definition of the avatar, situating it somewhere in between a cyborg, an amalgamation of the corporeal and the virtual, and a complete substitution. Gonzalez summarizes the general understanding of the avatar as "an object constituted by electronic elements serving as a psychic or bodily appendage, an artificial subjectivity that is attached to a supposed original or unitary being, an online persona understood as somehow appended to a real person who resides elsewhere, in front of a keyboard" (27–8). Applying this definition, the avatar offers an identificatory fantasy of appearance, constructed with elements of fashions in the corporeal world: industrial logos, Japanese *anime*, MTV, and Comix. Yet no code is more crucial in configuring the avatar than that of gender. As avatars represent the user in online chat rooms, the appearance of gender often determines with whom and how the players will chat. Note that the operating definition of the avatar still seems to be in relation to the user. Before moving away from that traditional understanding, a consideration of an actual online performance might aid in understanding how avatars function in cybersociety.

waitingforgodot.com

From the many possible uses of the avatar, I have selected an online performance entitled *waitingforgodot.com* for several reasons: first, for its familiarity of reference to those who study performance; second, because it represents an actual online performance piece; and finally, because it is designed to stage some of the issues crucial to this study. *Waitingforgodot.com* premièred at the Third Annual Digital

Storytelling Festival in Colorado in September 1997. It was created by Lisa Brenneis and Adriene Jenik. The performance takes place in a chat room at a site called The Palace.[9] In this space, where avatars roam and users seek chat-mates, two roundheads appear, reciting their version of some of the most familiar lines from Beckett's play. They do not announce their performance as such, but, as cyber-street theater, they simply perform in a public space. In fact, *waitingforgodot.com* could be perceived as a new kind of street theater in the cybersphere, erupting in social spaces where people pass through, or hang out. It offers a witty commentary on people hanging around in chat rooms with nothing to do or say and nowhere to go. However, as we will see, avatars resemble people, but do not necessarily represent them.

In Beckett's play, the tramps represent a minimalist, existential version of Everyman. Beckett's characters are literally Every*men*, in a world of men, retaining stable gender referents in his play.[10] In contrast, *waitingforgodot.com* deploys images derived from *pacman* video games and happy-face logos, which seem to suggest unmarked characters. They bear no markings of gender, or "race." Everyperson, then, or better, "Everysignifier," is a cartoon image, which was developed by the computer game industry and corporate ads to signify as neutral and happy. The two floating heads are literally severed from referents to corporeal existence. Their unmarked status is part of the strategy of this performance. As is evident in the accompanying illustration (Figure 6), the "performers" are quite unlike the other avatars in the chat space. "PalacePrincess" offers a scantily-clad female figure without a head, while "HedgeWitch" and "Jen" portray young, hip, seductive fashions. Those choosing to appear as male offer more Punk or Gothic versions of "self," identified as "BloodyRazors" and "ClanWolf." They are fully clothed, signaling masculinity through their bold looks out to the screen, or the tough violence suggested by their names. Interestingly, in this example, the masculinized avatars are composed of photos, while the feminized ones are cartoon-type characters. It is important to remember that this illustration represents an accidental grouping, merely archiving a moment in a chat room. The avatars, then, reveal a characteristic array of hyper-gendered features in their composition.

If we identify the roundheads in *waitingforgodot.com* as performers, what does their status imply about the nature of avatars in general? Are the other avatars in the chat room also performing? Do all avatars function like masks, or only when the user intends to perform? To understand the avatars as masks would agree with the received notion

Figure 6 waitingforgodot.com, © Adriene Jenik and Lisa Brenneis; digital capture by Adriene Jenik

that they function as identificatory images for the user. Two sets of problems militate against this interpretation. The first has to do with traditional assumptions about the nature of masking and the second with the nature of the online conventions of representation. First, the definition of character and mask depends on the opposite term of actor, or the indication of some "presence" behind the mask. Indeed, the sense of a subject as constituted before representation is what Judith Butler nominates as performance, against her concept of performativity.[11] Lurking behind the mask and the character is the "actual presence" that has somehow been altered, or represented by the mask. In other words, the mask depends upon some notion of the "real," or the "natural" for its function. Nietzsche, in his study of the classical Greek mask in *The Birth of Tragedy*, offers a hyper-image of the relation of the mask to the essential that emphasizes these qualities: "The Sophoclean hero – the Apolline mask[s] . . . are the inevitable products of a glance into the terrible depths of nature: light patches, we might say, to heal the gaze seared by terrible night" (46). For Nietzsche, as for the Hindu scholar Sankara, the notion of mask and avatar borders on incarnation – the idea that a god, or some figure of ideality, is corporealized in the process of making theater (51). In the cybersphere, the corporeal resides in the function of the user, with the avatar serving as her/his virtual mask. Either way, the sense of avatar as mask points us back to the play of essences, the necessary stipulation that there is a user, whose "real" self is altered by the avatar.

Much of the discussion about avatars does presume this relationship between avatar and user, subjecting the dynamics to a scrutiny of identificatory processes and masquerade. Utopic visions of a sphere where cross-gender identifications abound, appear alongside feminist warnings against any belief in the possibility of "free" play within the gender regime. Yet both sides would agree that the users are, somehow, performing versions of social identities and relationships in cyberspace. Anterior notions of "self," volition, or agency, and clear, stable attributes of social organization are required for the backdrop behind this theater of avatars. As I have argued more fully in my book *The Domain-Matrix*, many of these attributes are specific to an earlier form of capitalism and do not reflect the contemporary, corporate structuring of social relations.[12] Given the corporate, commercial take-over of what was once considered to be private space and discourse, the referents of the sign system no longer reside in the kind of natural environment Nietzsche and traditional studies of the avatar presume. Specifically in this study of the avatar, the signification of gender, or, as we will see, "race," has less to do with promoting an identificatory process between user and avatar than with finding a way to *promote* the avatar onscreen. In other words, avatars do not function as masks for users, but as brand names, or logos, competing in a commercial space.

Returning to those roundheads in *waitingforgodot.com*, whose function of Everysignifier is derived from computer games and corporate "happy faces," we can see how the avatar references structures of corporate branding and even the status of the technology itself. The cartoon avatar, such as a Disneyfied diva in the chat space, is drawn to resemble the private body of earlier capital relations, but, in its cartooned abstraction, signals the corporate reference at its root. The digital diva is a representation of gender codes used to articulate the interface between that anterior sense of the private and the live with new, corporate virtual systems. The diva is the hostess, so to speak, who promotes forms of interaction that seem familiar and enticing in the new cyberspace. The users who promote themselves through these avatars, such as "Jen," or "HedgeWitch," are animating the interface for themselves, seduced and seducing the users to use the new products of corporate technology.

In one sense, Mark Poster prefigured this notion in his theory of how something like a subject position appears within a database. Poster notes that when so much information about a person congeals in the data, a kind of "double" of the subject actually appears there, but that that subject is one completely interpellated, or overdetermined by dominant ideologies (97–8). I want to continue in this line of reasoning, but abandon any notion of a subject online; instead, I want to draw the relations among avatars on the screen as *interfetish object relations*. As data and functions congeal around an avatar, it acquires the seductive qualities of the fetish. Its seductive qualities serve to compete for focus with other online objects within the competitive, commercial relations of the cybersphere.

The cyber-world of inter-fetish relations is simply one of the final frontiers in the development of corporate uses of the logo. Rather than serving users as masks for their identificatory fantasies, avatars actually function as forms of logos. In her brilliant study *No Logo*, Naomi Klein offers a history of the rise of the corporate "branding" that ultimately produced the logo-centric surround of the new millennium. She notes that "the first task of branding was to bestow proper names on generic goods, such as sugar, flour, soap, and cereal. . . . Logos were tailored to evoke familiarity and folksiness" (6). Enter Uncle Ben, Aunt Jemima, and Old Grand-Dad, who substituted for rice, flour, and whiskey. As corporate branding became more sophisticated, actual people began to stand in for the logo, as well as the more cartoon characters. By now, we are accustomed to make a product association with movie stars, or sports stars, as well as talking Chihuahuas and Bart Simpson. The person-alized logos signify products, or the conglomerate behind products. Magic Johnson means Nike® and McDonald's® can extend its referent through any number of toys that resemble familiar cartoon characters. Klein further develops how logos are placed, within movies, novels, and other so-called cultural venues. Situating the logo within civic and cultural spaces spawned what the *Wall Street Journal* identified as the "experiential communication" industry; as Klein notes, "the phrase now used to encompass the staging of branded pieces of corporate performance art . . . ." (12). We now have branded hotels, theaters, theme parks, and even little villages. The brands loop back into their own worlds through synergies of entertainment and products, creating, as

Starbucks calls it, "a brand canopy" (148). Brands, then, Klein argues, "are not products but ideas, attitudes, values, and experiences . . . the lines between corporate sponsors and sponsored culture have entirely disappeared" (30).

Gendered characterizations, in particular those that are sexualized, have been promoted in this logo culture to create the logo, or in our case, the avatar as fetish. To reverse Freud's equation, the referents of sexual practices are made to serve as fetish object of product lines. Jean Kilbourne, a scholar of advertising, emphasizes that the average person in the United States is bombarded by 3,000 ads per day (*Ms. Magazine* 55). Kilbourne notes that many of these ads create what she terms a "synthetic sexuality" – one that designates a certain body type, gestural system, and fashion sense as sexy. The referent is not sex; on the contrary, sex is the referent for the product line, or more, the corporation behind various product lines. Hyper-feminized avatars, then, circulate among the other logos, competing for focus, and acting out corporate and technological relations as seductive and even as sexual. Their referent is not the user, but the corporate logos which are used to comprise the image of the avatar.

Astrid Deuber-Mankowsky has composed a sophisticated treatment of the avatar of Lara Croft, the protagonist of the computer game *Tomb Raider*, which illustrates how the sexified, powerful Lara stands in for corporate, technological success. In the narrative of the game, Lara appears as a "white," upper-class, British archaeologist off on adventures in the Third World. She is scantily clad, but tough, with weapons and martial arts in her arsenal against the Other. She is viewed from behind, suggesting that she represents, or works for, the game player. Many feminist treatments of Lara replicate the traditional focus on the user's identificatory processes, debating her subject/object status for the mostly male players, who both desire her and identify with her. Deuber-Mankowsky, however, argues that Lara Croft functions not as a character, a *Spielefigur*, but as a *Werbefigur*, an ad.[13] The composition and function of Lara serves to perform the imaging power of the 32-bit platform and the 3-D graphics card. She is the sexy diva that attests to the imaging power of the Sony Playstation®. In other words, an avatar of a heterosexualized, white woman offers a ground for the imaging of the new convergence of filmic and digital possibilities that made the game *Tomb Raider* popular. Lara represents the high level of 3-D simulation that the successful upgrading of the computer platform and graphics card allowed in the construction of the game. Her whiteness and gender work together to create an alluring and powerful image of new technologies at work in the world.

Cyber-minstrelsy

Like Lara, the majority of avatars on the net signify "whiteness," or stereotypical Anglo-American characteristics, yet there are also several uses for racial and ethnic markers in the logo-centric space. The earlier examples drawn from the initial stage of "branding," such as Uncle Ben and Aunt Jemima, present two logos based on racial stereotyping and nostalgia for the "old South." While today, the image of a "mammy," and a "house servant," may seem dated in their form of representation, Spike Lee's recent film *Bamboozled* attests to their continuing power of representation in the late twentieth century. *Bamboozled* tells the story of a TV executive who becomes successful by producing a new series called *Mantan: The New Millennium Minstrel Show*. A dancing Aunt Jemima, along with a chorus line of minstrels, helps to make the series a popular success. Lee suggests that the current enthusiasm for black performance in mass media entertainment is just another form of the minstrel show, with similar stereotypes still capable of drawing an enthusiastic audience.

Imagining that we are part of a contemporary sophisticated, urban audience, or buying public, it would seem that these antique markers of ethnicity would not produce much allure. Why would a minstrel masking of race be effective in this time of so-called multicultural social practices? The answer may lie, in part, in the kind of economic conditions that encourage such strategies of othering. In both the mid-to-late twentieth century and the mid-nineteenth century, when minstrel shows were invented, major shifts in capital investment and labor practices caused high anxiety in certain sectors of the population. In his book on minstrelsy, *Love and Theft*, Eric Lott locates the beginning of minstrel shows in the 1840s, during the depression that followed the panic of 1837 (137). According to Lott, the new consolidation of industrial capital caused high unemployment among the laboring classes. Lott argues that during industrialization, these minstrel shows, depicting "happy" slaves singing and dancing on the porch of the old cotton plantation, played out nostalgia for pre-industrial times (148). But this nostalgia for the time of the "happy old slave" did not operate through identification with the slave. Remember that minstrel shows were the product of white entertainers in the northeast, who portrayed black, slave culture in the "old South." The blacks were represented as unruly and uncivilized in their lusting after a good time. Their unruly behavior served two functions: to render the agrarian past as less structured and more fun than the new industrialized time, and to identify unruly behavior as specifically "black." Lott cites reviews of the minstrel shows that describe a "savage energy," with performers whose "white eyes [were] rolling in a curious frenzy" (140). He notes that when these performers cross-dressed as women, they portrayed the black women as enormous, gorging themselves on food and sex. In this way, Lott suggests, the minstrel shows displaced anxieties over unemployment to a performance of racial hierarchies. By encouraging racist and sexist prejudices, the enjoyment taken in the minstrel show displaced the uneasy contest among whites for low-level employment in the northeast onto contempt for blacks in the "old South." This form of working-class entertainment thus consolidated the audience, through their laughter, as "whites" (137). Further, their masculinity was shored up by the sexist rhetoric and the portrayal of heterosexual relationships as ones in which women were subordinate to men.

Many of the anxieties and solutions to the problems in the 1840s may also be identified within the current digital age. In the digital age, which arguably began in the 1980s with the invention of the internet, the "upload" of economic prowess and employment possibilities into the electronic sphere has caused similar kinds of anxieties among workers. New firms and new job descriptions are replacing old ones, while many kinds of companies and forms of employment are disappearing. Skills with new technologies and software are required for everything from job skills to personal communication, and entertainment. Economic envy and fear among white working-class sectors could be allayed by a form of entertainment that operates through stereotypes of black masculinity and white feminine allure. Sex and violence, those two markers of mass entertainment in the 1990s and onward, mask those anxieties through stereotypes that promise to initiate us into the land of the successful.

Imagining internet representation as a play of racial stereotypes, Guillermo Gómez-Peña and Roberto Sifuentes opened the online "Ethno-Cyberpunk Trading Post and Curio Shop on the Electronic Frontier." In 1994, Gómez-Peña announced that they were going to infiltrate cyberspace as "cyber-immigrants" or what Gómez-Peña calls "cyber-wetbacks." Their "Ethno-Cyberpunk" trading post traded in ethnic identities both as a gallery installation and on the internet. Avatars included "Cyber Vato," a "robo gang member," "el Postmodern Zorro" and "El Cultural Transvestite." Visitors to the website sent in images, sound, or texts about how Mexicans, Chicanos and Native Americans of the 1990s should look, behave, and perform.[14] The artists then reproduced these stereotypes to represent ethnic identities online. In other words, these artists only reproduced stereotypical notions of how Chicanos and Native Americans seem to appear, in order to compose their avatars, or the online representatives of these members of ethnic communities. Displayed within a trading post, the stereotypes are elements of exchange. Whatever seems to be a referent to ethnicity is used for its product value.

Once more, Jennifer Gonzalez offers an insight into the construction of the avatar – this time as racialized. Continuing to operate on the assumption that avatars represent identificatory fantasies, she notes that the elements of racial stereotyping seem appealing and without threat because "Race is understood not to 'matter'... in this online domain," which claims to be "outside" the economic and juridical systems. She continues, "The idea of not being oneself is intimately tied to the conditions of leisure and the activity of consumption" (45). Gonzalez concludes: "It is precisely through an experimentation with cultural and racial fusion and fragmentation, combined with a lack of attention to social process, a lack of attention to history... that a new transcendental, universal, and, above all, consuming subject is offered as the model of future cyber-citizenship" (48). Even though she proceeds from a study of the subject, Gonzalez concludes that the avatar circulates in a special economic zone of privileged consumption, unmarred by considerations of labor and legal practices.

So it seems that both in this study and in studies that imagine the avatar as a subject, racial and ethnic markers reference little else but market strategies. Yet to condemn all representations of ethnicity online would only affirm the Anglo, "white" economy of representation that controls most of the online figures, bolstering the dominant assumption that the unmarked space of representation is, indeed, "white." For an imaging of ethnicity that is funky and playful, rather than the sort deployed by corporations such as The United Colors of Benetton, we can return to another performance staged by Adriene Jenik. This time, Jenik uses the screen as a dreamscape, in which a player may narrate a dream that the others will inhabit and draw as it proceeds. The dream is called *riverofsalsa*.

Riverof Salsa

"Catwoman," coded Latina, enters the space. The space, the *mise en scène*, begins as a generic, unmarked road. "Scotty" appears in "*barrio*" wear, with a boom box. Catwoman narrates her dream, while a drawing on the screen visualizes it. The two avatars meet, a taco is suggested, then, suddenly, a river of salsa, flowing from the food, overtakes the space and the characters, immersing them (see Figure 7). Ethnicity is marked by the fashion in clothing, in the actual drawing of "Catwoman," in items such as the boom box, and in the references to a specific ethnic cuisine. Certainly, these are stereotypical images of ethnic subcultures. Perhaps they fill the formula that Gómez-Peña and Roberto Sifuentes would identify as trade in the "Ethno-Cyberpunk Trading Post."

Nevertheless, as Beth Kolko outlines in her discussion of the online site LambdaMOO, there is a "growing awareness that technology interfaces carry the power to prescribe representative norms and patterns, constructing a self-replicating and exclusionary category of 'ideal' user . . . " (318). In order to intervene in the construction of the

Figure 7   Riverofsalsa, © Adriene Jenik and Lisa Brenneis; digital capture by Adriene Jenik

ideal as "white," Kolko concludes that the user must somehow force an ethnic marking into the system by choosing a name with those specific associations, or by linguistic style, or by ethnic references (216). Kolko's work raises some key questions: how can we determine when these elements may be serving an identificatory function for the user; who does participate in the latino subculture; or when are they simply elements of ethnic fashion? Finally, would it matter whether the user who was manipulating these signs were actually within the latino subculture or not? Isn't the point to "color" the representational vocabulary of cyberspace?

Closing the window

As these examples have shown, the interrogation of how signs of gender and ethnicity operate online reveals less about the status of these codes in the "real" world than the basic change in the sign system of the cyber. As the frame of the real recedes from what are called immersive technologies, so, too, does its power as a referent. Cyberspace stages a theater of masks without actors, rendering the mask an antique form of the "live" that once presumed the taking on of social and private faces, different from one's own identity. Hyper-gendered avatars and the practice of neo-minstrelsy reveal a transitional phase, in which evocations of the "real" are still necessary to manage the new theater of logos. Gender codes are used to signify the allure and pleasure of new technological capabilities and product lines, while neo-minstrelsy masks the globalizing sameness of synergies with images of difference and diversity. The "happy face" logo/avatar registers the beginning of the transcendence of corporate representation in cyberspace, in which gender and minstrelsy will no longer be required for synergies to stage their competitive functions entirely without reference to social conditions.

However, while the residue of difference still plays in the increasingly monotone cyberworld, it may provide some small intervention into the upload of signification. Even if gender and ethnic codes serve only as fragments of identificatory processes for the ever-distant users, they might be used to signal the conditions of those who are not invited into the ranks of the privileged. Unfortunately, at this point, the sign for woman serves pretty much the same function of seductive hostess as in traditional uses, and ethnic markers seem to signal "hip," "young," and hyper-gendered users on the make. But what if users with more activist agendas began to people cyberspace with the images of the poor, the weak, and the disenfranchised? What if the body types of the avatars did not match the requirements of young, thin, toned, Anglo avahunks, or digital divas? What if they did not hang around chat rooms, but used them as sites to organize, to educate, and to radicalize? What if they could imagine the "discoursemachineweapon," as Kittler called it, as one of the most powerful tools available for intervention – turning it back onto the logos who would manage it?

What would it take to make that happen?

Notes

1. Elsewhere, I have argued for the vampire as a figure for appearance of lesbians in the system of representation. I think the work there amplifies this article's focus on gender rather than sexual practice. See "Tracking the Vampire," in *differences* 3:2 (1991): 1–20.
2. Interestingly, Bram Stoker served as secretary to the eminent actor/manager Henry Irving. The term "secretary" derives from the Latin "keeper of secrets." It had a more prestigious connotation for men in the Victorian era, when it suggested privy knowledge within the realm of public or governmental service. See *The History of the Secretarial Profession* on the official website of Professional Secretaries: www.iaap-hq.org.
3. See Grant Kestler's "Out of Sight is Out of Mind: the Imaginary Space in Postindustrial Culture," in *Social Text* 11:2 (Summer 1993): 72–92.
4. Nina Auerbach, in *Magi and Maidens: The Romance of the Victorian Freud*, notes that Bram Stoker took part in the Society for Psychical Research in 1893, where he became acquainted with the notion of female hysteria. *Critical Inquiry* 8, 290. In a chapter on "Victorian Mythmakers," Auerbach suggests that Svengali, from George DuMaurier's novel *Trilby*, inspired Stoker's Dracula. She compares an illustration of the unconscious Trilby on stage with the swooning figure of an "hysterical" woman exhibited by Charcot. *Woman and the Demon: The Life of a Victorian Myth* (Cambridge: Harvard University Press, 1982), pp. 15–34.
5. As we know, this practice persists today, with the taboo of illicit penetration providing a rationale for the murder of Matthew Shepard [a young student who was murdered in 1998, in Wyoming, because he was gay] among others.
6. I am indebted to Jeff Nyhoff for this clarification in his sophisticated, yet-unpublished work on performing the interface.
7. For a discussion of the multiple uses of the term "technology," see the introduction to *Processed Lives: Gender and Technology in Everyday Life*, eds Jennifer Terry and Melodie Calvert (London and New York: Routledge, 1997), pp. 1–19.
8. The visual elements of the performance described here are taken from a video of *Virtually Yours* performed at Josie's Juice Bar in San Francisco in 1994.
9. For a complete discussion of desktop theater, see Adriene Jenik's "Keyboard Catharsis and the Making of Roundheads," in *The Drama Review* 45.3 (Fall 2001): 95–112. To access the archived performances, go to leda.ucsd.edu/%eajenik/main/files.

10. On the point of gender, see James Knowlson's *Damned to Fame: The Life of Samuel Beckett* (New York: Simon & Schuster, 1996). "[Beckett] felt very strongly that the characters in his plays were either male or female and that their sex was not interchangeable. There were many requests, sometimes fervent personal appeals made directly to him, for women to be allowed to play the male characters in *Waiting for Godot*. Beckett (or his agents) always turned them down, though he himself showed signs of wilting several times under the intense emotional pressure that was brought to bear on him" (610).

11. See "Critically Queer." *Glq:A Journal of Lesbian and Gay Studies* 1:1 (1993): 258–308.

12. See, especially, the section entitled "Bringing Home the Meat," which traces the commodification of social relations.

13. Unfortunately, for some, Deuber-Mankowsky's monograph is in German. *Lara Croft: Modell, Medium, Cyberheldin: das virtuelle Geschlecht und seine metaphysischen Tücken* (Frankfurt: Suhrkamp, 2001).

14. For further information on this project and its attempt to "brownify" virtual space, see www.telefonica.es/fat/egomez.html.

Works cited

Bornstein, Kate, *Virtually Yours*. In *O solo homo*, ed. Holly Hughes and David Roman (New York: Grove Press, 1998), pp. 229–78.

Case, Sue-Ellen, *The Domain-Matrix: Performing Lesbian at the end of Print Culture* (Bloomington: Indiana University Press, 1996).

Gonzalez, Jennifer, "The Appended Subject: Race and Identity as Digital Assemblage." In *Race in Cyberspace*, ed. Beth E. Kolko, Lisa Nakamura and Gilbert B. Rodman (New York and London: Routledge, 2000), pp. 27–50.

Hanson, Ellis, "The Telephone and its Queerness." In *Cruising the Performative*, ed. Sue-Ellen Case, Philip Brett and Susan Leigh Foster (Bloomington: Indiana University Press, 1995), pp. 34–58.

Kittler, Friedrich, *Draculas Vermächtnis* (Leipzig: Reclam Verlag, 1993).

Klein, Naomi, *No Logo* (London: Flamingo, 2000).

Kolko, Beth, "Erasing @race: Going White in the (Inter)Face." In *Race in Cyberspace*, ed. Beth E. Kolko, Lisa Nakamura and Gilbert B. Rodman (New York and London: Routledge, 2000), pp. 213–32.

Lott, Eric, *Love and Theft: Blackface Minstrelsy and the American Working Class* (Oxford: Oxford University Press, 1993).

Ms. Magazine, December 2000/January 2001.

Nietzsche, Friedrich, *The Birth of Tragedy*, trans. Shaun Whiteside (New York: Penguin Books, 1993).

Parrinder, Edward Geoffrey, *Avatar and Incarnation* (New York: Barnes & Noble, 1970).

Poster, Mark, *The Mode of Information* (Chicago: University of Chicago Press, 1990).

Index

A Different Light   55–6
ACT UP   60–1, 108–9
acting   150–2
activism   14, 108, 123, 125
  Lysistrata   116
activist movements   1, 4, 60
addictions   22
Agamemnon   121
Aidoo, Ama Ata   127
AIDS   10, 60–1, 62, 82
  Geisha in Bath   160–1
alcoholism   20, 21
Alexander, Jacqui
  Feminist Genealogies, Colonial Legacies,
    Democratic Futures   131
Alien Resurrection   149
all-male culture   2
Allison, Dorothy
  Skin   51
  Trash   50
Althusser, Louis   31, 138
Angels in America   55
Anger, Kenneth   27
Anjaree   92
Antarctica   91
antipornography   33, 35
Anzaldúa, Gloria
  Los atravesados   125–6
Argentina
  Dirty War   129
Aryan roots   2
Asia-Pacific   159
Asian Lesbian Network   92
Aston, Elain
  Staging International Feminisms   12
Athenian culture   113
Atkinson, Ti-Grace   54
authors   50
avatars
  dualism   175

Ethno-Cyberpunk Trading Post and
    Curio Shop on the Electronic
    Frontier   183
gender coding   175
gender roles   178
gendered   185
incarnation   178
Lara Croft   180–1
object relations   179
race   178
users   178
waitingforgodot.com   176–7
white middle class   181
women   174–5
Avila, Teresa of   70

Bacchae, The   114
Bacon, Kevin
  Lysistrata Project   120
Baez, Joan
  hippie butch   28
Bakhtin, Mikhail   42
Bangkok   90
bar culture   21, 26, 40
Barbin, Herculine
  Brandon website   155
Barnes, Djuna
  Nightwood   44
Barthes, Roland   10, 90
  Empire of Signs, The   135
Baudelaire, Charles
  Femmes Damnées Delphine et
    Hippolyte   73
Baudrillard, Jean   39
  De la séduction   45–6
  Simulations   59
Because the Dawn   81
Beckett, Samuel
  Waiting for Godot   176
Bernal, Martin
  Black Athena   2

Berry, Chris
  *Mobile Cultures: New Media in Queer
    Asia* 95
bestiality 95–6
Beware a Holy Whore 78
Bingen, Hildegard von 70
black women 20
Blau, Herbert 37–8, 101
Bloch, Ernst 13, 141–2
  Utopian Function 139
Bloolips
  Belle Reprieve 136
Boal, Augusto 109, 141
body 151, 161
Boellstorff, Tom 93–4
Boone, Joseph
  homoerotics of Orientalism 90
  LGBT conference 12
Bornstein, Kate
  Hidden: A Gender 10
  Virtually Yours 153, 172, 173f5, 174
Braidotti, Rosi 126, 129
Brandon, Teena 154
Brandon website 154, 155–6, 157,
    167
Brecht, Bertolt 126, 152
Brenneis, Lisa
  waitingforgodot.com 176
Bronski, Michael 36
Bruss, Elizabeth
  *Beautiful Theories: The Spectacle of
    Discourse in Contemporary
    Criticism* 6
Bureau of Journalism 164
Bush, President George W. 140,
    142–3
butch 10, 20, 24, 28
butch-feminist 63–4
butch-femme
  camp discourse 35–6
  culture 18–19
  feminist subject 32
  Maud's 17
  mythology 26
  performance 43
  realism 46
  relations 8
  role-playing 33
  roles 41

seduction 47
subject position 39
womanliness masquerade 40
Butler, Judith 1–2, 116–17,
    177
Judy! 8

Caen, Herb 23
California 23
Cameron, Leon 11
Cammermeyer, Margarethe 29, 59
camp discourse 66, 77
camp style 4, 36–7, 46
capitalism 88
Case, Sue-Ellen
  *Domain-Matrix: Performing Lesbian at
    the End of Print Culture, The* 5,
    11, 178
  Performing Science and the Virtual
    13, 14
  Staging International Feminisms 12
  Tracking the Vampire 52–3
Castle, Terry
  Apparitional Lesbian, The 61
Cayman Islands 89
censorship 97, 143
Chao, Antonia 94
Chee, Alexander
  Queer Nation 62
Chicago, Judy 4
Chow, Rey 130–1
  Woman and Chinese Modernity 129
Christain, Barbara 49
Christian, Meg 20
Chronicle 23
Chuen-juei Ho, Josephine 95–7
Churchill, Caryl
  Top Girls 4
citizenship 143
civil disobedience 121
Cixious, Hélène
  Laugh of the Medusa 7, 105
  proximity 126
Clark, Danae
  commodity Lesbianism 57
class 31
class prejudice 35
Clinton, Hillary 128
cocaine 21

coffee houses   22
comedy   55
commodity fetishism   12, 21, 57,
   102, 168
communes   23
communism   11
corporate branding   178, 179–80
counterculture   4
critiques   12
cross-gender identification   66
cultural resources   55–6
culture   12, 131
cyber-Brandon   154, 155, 156
cyber-world   179
cyberspace   185

Daly, Mary
   GynEcology   105
Daly, Tyne   91
dancing   24
Daughters of Bilitis (DOB)   21, 33–4
Daughters of Darkness   81
Davis, Angela   18
Davis, Madeline
   Boots of Leather, Slippers of Gold:
      The History of a Lesbian
      Community   8
Dawn of the Dead   82
Day of the Dead   82
Deavere Smith, Anna
   Brandon's Virtual Court System
      157
Derrida, Jacques   42
   Grammatology   7
desire   70
Deuber-Mankowsky, Astrid   180–1
DeVeaux, Alexis   82
Diamond, Elin   101, 111
Diamond, Liz
   Brandon's Virtual Court System
      157
Dirlik, Arif   86–7
discourse of blood   71
Doane, Mary Ann   39
   Film and the Masquerade: Theorising
      the Female Spectator   41–2
   Woman   76
Dolan, Jill   33, 141, 143
   Feminist Spectator as Critic   102–3

dominant culture   43
drag kings   11
Drama Review, The   6
drug abuse   20, 21
Duncan, Nancy
   BodySpace   107
Duras, Marguerite
   India Song   127

Echols, Alice   33
Eco, Umberto
   Semiotics of Theatrical
      Performance   6
ecofeminism   14
ecology   91
El Ramly, Lenin
   Peace of Women, The   122–3
Elam, Keir
   Semiotics of Theatre and Drama,
      The   6
embodied knowledge   101
Eng-Beng Lim
   Glocalqueering in New Asia   92
Engels, Friedrich
   Holy Family, The   119
erotic spectatorship   78
Etheridge, Melissa   91
Ethnic Studies   103
ethnicity   181, 184, 185
European history   117–18
Evans, David
   Sexual Citizenship   143
Expressionists   152, 153

Fag Rag   36–7
Fassbinder, Rainer Werner
   Querelle   77
female masculinity   26
female subject   32
female-to-male transsexuals   10
feminism
   Alienation Effect   126
   butch-femme   39
   Chicana movement   130
   cloning   23, 25
   coalitions of women   26
   communism   11
   critical theory   5–6, 7, 31
   culture   131

discourse 49
embodied knowledge 101
equality 25
futures 133
historians 133
homophobia 34–5
interest in women 24
international 126
Lauretis, Teresa de 31–2
lesbians 33
nation-state 143–4
performance 125
personal as political 137
political change 32
politics 53–4
proximity 80
rejects lesbian subculture 8
research 125
scholars 101, 105, 111
sexuality studies 12
substance abuse 21
theatre 105
theatre studies 102
time 13
transnational 5
white middle class 35
feminist theory
heterosexual 42–3, 67
lesbian position 9
universal man 3
woman 78
feminists 129
femmes 20, 24, 41–2
Féral, Josette 141
Fernández, Charles
Undocumented Aliens in the Queer
Nation 62
film studies 7
Finley, Karen 107
flirtation 24
flower children 24
Foley, Helene 121
Females Acts in Greek Tragedy
114–15
Fornes, Irene
Mud 46
Foster, Jody
Contact 149

Foster, Susan Leigh see Leigh Foster,
Susan
Foucault, M. 31
France 6
Freeman, Carla 87
Freud, Sigmund 79–80, 135, 136
Futurists 152

Galapagos Islands 91
gallantry 24
Gallop, Jane
Daughter's Seduction: Feminism and
Psychoanalysis, The 7
Thinking Through the Body 75
Gandersheim, Hrotsvitha von 70
gang rape 27
Garland, Jack
Brandon website 155
gay male 9, 52, 54, 63, 67–8
gay politics 38
Gay Pride 57, 58
gender
biological body 154
ethnicity 125
local 87
new technologies 167, 185
performance 166
reassignment 152
representation 113
transnational identity 166
gender coding 134, 175, 178–9, 185
gender identification 10, 34
gender politics 131
gender-reassignment 10
gender roles 114, 116, 158
Genet, Jean
Blacks, The 37
Screens, The 37
ghetto 78
ghetto nature 22
Gide, André 90
Gilbert, Helen
Post-colonial Drama: Theory, Practice,
Politics 118
Ginsburg, Allen 29
Girl Scout counselors 19
global 87
global discourse 87
Global Feminist Workshop 126

globalization
  capitalism 58
  commodity marketing 131
  dynamics 5
  gender roles 87
  new technologies 11, 13
  sex 95
  transnational flows 86
"glocalization" 94–5
Golden Age 71
Gómez-Peña, Guillermo
  Ethno-Cyberpunk Trading Post and
    Curio Shop on the Electronic
    Frontier 182–3
Gonzalez, Jennifer 183
  Appended Subject, The 175
Grace, Delia
  Lagrace Volcano, Del 10
Grahn, Judy 20
Grosz, Elizabeth
  Volatile Bodies 107
Gulf War 112

Hair 106
Halberstam, Judith ("Jack")
  Female Masculinity 10
Hammer, Barbara 20, 25, 27
Hanson, Ellis
  Telephone and its Queerness,
    The 172
Haraway, Donna 3, 10, 13
Hardt, Michael
  Empire 86
Harris, Bertha 50, 51
Harvard Law School
  Brandon's Virtual Court System
    157
Harvey, David 86
Hawaii 91
Hayles, Katherine 13
Heaven's Gate 150
Henley, Beth
  Crimes of the Heart 46
heteronomous position 31
heterosexism 68
heterosexual relations 161
heterosexuality 131, 159
Highway, Tomson
  Rez Sisters, The 126–7

hippie butch 28
hippie dykes 17–18, 26
hippie neo-butches 18
hippies 20, 23, 25, 29, 30
history 3, 54
Hitler, Adolf
  Mein Kampf 71–2
Hoffman, Abbie
  Free Speech Movement 103
Hollibaugh, Amber 35
Holst-Warhaft, Gail
  *Dangerous Voices: Women's Laments and
    Greek Literature* 111
homophobia 27, 33, 37
homosexual lifestyle 32
homosexual sex 69
homosexuality
  discourses 52
  German Democratic Republic
    (GDR) 164
  Germany 164
  identity 167–8
  performance 166
  semiosis 135
  Thailand 165
  transnational zone 163
homosexuals 69
Hooks, Bell 126
Huerta, Dolores 91
Hughes, Holly 139–41
Hwang, David Henry
  Golden Child 129–30
  M. Butterfly 165–6

identity 94, 128, 172
ideology 32
individuals
  Queer Nation 62
Indonesia
  Lesbian and Gay Congress 92
International Conference for Women
  (Beijing, 1995) 128
International Feminist Working
  Group
  International Federation of Theatre
    Research 12
internet 95, 96
  Lysistrata Project 122

invisibility   8
Iraq war   120
Irigary, Lucy   126

Jacobs, Katrien   97
James, Henry   10
Jameson, Frederic   86
Japan   159
   Occur   92
Jelinek, Elfriede
   Illness or Modern Women   142
Jenik, Adriene
   riverofsalsa   183–4
   waitingforgodot.com   176
John of the Cross   71
   Dark Night of the Soul, The   70
   Living Flame of Love   70
   Spiritual Canticle, The   70–1
Johnson Reagon, Bernice   59
Jones, Jordy   156–7
   Injectable Man   153
Joplin, Janice   19, 28
Jorgensen, Christine   153
Joseph, Miranda
   Queer Globalizations   87–8
Journal of Consumer Marketing   56
Judy!
   Butler, Judith   8
Jung Soon Shim   12

Kabuki theatre   160
Kane, Sarah   13
   4:48 Psychosis   138–41
Karge, Manfred
   Medea   119
Kennedy, Elizabeth Lapovsky *see*
   Lapovsky Kennedy, Elizabeth
Key West, Florida   91
Kilbourne, Jean   180
King, Katie   93
Kittler, Friedrich   186
   Dracula's Legacy   13, 170–1
Klein, Naomi
   No Logo   179–80
knowledge   102
Kolko, Beth
   LambdaMOO   184–5

Kollentai, Alexandra   128
   *Sexual Relations and the Class
      Struggle*   125
Kotzamani, Marina
   Lysistrata   122

La Malinche   130
Lacan, Jacques   6, 7, 135, 158
   Seminar XI   7
Lacy, Suzanne   105
Lagrace Volcano, Del   10–11
Lakich, Lili   20
laments   111–15, 120
Langhoff, Matthias
   Medea   119
Lapovsky Kennedy, Elizabeth
   *Boots of Leather, Slippers of Gold:
      The History of a Lesbian
      Community*   8
*Last Call at Maud's/The Maud's
   Project*   17
Lauretis, Teresa de   8
   *Alice Doesn't: Feminism, Semiotics,
      Cinema*   7, 134
   Queer Theory: Lesbian and Gay
      Sexualities   52
   Sexual Indifference and Lesbian
      Representation   9, 68
   Technology of Gender, The   31
Le Fanu, Sheridan
   Carmilla   72
Lee, Spike
   Bamboozled   181
Leigh Foster, Susan   108
lesbian
   feminist movement   27,
      67–8
   history   52
   identification   24
   identities   131, 163–4
   life   4
   relationships   26, 128
   representation   68
   scene   17
   sexuality   76, 164
   space   22
   theory   3
   voice   3
   work   5

Lesbian and Gay Congress   92
lesbians   20–1, 33–4, 52–3
lesbians and gay men   57, 89
LGBT (Lesbian, Gay, Bisexual and
    Transgender)
    conference   8, 12
Libation Bearers, The   113
Living Theatre
    Paradise Now   106
logo culture   180
Lorde, Audre   22, 105
Lori-Parks, Suzan
    Venus   107
Lott, Eric
    Love and Theft   181–2
Lyon, Phyllis
    Lesbian/Woman   33–4
Lysistrata   116, 117, 121, 122
Lysistrata Project   112, 117, 120–3

male-to-female (M to F) transsexuals
    10, 153
Marcuse, Herbert   18
Margolin, Deborah   141
    Upwardly Mobile   45*f1*
Martial Law   164
Martin, Del
    Lesbian/Woman   33–4
Martin, Fran
    *Mobile Cultures: New Media in Queer
        Asia*   95
Marx, Karl   88
    Holy Family, The   119
Marxism
    Medea   117, 119
masculinity   9, 10, 11, 24, 28
mass entertainment   182
Maud's
    drag party   26
    Jo: A Lesbian History Play   20
    Last Call at Maud's/The Maud's Project
        30*n1*, 55
    lesbian   19
    lesbian bar   17
    location   23
    social coding   27
    white customers   20
Mayne, Judith   79

McLaughlin, Ellen
    Lysistrata Project   120
Medea   116, 117
Mediterranean   90
memory   134
Metropolis   152, 171
Meyer, Richard   140
Miller, D. A.   10
    Bringing Out Roland Barthes   135
Miller, Tim   107
Millett, Kate   25
mimesis   111
minstrel shows   181–2
Modleski, Tania   12
Mohanty, Chandra
    *Feminist Genealogies, Colonial Legacies,
        Democratic Futures*   131
monogamy   25
monster   76
Moon, Michael   9, 10
Moraga, Cherríe   35, 61
    Giving Up the Ghost   126–7
morality   27, 97
Mueller, Heiner
    Cement   11
    Construction, The   11
Müller, Heiner   112
    Medea   117–20
Mulryan/Nash   57
Muñoz, José Esteban   136, 139

National Gay and Lesbian Task Force
    154
national identity   128
natural resources   14
nature   81–2
Negri, Antonio
    Empire   86
nelly butches   25
neo-femmes   19
Nestle, Joan   43
    Lesbian Herstory Archives (New
        York)   35
    Restricted Country, A   8
Netherlands   91
new media studies   5
New Mexico   23

new technologies
  avatars 185–6
  employment 167
  feminism 13
  gender coding 185
  globalization 95
  information culture 11
  representation 184
  skills 182
  social processes 149
  transgender 154
  transnational interests 167
Newton, Esther 22, 36, 39
Nietzsche, Friedrich
  Birth of Tragedy, The 177–8
  Ecco Homo 108
Night of the Living Dead 82
Norman, Marsha
  'night Mother 46
nude body 106–7, 161

Oakland 20
Occur 92
Oedipal triangle 76–7
Oedipus 114
Olalquiaga, Celeste
  Megalopolis 63–4
ontology 71
Onwueme, Tess
  Tell It to Women 127–8
Oregon 23
Oresteia 115
Orlan 151

Panda, Ashe 12
Paris is Burning 155
Parker, Andrew
  Nationalisms and Sexualities 143
performance
  animation 156
  arts 103
  butch-femme 8
  critical approach 7
  discursive 108
  gender representation 132
  interpretation 7
  M to F transsexuals 10
  new technologies 152
  as politics 60

production of meaning 6
  strategy 8
  studies 134
  text 18
  training practices 101
Performance Group
  Dionysus in '69 106
performance practices 32, 172
performative language 3
performative voice 5
Phelan, Peggy 141
  *Unmarked: The Politics of
    Performance* 8
Philippines
  Progressive Organisation of Gays 92
Plato 68
political action 113
popular culture 2
post-disciplinary 108, 109
Poster, Mark 179
Praz, Mario
  Romantic Agony, The 72
prejudice 182
Pride Parade 9
Progressive Organisation of Gays 92
protests 103
Proust, Marcel
  Captive, The 36
  Remembrance of Things Past 134–5
proximity 102
psychoanalytic theory 137

queer 66, 68, 69
  alliance 8
  desire 78
  discourse 69, 89
  identity 93, 94, 95
  performativity 58
  politics 12
  studies 88, 97, 134
Queer Nation 62
queer theory 5, 51, 52, 53, 67, 68
queer tourism 89–90

rape 104–5, 126, 129
Reagon, Bernice Johnson *see* Johnson
  Reagon, Bernice
realism 46–7

Reinshagen, Gerlind
  Sunday's Children 126
Reno
  Rebel without a Pause 143, 144
representation 81, 82, 134, 168, 181
research 96
Rich, Adrienne
  Dream of a Common Language, The
    105
Rimbaud, Arthur 66
  Illuminations 72–3
  Season in Hell 72
riverofsalsa 184*f*7
Riviere, Joan
  Womanliness as a Masquerade
    39–40
Roach, Joseph
  Cities of the Dead 134
  Tulane University 1992 9
Roadkill
  Brandon website 155
role-playing 8, 25
Román, David 143
Rosenberg, Tina 12
Ruehl, Mercedes
  Lysistrata Project 120
Russo, Mary 39, 42
  Nationalisms and Sexualities 143

Salmagundi
  sexual politics 37–8
Samaras, Connie
  Is it Tomorrow or Just the End of
    Time? 150
same-sex desire 82
San Francisco 17, 26, 55
San Francisco Chronicler 20
San Francisco State College 18, 20,
  21, 103
Sankara 175, 177–8
Schleef, Einar
  Betrayed People, A 108
Schneeman, Carolee
  Interior Scroll 106
  Meat Joy 106
scholarship 102
Schulman, Sarah
  management class 56–7
  My American History 62, 143

science 152
science fiction 167
scopophilia 76
Sedgwick, Edie
  Edie 21
Sedgwick, Eve 9, 10, 37, 137
seduction 45–6
self-representation 28
semiotics 6
sex 95
  trade 90
sexual citizenship 143
sexual desire 122
sexual identities 57
sexual interest 76
sexual movement 58
sexual orientation 93
sexual politics 53, 64
sexual practices
  AIDS 60
  censorship 95
  ethnicity 125
  feminism 128
  globalization 88
  national identity 128
  self-representation 106
sexual promiscuity 54
sexual revolution 18, 25
sexual subcultures 4
sexuality 7, 31, 33, 158, 166, 167
sexuality studies 9, 12
Seyrig, Delphine
  Daughters of Darkness 81
Shakespeare, William 10
Shaw, Peggy 7, 55, 136
  Beauty and the Beast 43–5
  Belle Reprieve 155–6
  Upwardly Mobile 45*f*1
Shepard, Sam
  Lie of the Mind, A 46
Sherman 24–5
Shu Lea Cheang
  Brandon website 154, 157
  IKU: A Japanese Cyber-porn
    Adventure 97
Sieg, Katrin
  Sexual Subjects of the Cold War
    164

Sifuentes, Roberto
  Ethno-Cyberpunk Trading Post and
    Curio Shop on the Electronic
    Frontier 182–3
Signs
  Women's Studies 104
Silverman, Kaja
  Fassbinder and Lacan: a
    Reconsideration of Gaze, Look
    and Image 77–8
  Subject of Semiotics, The 7
Sinfield, Alan 10
Singapore 92
Sobchack, Vivian 13
sober dykes 21
social agency 107
social agendas 1
social coding 7
social communication 11
social dynamics 33
social identity 66, 94
social intercourse 26
social issues 105
social life 21, 22
social relationships 22, 178
Socrates
  Republic, The 112
Solon 111, 113
Sommer, Doris
  Nationalisms and Sexualities 143
Sonoma Country 23
Sontag, Susan 36
Spivak, Gayatri 7
Split Britches 7–8
  Beauty and the Beast 43
  Belle Reprieve 136
Sprinkle, Annie 107
Stein, Arlene 28
Stein, Gertrude 68
Stepford Wives, The 171
Stoker, Bram
  Dracula 170
Stone, Allucquere Roseanne
  Empire Strikes Back: a
    Posttranssexual Manifesto,
    The 10
Stryker, Susan 153
  Christine Jorgensen's Atom Bomb
    151–2

Stuart, Andrea
  Diva 20
student activism 18
subcultural practices 4, 23, 26,
    28, 29
subject position 32
subjectivity 151
surgery 10
surveillance 95
Sweden 166
symbolism 31
  Beauty and the Beast 43

Tadiar, Neferti
  Sexual Economies in the Asia-Pacific
    Community 158–9
Taiwan 94, 163–4, 165
Taylor, Diana 129
  *Archive and the Repertoire: Performing
    Cultural Memory* 141
Teena, Brandon 154
telephone 172
Teraoka, Masami
  Adam and Eve/Mousetrap 161,
    163f4
  Eve with Three Blind Mice 161, 162f3
  Geisha in Bath 160f2
  McDonald's Hamburgers invading
    Japan 159–60
terminology 7
Terry, Jennifer
  Deviant Bodies 107
Thailand 90, 165
Theatre Journal 6
theatre studies 103, 104
theatres 7, 13, 101, 126, 150–1
theory 5, 6, 7
Thongthiraj, Took Took 165
Todorov, Tzvetan 79
Toklas, Alice B. 68
Tomb Raider
  Lara Croft 180–1
tomboys 92–3, 94, 164
Tompkins, Joanne
  *Post-colonial Drama: Theory, Practice,
    Politics* 118
tourism 89–92
traditions 3
tragic form 111, 112, 113, 114

training practices   101
transgender identification   9
  Cold War   164
  cultural memory   135
  feminism   10
  local traditions   94
  masculinity   10
  queer voice   92
  role-playing   8
  Taiwan   164–5
transgender politics   11, 153
transnational contact   161
transnational corporations   158–9
transnational studies   5
transsexual   9, 10, 151–2
transvestites   41

Urla, Jacqueline
  Deviant Bodies   107

vampire
  configuration of proximity   79–81
  discourse of blood   72
  image of perversion   9
  invisibility   52, 67
  as lesbian   81
  narcissism   142
  queer theory   74–5
  representation   75, 82–3
  same-sex desire   81
  undead   82
Vampire Lovers   81
Venkataraman, Padma   12
vice police   27
Vietnam War   26
visibility   8
vocabulary   6

waitingforgodot.com   177*f*6
  performance   175–6
Warhol, Andy   27
Warner, Michael
  Fear of a Queer Planet   61
water   14
Weaver, Lois   7–8
  Beauty and the Beast   43–5
  Upwardly Mobile   45*f*1
Weldon, Ann   26

Western culture   2
Whitman, Walt   10
Wilde, Oscar   10, 36, 37, 68
  Salome   73
Williams, Linda
  When the Woman Looks   75–7
Williams, Tennessee
  Streetcar Named Desire, A   136
Wittgenstein, Ludwig
  Tractatus Logico-Philosophicus   137–8
Wittig, Monique   54–5
  Lesbian Body, The   32
womanliness   40
women
  cyberspace   174
  demonstrations   2
  ethnic spectator   130–1
  free trade zones   159
  laments   111–12
  modern and traditional   130
  new technologies   120, 170–1, 185
  outside the state   125
  power of organization   128
  representation   134
  sexual objectification   127
  signify disorder   115
  Special Economic Zones   170
  subject position   31
  woman   111
Women in Theater   7
Women's centre   22
Women's Studies   103–4
Woolf, Virginia   24
  Three Guineas   125
Word is Out, The   19
working class   4, 34
world wide web   150, 158, 168
WOW (Women's One World)   7
writing   50–1, 102

Yaeger, Patricia
  Nationalisms and Sexualities   143
Yengning Chao   163–4
Yoshimoto, Mitsuhiro
  Real Virtuality   158
Yue, Audrey
  *Mobile Cultures: New Media in Queer
    Asia*   95